FINANCIAL ACCOUNTING

An intro

Hutchinson Management Studies

Series editor: Peter Lawrence, Senior Lecturer, Loughborough University of Technology

FINANCIAL ACCOUNTING
An introduction

John Blake
Lecturer in Accountancy, Loughborough University of Technology

Hutchinson
London Melbourne Sydney Auckland Johannesburg

Hutchinson & Co. (Publishers) Ltd
An imprint of the Hutchinson Publishing Group
17-21 Conway Street, London W1P 6JD

Hutchinson Publishing Group (Australia) Pty Ltd
16-22 Church Street, Hawthorn, Melbourne, Victoria 3122

Hutchinson Group (NZ) Ltd
32-34 View Road, PO Box 40-086, Glenfield, Auckland 10

Hutchinson Group (SA) Pty Ltd
PO Box 337, Bergvlei 2012, South Africa

Brookfield Publishing Co., Inc.
Old Post Road, Brookfield, Vermont 05036 USA

First published 1985

Set in Plantin 10 on 12pt by AKM Associates (UK) Ltd
Ajmal House, Hayes Road, Southall, London

Printed and bound in England by
Anchor Brendon Ltd, Tiptree, Essex

British Library Cataloguing in Publication Data

Blake, John, *1950–*
Financial accounting: an introduction. –
(Hutchinson management studies series)
1. Accounting
1. Title
657'48 HF5635

ISBN 0 09 161641 7

CONTENTS

Acknowledgements

I would like to express my thanks to my colleague Peter Lawrence, the series editor, for his advice and support. Also I thank the following for permitting me to use their examination questions:

The Association of Certified Accountants
The Society of Company and Commercial Accountants
University College of Wales, Aberystwyth
University College of Wales, Bangor
Queen's University, Belfast
University of Bristol
University College Cardiff
Hatfield Polytechnic
Heriot Watt University, Edinburgh
Huddersfield Polytechnic
Kingston Polytechnic
University of Lancaster
University of Manchester
Oxford Polytechnic
Portsmouth Polytechnic
Preston Polytechnic
University of Southampton
University of Stirling
Sunderland Polytechnic
Trent Polytechnic
Ulster Polytechnic
University of Warwick
Wolverhampton Polytechnic

1

THE NATURE AND ENVIRONMENT OF ACCOUNTING

Objectives

The basic objectives of this chapter are:

1 To introduce the environment of accounting.
2 To consider in more detail the background to the specific subject matter of this book, financial accounting.

Specifically we consider:

1 An introductory definition of the term 'accounting'.
2 The disciplines that overlap with accounting.
3 The structure of the accounting profession in the UK.
4 The range of work undertaken by accountants in the UK.
5 The sources of authority which influence the way in which published accounts are prepared and presented.
6 The users and uses of published accounts.

Definition

There is no standard, generally agreed, definition of what is meant by the term 'accounting'. However the American Accounting Association drew up a definition in 1966, and it is as follows:

> The process of identifying, measuring, and communicating economic information to permit informed judgements and decisions by users of the information.

Exploring some key words from this definition:

1 'Process' embraces both the *techniques* used by accountants and the *principles* which determine the way accountants do their job.
2 'Identifying' refers to the process by which data is collected.
3 'Measuring' is the process of analysing data in a meaningful way. As we will see throughout this book, the process of measuring often involves difficult professional judgements and estimates.
4 'Communicating' involves the presentation of the analysis of data.
5 'To permit informed judgements and decisions' involves this definition in identifying the *objectives* of accounting. The judgements and decisions will relate both to an assessment of the outcome of past activities and decisions on current action intended to affect the future.
6 'Users' is a term which leaves open the question as to which users the accountant should seek to serve. Originally accounting was envisaged as serving the needs of the proprietors of a business, but as we shall see below accounting information can be of use to anyone who makes decisions relating to a business.

Below we consider the various disciplines which overlap with accounting. Because accounting is a discipline with very open boundaries, the role of the accountant is difficult to pinpoint and varies enormously between different countries. In the UK and indeed in the English-speaking world as a whole, accountants have tended to take a wide range of roles. By contrast, in many countries the accountancy profession, in so far as it can be identified at all, has a very narrow role, with many functions being carried out by economists, lawyers, behavioural scientists, or quantitative specialists.

Overlapping disciplines

In order to appreciate the nature of accountancy it is important to be aware of the wide range of disciplines with which accountancy is linked.

Economics

The economist is concerned with understanding the economic relationships which the accountant is trying to measure and report. For example, the accountant will be trying to measure 'income' and 'capital', concepts which the economist is concerned to define. Aspects of the economic environment, such as inflation, have an impact on the financial position of a business which can only be measured properly by the accountant if the underlying economic causes are understood. Finally, the accountant presents reports on the basis of which users will make decisions; thus the information presented by the accountant can itself have economic consequences.

Behavioural Science

The way in which the accountant presents information can have a powerful influence on the way people behave in an organization. Thus an understanding of how individuals and groups respond to information can be important in designing an information system that will promote the objectives of the enterprise.

Quantitative analysis

There are a wide range of quantitative techniques available to help in business decision making, which involve the use of accounting data.

Law

Law is an essential related discipline because the accountant works in an environment where the form and content of many accounting reports is prescribed by law. Moreover there are some transactions which can only be accounted for properly if their legal implications are fully understood. In several of the areas in which accountants in the UK have developed expertise, such as taxation and insolvency, there is a specialized body of legal knowledge which must be understood.

Data processing

The accountant's involvement in data collection requires an understanding of data processing systems. Such systems can be manual, machine based, or computerized; the latter, in particular, involves the accountant in some very technical skills.

The accounting profession

Most accountants in the UK are members of one of the professional accounting bodies, each of which has its own rules requiring both practical experience and success in a series of examinations as a condition of entry. They are employed either by firms of accountants in public practice or directly by industrial, commercial or financial organizations (hereafter referred to as commercial organizations).

There are six UK accounting bodies which are incorporated by Royal Charter, and which have joined together to form the Consultative Committee of Accounting Bodies (CCAB). These are:

1 The Institute of Chartered Accountants in England and Wales (ICAEW).
2 The Institute of Chartered Accountants in Scotland (ICAS).
3 The Institute of Chartered Accountants in Ireland (ICAI).

These three bodies are each independent, but in practice are very similar in character. They require their students to train in public practice, but once qualified about half their members remain in public practice, while the other half are directly employed by commercial organizations.

4 The Association of Certified Accountants (ACA). The Association allows students to train either in public practice or in commercial organizations. The majority of the Association's members are

in fact directly employed by commercial organizations.

Under the Companies Acts members of each of these four bodies may be appointed to audit the accounts of limited companies.

5 The Institute of Cost and Management Accountants (ICMA). The ICMA requires its students to train in commercial organizations, where most of its members are employed.
6 The Chartered Institute of Public Finance and Accounting (CIPFA). This Institute requires its students to train in the public sector, and most of its members are employed in local government.

These six bodies have over 150,000 members and over 120,000 registered students between them. Together they have set up the Association of Accounting Technicians (AAT), intended to be a 'second tier' body for junior staff, which currently has nearly 10,000 members and over 15,000 registered students. There are a number of other professional accounting bodies in the UK, including the Institute of Administrative Accountants, the Society of Company and Commercial Accountants, the Association of Cost and Executive Accountants, and the Association of International Accountants, which together have over 20,000 members. In addition there are a number of accountants working in the UK who are not members of any professional body.

The work of accountants

In the UK the accountancy profession has become involved in a wide range of roles. These include:

The accounting system

Accountants are involved in designing and administering the systems used by enterprises to record and control the movement of resources through the business. The job of operating the accounting system is known as book keeping.

Preparation of accounts for publication

Accountants are responsible for the preparation of the accounting statements which are presented to the outside world. The basic accounting statements are the *profit and loss acount*, (sometimes called an *income statement*), and the *balance sheet*. In the case of a limited company these accounts are filed with the registrar of companies, and are available for public inspection. This function is often referred to as *financial accounting*.

Auditing

Auditing is a process of independent review of the accounting system and the accounting statements derived therefrom. The *external audit* is performed by an accountant who is independent of the business, and who attaches to the financial statements an audit report. All limited companies are required by law to appoint an independent auditor, and in practice many other businesses do so as well. A business may also arrange for *internal audit*, a process of review of operations by staff directly employed by the business. To be effective an internal audit department must be independent of other sections of the business, reporting directly to senior management. Internal audit is most commonly thought of as a process of controlling the accounting systems of a business, but in principle can be employed to control any aspect of the business operations. For example, some internal audit departments employ engineers to check on the efficiency of energy consumption by the business.

Taxation advice

This is an area of activity with which accountants are particularly associated in the public mind. The role of the accountant has two distinct aspects:

1 *Compliance work*, assisting the taxpayer to disclose all relevant information to the tax authorities so that the correct tax liability is computed.
2 *Planning* work, advising the taxpayer on how to arrange affairs so as to minimize the tax liability. This is known as *tax avoidance*, and is legal. By contrast no reputable accountant will become involved in *tax evasion*, which involves concealing taxable income from the authorities in order to evade taxation and is highly illegal.

The costing system

Costing involves the process of allocating the various expenses of the business to *cost centres* and eventually to units of output. This role of the *cost accountant* is clearly vital in the management of the business.

Management accounting

The *management accountant* is concerned with the preparation of reports for internal use by the management of the business. In practice the cost accounting and management accounting roles are often combined.

There are a number of important differences between financial accounting and management accounting reports:

1 Financial accounts are employed by a range of users, discussed below, and have to balance the needs of different kinds of user. Management accounts are designed for the specific objectives of management.
2 Financial accounts are subject to various regulations as to how they should be prepared and presented; an outline of the range of sources of authority is presented below. By contrast the business is free to consider internal reports in whatever form management choose.
3 The conventions that underlie financial accounts emphasize the need for prudence. By contrast for management purposes it is important that all estimates should represent the best estimate of the position of the business, without bias.

Trust accounts

A special type of work which combines accounting and taxation skills arises in relation to trusts. The accountant will be involved not only in the preparation and audit of the trust accounts, but also in advising on how to set up and administer the trust in a tax-efficient way.

Insolvency work

Accountants are often employed as *liquidators*, responsible for winding up the affairs of a company in liquidation and distributing the assets realized to those with a claim on the company. A more delicate task is that of the *receiver*, who takes over the management of an ailing company and tries to reorganize its affairs so as to put it on a sound footing.

Investigation work

The term 'investigation' is commonly used to describe various types of special assignment on which an accountant can be employed. An example is that when a company is considering a major acquisition it will normally employ accountants to investigate the accounts and general financial background of the firm being acquired. Accountants are also involved in the preparation of such documents as the *prospectus* which a company is required to issue when raising funds from the public.

Financial management

This term is used to describe the task of organizing the financial resources of the business. It involves planning how to meet the financial requirements of the business and how best to employ its resources.

Financial analysis

A wide range of organizations, such as banks, stockbrokers and financial institutions, employ accountants to analyse the accounts of companies in which they are interested.

General management

Training as an accountant has often proved a useful entry to a senior role in general management. In addition to the importance of the finance function, the status of accountants has been enhanced by the rigorous training and admission requirements of the major accounting bodies.

Sources of authority in published accounts

The aspect of the accountant's work with which this book is particularly concerned is financial accounting. The major sources of authority which give the accountant guidance on the preparation of published accounts are:

Company Law
Limited liability companies (discussed in detail in Chapter 5 below) are subject to detailed requirements relating to required practice and disclosure in their published accounts, contained in the Companies Acts of 1948, 1967, 1976, 1980 and 1981. There are also legal requirements prescribed for certain specific types of organization, e.g. building societies. The accounting practices of organizations not governed by the Companies Acts may be influenced to some extent by the example set by limited companies.

Statements of Standard Accounting Practice (SSAPs)
These SSAPs, often referred to as *accounting standards*, are formulated by a body called the Accounting Standards Committee (ASC) which is made up of representatives of each of the six CCAB bodies (see 'The accounting profession' above). Each accounting standard is preceded by an *Exposure Draft* (ED) which represents the ASC's proposals. Exposure Drafts are published and any interested party has the right to comment on them. Because four of the CCAB bodies together have a virtual monopoly of the audits of limited companies, such companies must either comply with SSAPs or face comment on their failure to do so in the audit report. Thus there is a strong motive for limited companies to comply with SSAPs, even though these have no legal authority.

International Accounting Standards (IASs)
These are formulated by the International Accounting Standards Committee (IASC), which is made up from representatives of the national accounting standard setting bodies of over 60 countries. IASs are intended to guide national accounting standard-setting bodies in the way in which they formulate their own national accounting standards, and do not apply directly to individual companies. The objective of the IASC is to promote international harmonization of accounting practice, which has become increasingly sought after with the growth of multinational business.

EEC directives
The EEC has a programme of harmonizing national company law requirements throughout the EEC. EEC directives, when agreed by the Council of Ministers, bind each national government to introduce their content into their national legislation. The EEC fourth directive, implemented in the UK by the Companies Act 1981, included detailed requirements on the form and content of company accounts.

Tax law
In some countries businesses are required to present their accounts in line with the way in which income is computed for tax purposes. This is not the case in the UK, but in practice an accountant will normally present accounts in such a way as to include most of the information required for tax purposes.

Private agreement
The way in which accounts are presented by a business may be affected by some form of private agreement. For example, it is common practice for the articles of association of a property investment company to include provisions stating how surpluses on the sale of properties should be accounted for. Such an agreement may be made between the different proprietors of the business, or between the owners of the business and outsiders.

Regulatory bodies
In certain kinds of commercial and professional activity firms are required to present accounts in a prescribed form by their regulatory body. Stockbrokers and solicitors both fall into this category.

Tradition
Certain accounting practices have become established by tradition, and continue to be followed because it is convenient that all businesses should follow consistent practice.

The users of published accounts

We have seen that the accounts of a limited

company are filed with the Registrar of Companies and are therefore available to any interested party. Anyone having any form of dealing, direct or indirect, with the company may be a potential user of the accounts. The range of potential users includes:

Shareholders

Shareholders have two kinds of interest in the accounts of the company:

1 Stewardship decisions. Shareholders will wish to see what the directors of the company have done with the funds entrusted to their stewardship, and make decisions on whether they are satisfied with the conduct of the directors.
2 Investment decisions. Shareholders will also make decisions on whether to buy more shares, sell the shares they have, or hold their existing shareholding. Potential shareholders considering buying shares also have this interest in the accounts.

Creditors

Anyone who is owed money by the company, or is considering allowing themselves to be put in that position, will be interested in assessing the company's ability to meet the terms of repayment in full on the due dates. Creditors fall into three broad categories:

1 Banks and financial institutions.
2 Investors acquiring debentures in the company.
3 Trade creditors, who supply goods to the business on credit terms.

Employees

Employees will be interested in assessing the security of future employment prospects, and the company's ability to offer pay rises in the future. Individuals considering employment in a company might look at the accounts, both to assess job security and to familiarize themselves with the company's position in preparation for interviews.

Trade contacts

Trade contacts can be divided into three broad headings:

1 Suppliers, who may look at the accounts of a customer both to make decisions on trade credit terms and also, in the case of a major customer, to assess likely future demand.
2 Customers, who may look at the accounts of a major supplier to assess the likelihood of the business continuing in existence. In cases where a supplier performs work under a long-term contract, receiving payment on account as successive stages of the work are completed, an assessment of the contractor's financial position will be particularly important.
3 Competitors, who will try to learn as much as they can about the financial strength and future prospects of rivals.

Non-executive directors

The full-time management of a business will not normally use the published accounts of their own business for decision-making purposes, because they have access to the detailed internal accounting records of the business. However non-executive directors may find the published accounts useful, especially as they will have been subject to an independent audit.

Government departments

The government is a significant potential user of accounts for a wide range of purposes. These might be classified under three broad headings:

1 Regulatory, e.g. assessment of taxation liabilities, administration of price controls where these apply, decisions on whether or not to permit mergers which tend towards the creation of monopolies.
2 Statistical analysis. The government statistical services analyse and publish a range of statistics based on published accounts.
3 Policy making. For example the government may be influenced by published accounts in deciding on appropriate levels of taxation or incentives to industry.

Regulatory bodies

A range of non-governmental regulatory bodies, such as the Stock Exchange, may have an interest in the published accounts of the enterprises they regulate.

Investment advisers
Investment advisers, such as stockbrokers, will have a very close interest in the published accounts of companies.

Trade unions
Trade unions have an obvious interest in the accounts of companies in their role as employee representatives. A sophisticated trade union may use published accounts to help decide on the appropriate time to press companies for improved remuneration and conditions of service.

General public
The activities of companies raise a number of issues which are regarded as being of interest to the general public. Politicians and pressure groups frequently use published accounts as evidence for a case which they wish to argue.

Journalists
Published accounts are frequently used by journalists, both in the financial press aimed at those involved in investment decisions and in general news reporting relating to matters of public interest.

Researchers
Both academic and commercial users will analyse company accounts and publish any conclusions they reach as to the state of specific industries or the economy as a whole.

This is, of course, a list of *potential* users, and does not imply that all the parties listed above necessarily make full use of published accounts. Few individual employees, for example, will make a detailed examination of their employer's published accounts. Nevertheless potential users may well be influenced by adviser groups interpreting accounts on their behalf. Thus employees may be indirect users of accounts through their trade unions.

An understanding of the wide range of users and potential users of accounts is important because:

1 Accounts influence the decisions not only of the owners of the business, to whom they are formally addressed, but of all those who have any kind of dealings with the business. This is important in appreciating the potential economic consequences of accounting reports, considered in detail in Chapter 10 below.
2 Different users have different needs. The question therefore arises for those who are responsible for deciding on accounting practices and disclosure as to which users should be considered.
3 Even if the most narrow view of the responsibility of the accountant is taken, and accounts are regarded as meeting only the needs of the proprietors of a business, the fact remains that the accounts will be used for more than one purpose. Therefore decisions on the nature and method of accounting disclosure will necessarily represent a compromise between different objectives.

Conclusions

Accounting is concerned with the collection, analysis, and presentation of data for the purposes of decision making. This function overlaps with a number of other disciplines, and the role of the accountant varies enormously between different countries. In the UK a powerful accounting profession has succeeded in establishing a wide number of areas of work covered by accountants. The area of accounting considered by this book is financial accounting, the preparation of accounts in a form suitable for publication. Such accounts have a wide range of potential users.

Questions

1 To what extent has the definition of accounting been influenced by the professional accountancy bodies?

2 How would you explain the role of the accountant and what is his contribution to the individual company, and to the community at large?

3 The published accounts of a limited company are filed with the registrar of companies and are available for inspection by any member of the public. List the parties who you think might use published accounts, and the purpose for which they will be used.

2

INTRODUCTION TO THE DOUBLE ENTRY BOOK-KEEPING SYSTEM

Objectives

The preparation of accounts is normally based upon the double entry book-keeping system. The objectives of this chapter are:

1. To explain the principles which underlie the double entry book-keeping system and how these relate to the two basic financial statements, the profit and loss account and the balance sheet.
2. To describe the operation of the double entry book-keeping system in the ledger.
3. To introduce the trial balance and to show how this links the ledger to the financial statements.

The basic accounting statements

Before accounts can be prepared it is necessary to identify the *entity* which we are accounting for. When accounting for a business it is normal to treat the business itself as the entity to be accounted for, independently of the personal resources and obligations of the proprietors. This 'entity concept' underlies the preparation of all accounts.

Virtually any business will need to employ resources; the resources owned by a business are called *assets*. The acquisition of assets must be financed from one of two sources:

1. Amounts borrowed from outsiders (as distinguished from the owners). These amounts are called *liabilities*.
2. The proprietors of the business themselves. Accountants call the proprietors' interest in the business *capital*.

A *balance sheet* is a statement which shows for a given point in time the resources of the business and where they have been derived from. The balance sheet equation can be summarized as:

Capital + Liabilities = Assets

When presenting a balance sheet it is normal to list assets in inverse order of liquidity, so that those assets which are expected to take the longest time to be converted into cash are shown first; this is often known as 'marshalling' the assets.

To illustrate the workings of the balance sheet equation we will consider how the balance sheet of John Sinclair would appear after each of the transactions listed in Example 1.

Example 1

John Sinclair decided to set up a furniture retailing business. In January 1985 the following transactions occurred:

1. On 1 January he paid £10,000 into a newly opened bank account.
2. On 4 January he borrowed £6,000 from Jane Dundas; the loan is interest-free, to be repaid on 31 December 1990.
3. On 6 January he paid £13,000 for the freehold of a small lock-up shop.
4. On 7 January he paid £1,000 for furniture which he planned to resell.

5 On 8 January he bought furniture for resale from Arthur Young for £1,500, agreeing to pay for these goods in 15 days time.
6 On 10 January he sold furniture which had cost £600 for cash £900.
7 On 15 January he sold furniture, which had cost £1,100, for £1,700 to Mary Baker, who agreed to pay the amount due within one month.
8 On 23 January he paid £1,500 to Arthur Young.
9 On 29 January Mary Baker paid £800 of the amount she owed.

Assume that all cash items passed in and out of the bank account.

The successive balance sheets are shown in Figures 1 to 9

Transaction 1
This is the transaction which effectively launches the business. Because of the entity concept, the balance sheet only deals with this particular operation and tells us nothing about John Sinclair's personal assets and liabilities.

Transaction 2
The balance sheet records that an amount of £6,000 has been borrowed. It is not normal to show on the face of the balance sheet who the loan has been borrowed from, although clearly this information has to be noted somewhere in the records of the business. Another important piece of information is the date when the loan is repayable; although this information is not disclosed by the balance sheet equation, it is normal for accounts to distinguish between long-term liabilities, repayable more than one year from the balance sheet date, and current liabilities, repayable within one year. Often a business will disclose more detailed information on the repayment date for long-term loans.

Transaction 3
Note that in the balance sheet freehold property is listed above the bank balance because clearly the bank balance is a more liquid asset.

Transaction 4
Goods purchased for resale are called *stock*.

Transaction 5
Anyone to whom the business owes money can be described as a *creditor*. In particular a supplier to whom money is owed is described as a *trade creditor*; confusion can arise because often in practice accountants use the term 'creditor' to describe a trade creditor.

Transaction 6
Previous transactions have involved simple exchanges between various parts of the balance sheet equation. In this case the business has managed to exchange a £600 asset (stock) for a £900 asset (cash); the £300 surplus is a profit. Since any profits or losses fall to the proprietors of the business, this profit is added onto the capital of the business.

Transaction 7
This is a similar transaction to 6 except that the sale is on credit terms. Anyone who owes money to the business is called a debtor.

Transaction 8
This payment happens to clear the entire balance owed to the only trade creditor.

Transaction 9
This represents receipt of part of the amount owed by Mary Baker.

Figure 1 *Transaction 1*

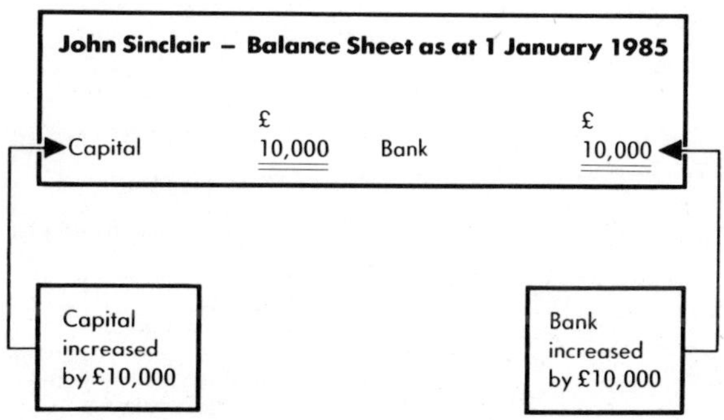

Figure 2 *Transaction 2*

John Sinclair – Balance Sheet as at 4 January 1985

	£		£
Capital	10,000	Bank	16,000
Loan	6,000		
	16,000		16,000

Liability increased by £6,000

Asset increased by £6,000

Figure 3 *Transaction 3*

John Sinclair – Balance Sheet as at 6 January 1985

	£		£
Capital	10,000	Freehold property	13,000
Loan	6,000	Bank	3,000
	16,000		16,000

Asset decreased by £13,000

Asset increased by £13,000

Figure 4 *Transaction 4*

John Sinclair – Balance Sheet as at 7 January 1985

	£		£
Capital	10,000	Freehold property	13,000
Loan	6,000	Stock	1,000
		Bank	2,000
	16,000		16,000

Asset decreased by £1,000

Asset increased by £1,000

Figure 5 *Transaction 5*

John Sinclair – Balance Sheet as at 8 January 1985

	£		£
Capital	10,000	Freehold property	13,000
Loan	6,000	Stock	2,500
Trade creditor	1,500	Bank	2,000
	17,500		17,500

Liability increased by £1,500

Asset increased by £1,500

Figure 6 *Transaction 6*

John Sinclair – Balance Sheet as at 10 January 1985

	£		£
Capital b/fwd	10,000	Freehold property	13,000
Surplus on sale	300	Stock	1,900
Capital c/fwd	10,300	Bank	2,900
Loan	6,000		
Trade creditor	1,500		
	17,800		17,800

Asset increased by £900

Capital increased by £300

Asset decreased by £600

Figure 7 *Transaction 7*

John Sinclair – Balance Sheet as at 15 January 1985

	£		£
Capital b/fwd	10,000	Freehold property	13,000
Surplus on sale	600	Stock	800
Capital c/fwd	10,900	Debtor	1,700
Loan	6,000	Bank	2,900
Trade creditor	1,500		
	18,400		18,400

Asset increased by £1,700

Capital increased by £600

Asset decreased by £1,100

Figure 8 *Transaction 8*

John Sinclair – Balance Sheet as at 23 January 1985

	£		£
Capital	10,900	Freehold property	13,000
Loan	6,000	Stock	800
		Debtor	1,700
		Bank	1,400
	16,900		16,900

Liability decreased by £1,500

Asset decreased by £1,500

Figure 9 *Transaction 9*

John Sinclair – Balance Sheet as at 29 January 1985

	£		£
Capital	10,900	Freehold property	13,000
Loan	6,000	Stock	800
		Debtor	900
		Bank	2,200
	16,900		16,900

Asset increased by £800

Asset decreased by £800

In our examples we have shown the balance sheet in 'horizontal' form, with capital and liabilities listed on the left and assets listed on the right. Matters of presentation are covered in detail in Chapter 9 but at this stage the following points are worth noting:

1 It is common to show current liabilities as a deduction from assets rather than with capital and other liabilities; sometimes all liabilities are shown as a deduction from assets.

2 A 'vertical' form of presentation is often used, whereby the two halves of the balance sheet are shown one above the other instead of side by side. In this case there is no established convention as to which half of the balance sheet is shown first.

3 In many countries, including the USA, it is normal when presenting a balance sheet in the horizontal format to show the list of assets on the left and the list of capital and liabilities on the right.

Our example has illustrated how the balance sheet of a business shows the resources owned by the business and how these have been financed at a given point in time. We have seen that when each transaction occurs the accounting equation continues to balance, either because the movement of resources occurs between items on the same side of the equation or because there is an equal adjustment on each side of the equation. However, in practice the repeated preparation of a balance sheet after each transaction would be unacceptable as a method of accounting being absurdly cumbersome and unwieldy. Accordingly the balance sheet of a business is only published at regular intervals, and a record of transactions between balance sheet dates is made to enable preparation of each balance sheet; the system of recording is considered in detail below.

In Example 1 we have seen two examples of transactions involving trading activity; in each case the surplus generated by trading was recorded as an increase in capital. At the end of an accounting period information on all trading transactions has to be collected; the net surplus or deficit arising on trading is computed; then the capital account can be adjusted accordingly. A summary of the income and expenditure during the accounting period called the *profit and loss account* will be presented. The balance sheet and the profit and loss account together then form the basic accounting statements.

The ledger

We have seen how each transaction involves a transfer between the various parts of the balance sheet, and that it is not practical to prepare a new balance sheet each time a transaction occurs. The method normally used to record the effects of each transaction is the *double entry book-keeping system.* Under this system a record called an *account* is maintained in respect of each type of balance sheet or profit and loss item; the collection of all the accounts is known as *the ledger.*

In its simplest form an 'account' can be envisaged as a sheet of paper with dividing line drawn down the middle of the page from a heading at the top to the bottom, forming a 'T' shape. On the left hand side are recorded all transfers of resources *to* the aspect of the business represented by the account, and this is known as the *debit* side. On the right hand side are recorded all transfers of resources *from* the aspect of the business represented by the account, and this is known as the *credit* side. The difference between the totals of each side is known as a *balance,* so that accounts representing items which absorb or consume the resources of the business will show a debit balance while accounts representing items from which the business derives resources will show a credit balance. On each side of the T account will be shown three columns, the first giving the date, the second showing the details of the transaction, and the third column showing the amount involved.

Let us consider Transaction A in Example 1. On 1 January 1985 £10,000 was paid into the bank. This represents resources going *to* the bank, the account for which will be *debited,* and derived from the proprietor, so that the capital account will be *credited.* Thus:

Bank	
1.1.85 Capital 10,000	

Capital	
	1.1.85 Bank 10,000

Students often have difficulty in the early stages of learning when to debit and when to credit an item. There are two ways in which the principles can be approached:

1 The principle of the double entry system is that each transaction represents a transfer of resources, so that we debit the account to which resources are transferred and credit the account from which resources are transferred. This is often expressed in simplified terms as, 'credit the account which gives, debit the account which receives'. Figure 10 describes an accounting entry.

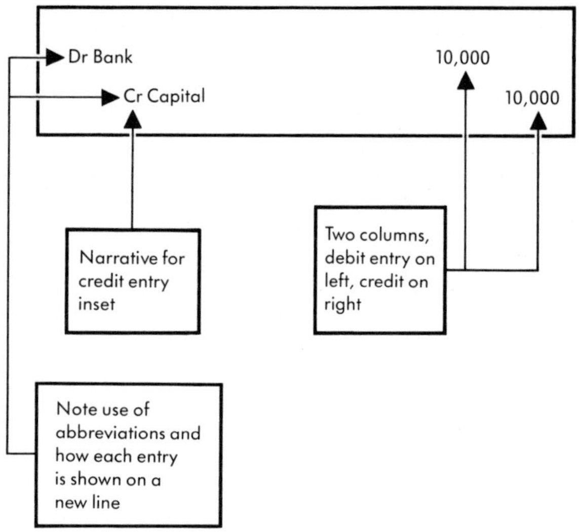

Figure 10 *Description of an accounting entry in narrative form*

2 Some students prefer to learn how to apply the double entry system by learning the effect of different types of transaction on different accounts. The resources of a business will be absorbed by assets and by items of expenditure, so any increase in these items will involve a debit entry, and any decrease a credit. Conversely the resources of a business will be derived from capital, liabilities, or income, so any increase in these items will involve a credit entry and any decrease a debit. This is summarized in Figure 11.

Figure 11 *Summary of accounting entries related to different categories of accounting item*

	Increase	*Decrease*	*Balance (normally)*
Asset	Debit	Credit	Debit
Liability	Credit	Debit	Credit
Capital	Credit	Debit	Credit
Income	Credit	Debit	Credit
Expenditure	Debit	Credit	Debit

To illustrate the workings of the double entry book-keeping system, the various transactions in Example 1 have been recorded in accounts shown in Figure 12. Considering each transaction in turn:

Transaction A

This transaction involves a transfer of resources to the bank (debited) from the proprietor (credit capital account). This is an increase in an asset and an increase in capital.

Transaction B

This is a transfer of resources to the bank (debited) from borrowing (credit Jane Dundas, the individual creditor), being an increase in an asset and an increase in a liability. When reflecting this transaction in the balance sheet (Figure 2 above) we saw that it was necessary to record somewhere in the system the person to whom each liability is owed; this record is normally kept in the ledger.

Transaction C

This is a transfer of resources to freehold property (debited) from the bank (credited), being an increase in one asset and a decrease in another.

Transaction D

In the balance sheet we showed this transaction as an increase in stock. In the ledger, however, it is normal to record all acquisitions of goods for sales in an expenditure account called 'purchases'. Accountants normally reserve the terms 'purchases' and 'sales' to describe transactions in goods bought and sold in the course of trading. Thus this will be regarded as a transfer of resources to the expenditure item purchases from the bank (credited), an increase in expenditure and a decrease in an asset.

Transaction E

This is a transfer of resources to purchases (debit) from an individual trade creditor, A. Young (credit), being an increase in an expense and an increase in a liability.

Transaction F

When preparing a balance sheet following this transaction (Figure 6) it was necessary to compute and account for the profit on the transaction. However, such calculations are normally only made in the ledger at the end of the accounting period. Thus at this stage the ledger will show that £900 has gone to the bank account (debit) from sales (credit) being an increase in an asset and an increase in an income item.

Transaction G

This is a transfer of resources of £1,700 to the debtor, Mary Baker (debit) from sales (credit), an increase in an asset and an increase in an income item.

Transaction H

This is a transfer of resources to the creditor, A. Young (debit) from the bank (credit), a decrease in an asset and a decrease in a liability.

Transaction J

This is a transfer of resources to the bank (debit) from the debtor, Mary Baker (credit), an increase in one asset and a decrease in another asset.

When first introduced to the double entry book-keeping system there are two points which often confuse students:

1 In everyday language the word 'debit' is often used to indicate a disadvantage, as in 'on the debit side we must bear in mind . . .', and the word 'credit' is often used to indicate a benefit. It is important not to try and link this everyday usage with the accountant's meaning.

Figure 12 *Extracts from the ledger of John Sinclair*

Capital

				(a)	1.1.85	Bank	10,000

Bank

(a)	1.1.85	Capital	10,000	(c)	6.1.85	Freehold property	13,000
(b)	4.1.85	Jane Dundas	6,000	(d)	7.1.85	Purchases	1,000
(f)	10.1.85	Sales	900	(h)	23.1.85	Arthur Young	1,500
(j)	29.1.85	Mary Baker	800				

Jane Dundas

				(b)	4.1.85	Bank	6,000

Freehold property

(c)	6.1.85	Bank	13,000				

Purchases

(d)	7.1.85	Bank	1,000				
(e)	8.1.85	Arthur Young	1,500				

Arthur Young

(h)	23.1.85	Bank	1,500	(e)	8.1.85	Purchases	1,500

Sales

				(f)	10.1.85	Bank	900
				(g)	15.1.85	Mary Baker	1,700

Mary Baker

(g)	15.1.85	Sales	1,700	(j)	29.1.85	Bank	800

2 In the account which records transactions with the bank a business will show receipts of money as a debit and payments of money as a credit. This is the opposite to the way in which these items will appear on the statement received from the bank. This is because a bank statement is a copy of the customer's account as recorded in the bank's own ledger. Thus an amount paid in by a customer which represents an *increase in the customer's asset* cash held at bank represents an *increase in the bank's liability* to the customer, and conversely a payment from the bank account by a customer represents a decrease in the customer's asset and a decrease in the bank's liability.

Figure 13 *Formal ledger account*

Mary Baker							
Date	*Particulars*	*Fo*	*£*	*Date*	*Particulars*	*Fo*	*£*
15.1.85	Sales	29	1,700	29.1.85	Bank	4	800

We have seen the ledger accounts presented in a simple format, the 'T' account. This is a very useful device for teaching and examination purposes, but in practice a more formal presentation would be used. Figure 13 gives an example of how the account for Mary Baker might be presented in a formal ledger. Note that the 'Folio' column (abbreviated to *Fo*) gives a reference to the account in which the other side of the accounting entry has been recorded. Thus in our example, the bank account appears to be on page 4 of the ledger, and the sales account on page 29.

Another common form of the ledger is the three-column format illustrated in Figure 14. A great advantage of this system is that the balance on the account can be identified immediately at any point in time. This form is particularly suitable where some type of mechanical system for writing up the ledger accounts is in use, so that the balance can be computed after each entry without additional labour.

It should be noted that the form of the ledger account might be varied considerably, particularly where a computer system is in operation, but the basic principles remain unchanged.

The trial balance

At the end of each accounting period it is necessary to extract a summary of the data contained in the ledger in order to prepare the accounts. In order to do this it will first be necessary to compute the balance on each ledger account, unless a three-column format is used in which case the balance will already be shown (see Figure 14). The formal method for presenting the computation of the balance on an account is illustrated by reference to

Figure 14 *Three-column form of the ledger*

Mary Baker					
Date	*Particulars*	*Fo*	*Dr*	*Cr*	*Balance*
15.1.85	Sales	29	1,700		1,700 Dr
29.1.85	Bank	4		800	900 Dr

the bank account of John Sinclair, shown in Figure 15. In this case the total on the debit side exceeds the total on the credit side by £2,200, so this is the debit balance on the account. Having computed the balance, we enter it on the *opposite* side so that the two sides each add up to the same total, which is then shown at the foot of each column. The balance is described as 'Balance carried forward' (often abbreviated to Bal c/f) and the date at which the balance is extracted is shown. Underneath the totals the account for the next accounting period is shown brought forward on the first day of the period, on the appropriate side, i.e. debit balances on the debit side, credit balances on the credit side. Some accountants prefer to refer to balances 'carried down' and 'brought down' (abbreviated to c/d and b/d) rather than 'carried *forward*' and 'brought *forward*'.

In practice at the end of an accounting period certain adjustments will be necessary before all the movements of resources in the period can be accounted for; these are discussed in Chapter 4. Therefore at the end of an accounting period it is normal to compute the balance on each account without formally closing the account, so that if any adjustment is necessary this can still be made. Whether the balances have been computed formally or informally they will then be listed in a *trial balance*. The trial balance is a list of the balances on each account extracted from the ledger, presented in two columns. Debit balances are listed in the left-hand column and credit balances in right-hand column. The trial balance for John Sinclair at 31 January 1985 is shown in Figure 16.

The two columns of the trial balance should each add up to the same total since in the double entry book-keeping system the total of each debit entry should be balanced by a corresponding credit entry. If the trial balance does not in fact balance this indicates that there has been some error. The following are the major potential sources of error:

1 An amount may have been included in the wrong column of the trial balance.
2 The trial balance columns may have been added incorrectly.

Figure 15 *Formal presentation of the balance on an account*

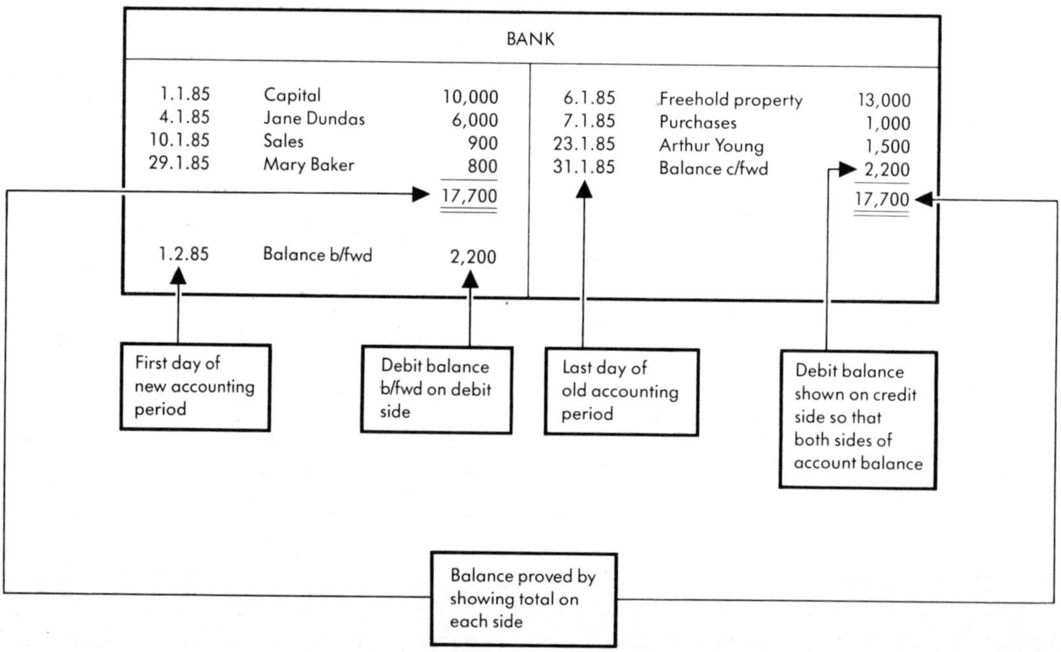

John Sinclair – Trial balance at 31 January 1985

	Dr £	*Cr* £
Capital		10,000
Bank	2,200	
Jane Dundas – Loan		6,000
Freehold property	13,000	
Purchases	2,500	
Sales		2,600
Mary Baker	900	
	18,600	18,600

Figure 16

3 There may have been an error in transferring the amount of balances from the ledger to the trial balance.
4 There may be an error in the computation of balances within the ledger.
5 There may be an error in the amounts of the entries made in the accounts in the ledger such that the totals of debit and credit are not equal.

The balancing of the trial balance does not necessarily prove the accuracy of the accounts. For example:

1 An entire transaction may be omitted.
2 Both sides of an entry might be entered more than once in error.
3 An entry might be incorrect, although both sides are properly entered.
4 A debit or credit entry might be entered in the wrong account in error.

Thus the trial balance is a useful but not infallible tool for controlling the accuracy of the accounts. Procedures for using the trial balance effectively as a control mechanism are considered under the heading 'control accounts', and the correction of errors under the heading 'suspense accounts', both covered in Chapter 3 below.

Apart from its function as a control mechanism, the trial balance is also used as a tool in the process of preparing the accounts. We have already seen that at the end of an accounting period a statement called the *profit and loss account* is presented, showing a summary of income and expenditure for an accounting period. In our trial balance there are two accounts which relate to income and expenditure, the sales account and the purchases account. There is a problem with the purchases account because part of the purchases will have been consumed during the year, and therefore should be shown as an expense, while part will be retained in stock to be sold in the following year and should therefore be shown as an asset in the balance sheet. The solution to this problem is to show the whole of the purchases as an expense in the profit and loss account, but to deduct the closing stock in order to arrive at a 'cost of sales' figure; the closing stock will then be shown in the balance sheet.

In our example 'John Sinclair' we are told that the total cost of the goods sold is £1,700 (total of items 6 and 7), and the trial balance shows total purchases £2,500. Thus closing stock must be 2,500 — 1,700 = £800. The profit and loss account will therefore report:

	£	£
Sales		2,600
Less:		
Purchases	2,500	
Less:		
Closing Stock	800	
		1,700
Profit		900

The balance sheet will appear as in Figure 9. In the following years the 'cost of sales' will be computed as:

Opening stock + Purchases – Closing stock, the closing stock being shown as an asset in the balance sheet.

So far we have only shown in the ledger the transactions during the accounting period. In order to allow the ledger to contain a complete record of the position of the business the following steps are necessary:

1 Any adjustments for movements of resources not evidenced by transactions must be made.
2 The balances on all income and expenditure accounts are transferred to the profit and loss account in the ledger. The profit and loss

account in the ledger is recorded in ledger account format. For our example John Sinclair, the transfers necessary will be:

Dr Sales	2,600	
Cr Profit and Loss (often abbreviated to P & L)		2,600
Dr Profit and Loss	2,500	
Cr Purchases		2,500

3 An account for stock is kept in the ledger. Any balance on the account at the beginning of the year is transferred to the profit and loss account, and the year end stock is debited to the stock account and credited to profit and loss. For John Sinclair the only entry necessary will relate to closing stock:

Dr Stock	800	
Cr Profit and Loss		800

4 The balance on the profit and loss account is transferred to the capital account. In our example this entry will be:

Figure 17 *Extracts from the ledger of John Sinclair*

Capital

	31.1.85	Bal. c/fwd	10,900	(a)	1.1.85	Bank	10,000
					31.1.85	P & L	900
			10,900				10,900
					1.2.85	Bal. b/fwd	10,900

Purchases

(d)	7.1.85	Bank	1,000		31.1.85	P & L	2,500
(e)	8.1.85	Arthur Young	1,500				
			2,500				2,500

Sales

	31.1.85	P & L	2,600	(f)	10.1.85	Bank	900
				(g)	15.1.85	Mary Baker	1,700
			2,600				2,600

Profit and loss account

31.1.85	Purchases	2,500	31.1.85	Sales	2,600
31.1.85	P & L	900	31.1.85	Stock	800
		3,400			3,400

Stock

31.1.85	P & L	800	31.1.85	Bal. c/fwd	800
1.2.85	Bal. b/fwd	800			

Dr Profit and Loss	900	
Cr Capital		900

5 The balances left in the ledger should now be those shown in the balance sheet. These are carried forward to the commencement of the next accounting period as illustrated in Figure 15.

Figure 17 shows how the accounts of John Sinclair affected by the closing entries will be written up.

The profit and loss account in the ledger constitutes a formal record of the income and expenditure for the accounting period. The profit and loss account as presented in the financial statements will contain the same information but will not normally be presented in a double entry format. The balance sheet lists the balances carried forward on the various accounts in the ledger. In the accounts of a private individual it is normal to show on the face of the balance sheet an explanation of the change in capital during the accounting period. This will normally be made up of:

Capital b/fwd	X
Profit	X
	X
Less: Drawings	X
	X

Drawings are amounts withdrawn by the proprietor during the year. In addition, the proprietor may have introduced new capital during the year.

Conclusion

In Chapter 1 we have seen that the role of the accountant includes the collection, processing, and analysis of financial data. The double entry book-keeping system is the mechanism whereby data is collected and processed.

Questions

1 Identify in respect of each of the following items whether it represents an asset (A), a liability (L), capital (C), income (I), or expenditure (E).

(a) A motor van used for delivering goods.
(b) A loan from the owner's mother-in-law.
(c) Wages.
(d) Rent paid.
(e) A motor car bought for resale.
(f) A bank overdraft.
(g) A bank deposit account.
(h) Sales.

2 Draw up a balance sheet for S. Perceval at 30 September 1985 based on the following list of items he owned and owed at that date:

	£
Building	20,000
Plant	51,000
Trade creditors	10,000
Stock	24,000
Bank deposit	7,000
Loan from brother	22,000
Debtors	15,000
Cash in hand	1,000

3 In respect of each of the following transactions state which accounts should be debited and which credited:

(a) John Brown commenced business and paid £20,000 into the bank.
(b) Bought goods for £12,000 from Fred Green on credit.
(c) Bought van from Jane White for £14,000, paying half in cash and agreeing to pay other half in three months' time.
(d) Sold goods on credit to Alan Pink for £5,000.
(e) Borrowed £10,000 from Mary Black and paid this amount into the bank.
(f) Withdraw £400 from bank for use as petty cash.

(g) Paid Fred Green £7,000 by cheque on account.
(h) Paid wages £800 by cheque.
(j) Paid cleaner £50 out of petty cash.
(k) Made an offer of £15,000 to Roger Red to buy his lock-up shop.

4 Joseph Anton set up in business as a consultant surveyor in July 1985. During that month he had the following transactions:

(a) 1 July he paid £5,000 of his own money in a business bank account.
(b) 2 July he paid rent on an office for the month of July £250.
(c) 3 July he purchased equipment for use in the business for £4,000.
(d) 12 July he sent an invoice to a client, Frank Williams for work done, £800
(e) 19 July he paid wages for the month of July to an assistant, £300
(f) 28 July, received an invoice for £400 for goods consumed during the month from J. Austen, payable in six weeks' time.
(g) 29 July received payment on account from Frank Williams £450.
(h) 30 July, he sent an invoice to a client, Catherine Sinclair, for work done £940

You are required:

(a) To write up the above transaction in the accounts of Joseph Anton.
(b) To extract a trial balance as at 31 July 1985
(c) To prepare a profit and loss account for the month to 31 July 1985 and a balance sheet as at that date.
(d) To complete the entries in the ledger and carry down the new balances as at 1 August 1985.

3

OPERATING THE DOUBLE ENTRY SYSTEM

Objectives

This chapter is concerned with some detailed aspects of the way in which the double entry book-keeping system is operated. The objectives are:

1 To give a broad view of the way in which the double entry book-keeping system is operated.
2 To explain the way in which transactions are summarized prior to entry in the ledger.
3 To discuss the special mechanisms developed for recording bank and cash transactions, and to look at the bank reconciliation statement.
4 To consider ways in which the ledger can be broken down and the uses of control accounts.
5 To explain how the suspense account is used as a tool for the correction of errors.

Overview of the recording system

Figure 18 gives an overview of the accounting system:

1 The record of the position of the business at the commencement of the accounting period is brought into the ledger in the balances brought forward.
2 As transactions during the period occur it is normal, in most accounting systems, to make a summary of these in what are called 'books of prime entry'. The reason for this is that it would normally be inconvenient to require access to the ledger in order to record each individual transaction. These books of prime entry are often referred to as 'day books' or 'journals', and are considered in detail below.
3 The summary of transactions will be entered periodically in the ledger; the process of making an entry in the ledgers is termed 'posting'.
4 As we have already seen in Chapter 2 above, at the end of an accounting period a list of balances is extracted from the ledger.
5 Following the extraction of a trial balance it is normally necessary to make adjustments to account for any movement of resources which has not been evidenced by a transaction. These adjustments are normally made initially in some type of working schedule outside the ledger. The nature and purpose of these adjustments is considered in detail in Chapter 4 below.
6 Following the adjustments a profit and loss account for presentation is prepared, together with a balance sheet.
7 When the profit and loss account and balance sheet have been prepared, all the adjustments following extraction of the trial balance are entered in the ledger and balances are carried forward.

Books of prime entry

As we have seen, it is normal to summarize the transactions of a business in books of prime entry prior to entry in the ledger. The books of prime entry which are used will depend upon the nature of the business, but can be considered under three broad headings:

Figure 18 *Overview of the recording system*

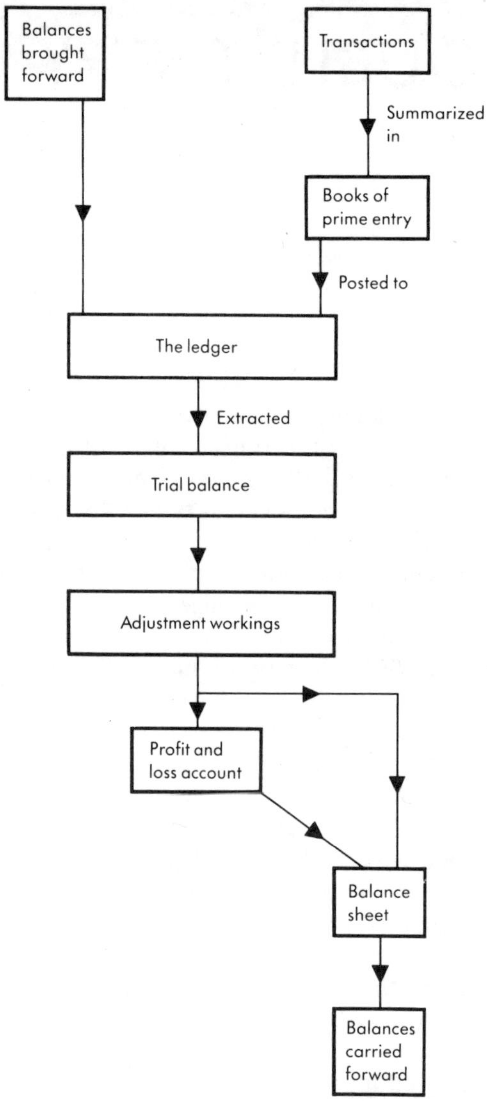

1 Records of payment and receipts of cash, whether going through the bank or petty cash. These are considered in detail later in this chapter.
2 Records of sale or purchase transaction on credit terms.
3 Records of assorted other entries, summarized in one book, 'the journal'.

Credit purchase and sales transactions are normally evidenced by a document known as an *invoice*. The invoice is a document sent from a supplier to a customer showing details of the transaction. Figure 19 shows an illustration of how an invoice might appear. A customer will retain the invoice received as evidence of the transaction and as the basis of the accounting records; often the recipient of an invoice will attach their own sequential number to the document on receipt as a way of identifying it and also as a control mechanism. A supplier will send the original copy of a sales invoice to the customer but will normally retain one or more copies for recording purposes; normally the supplier will control the issue of invoices by numbering them sequentially prior to issue.

It sometimes happens that by agreement between a customer and a supplier goods bought on credit are returned to a supplier. In this case a *credit note* would be issued by the supplier to the customer, abating the original charge for the goods.

The specimen invoice in Figure 19 uses the term 'discount' in two different ways:

1 *Trade discount* is an abatement of price allowed by a supplier to specific customers. It is a device which makes it possible for a supplier to charge different prices to different customers, normally related to the volume of purchases by the customer. From the point of view of the purchaser the cost of goods is regarded as the price net of trade discount.
2 *Cash discount* is a reduction in price allowed if an invoice is paid within a specified period of time. From the point of view of both seller and purchaser it is normal to regard cash discount as a separate item of expenditure or income, not as constituting a reduction in sales or purchases.

The data on the invoice is summarized in a 'purchase day book' or 'sales day book' as appropriate. The data on credit notes can be summarized as negative items in the purchase or sales day book. Where the size of the business is such that there are a large number of credit notes they may be separately summarized in a 'returns inwards book' (for returns from customers) and a 'returns outwards book' (for returns to suppliers).

Example 2 summarizes the data on five invoices:

Figure 19 *Example of a purchase invoice*

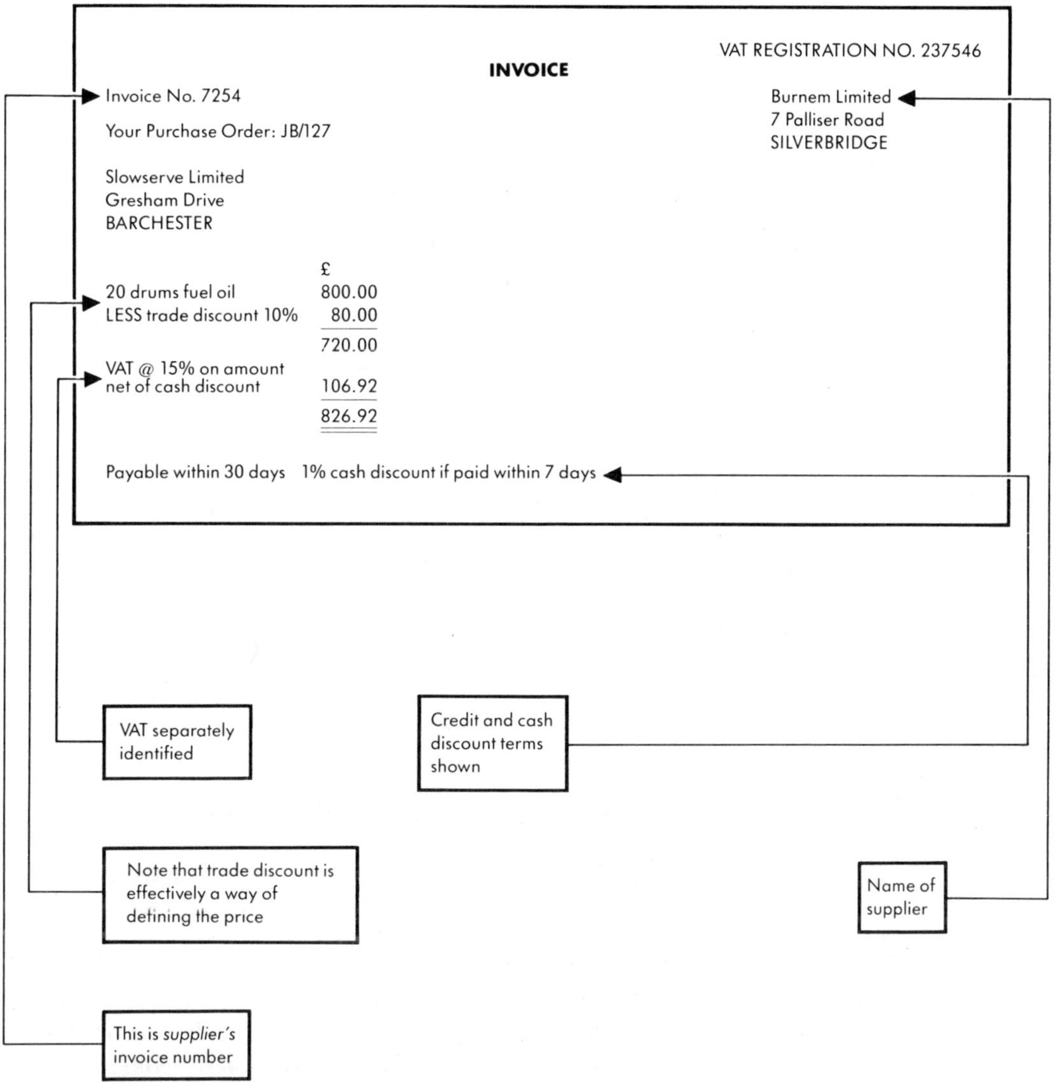
VAT REGISTRATION NO. 237546

INVOICE

Invoice No. 7254

Your Purchase Order: JB/127

Burnem Limited
7 Palliser Road
SILVERBRIDGE

Slowserve Limited
Gresham Drive
BARCHESTER

	£
20 drums fuel oil	800.00
LESS trade discount 10%	80.00
	720.00
VAT @ 15% on amount net of cash discount	106.92
	826.92

Payable within 30 days 1% cash discount if paid within 7 days

Example 2

Slowserve Ltd is a company owning a retail store which sells both food and a range of household goods. In the first week of September 1985 the following purchase invoices were received:

3 September – Burnem Ltd. for heating fuel, £600 plus £90 VAT (B3/157)

3 September – Frost Food PLC for supplies of food £2,900 (no VAT) (F8/158)

5 September – J. Shoddy, repairs to company van, £400 plus £60 VAT (S4/159)

6 September – Fabricators Ltd, supply of towels for resale £700 plus £105 VAT (F7/160)

7 September – Food Supplies Ltd, Dairy Products £1,500 and Carrier Bags £100, plus

£15 VAT on the carrier bags (F4/161)

After each transaction the customer account reference and the internal invoice number are shown.

Figure 20 shows how this data would be summarized in a day book:

1 The data recorded would normally be the date of receipt of the invoice rather than the date of despatch by the supplier.
2 The invoice number would normally be the number allocated by the business itself.
3 Particulars show the name of the supplier.
4 The folio (Fo) column shows the reference to the account of the individual supplier.
5 The 'total' column shows the total amount owing to the supplier. Each amount in the total column will be posted to the credit side of the individual supplier.
6 The analysis column gives a breakdown of the type of expense represented by each invoice. The total of each analysis column will be debited to the appropriate ledger account for that expense.

Thus we can see that the total debits will be equal to the total credits.

The sales day book can similarly be analysed according to the information needed by the business, e.g. type of goods sold, geographical area of sale.

The form in which the day books are written up will depend on the nature of business.

The word 'journal' can be used as an alternative to the word 'day book', so that we can speak of a 'sales journal' or 'purchase journal'. However, when accountants refer to 'the journal' they are referring to a special book which embraces all accounting entries not covered by any other book of prime entry.

Since transactions which recur frequently will normally be summarized in their own book of prime entry the journal normally covers items which only have to be considered occasionally, such as:

1 Corrections of errors, a topic considered in depth under the heading 'suspense accounts' below.
2 Closing entries, when the accounts for the year are finalized.
3 Items which arise from transactions not evidenced by documentation.

Figure 21 shows an example of how a journal entry might be presented. The 'folio' (fo) column shows the reference to the page of the ledger to which the entry is to be posted. Traditionally debit entries are shown first preceded with the word 'by', credit entries are preceded by the word 'to', and the ensuing explanation commences 'being'; in modern practice this convention is often dispensed with.

Bank and cash transactions

The term 'cash book' is commonly used to describe the book in which a record of bank transactions is kept, while the term 'petty cash book' is commonly used to describe the book in which cash transactions are recorded. Often these books are kept in a form that allows the balance at the bank or of petty cash to be identified, so that these books are regarded as

Figure 20 *Example of a columnar purchases day book*

Date	*Invoice number*	*Particulars*	*Fo*	*Total*	*Food purchases*	*Non-food purchases*	*Motor expenses*	*Heating fuel*	*Sundries*	*VAT*
3.9.85	157	Burnem Ltd	B3	690				600		90
3.9.85	158	Frostfood PLC	F8	2,900	2,900					
5.9.85	159	J. Shoddy	S4	460			400			60
6.9.85	160	Fabricators Ltd	F7	805		700				105
7.9.85	161	Foodsupplies Ltd	F4	1,615	1,500				100	15
				6,470	4,400	700	400	600	100	270

Figure 21 *Example of a journal entry*

Date	Particulars	Fo	Dr £	Cr £
30 June 1985	By interest payable	27	50	
	To H. Jones	34		50
	Being a half year's interest at 10% p.a. on loan from H. Jones			

Note that 'by', 'to' and 'being' are rather antiquated and often dispensed with.

the ledger accounts for bank and cash amounts while at the same time serving as books of prime entry for the purpose of posting the other side of each entry.

Frequently the cash book is split into a cash payments book and a cash receipts book, with analysis columns similar to those provided in purchase and sales day books. The cash book will also include a 'discount' column, showing the cash discount related to sums paid and received; the discount is posted to the individual debtor and creditor accounts, and in total to the discount allowed or discount received account.

A form of cash book which may be used in a business with relatively few cash and bank transactions is the three-column cash book, whereby on each side of a folio of a ledger there are shown three columns, one each for discount, cash, and bank items. The operation of a three-column cash book is illustrated with Example 3:

Example 3

In the first week of July 1985 Slowserve Ltd had the following cash and bank transactions:

1 At 1 July 1985 cash in hand was £50, the bank account was £1,150 overdrawn.
2 On 2 July 1985 takings of £2,400 were paid straight into the bank.
3 On 3 July 1985 £28 was paid in cash to the cleaners; also an amount of £1,000 owed to a supplier J. Austen was paid with a cheque for £990, a discount of £10 for prompt payment being taken.
4 On 4 July a debtor W. Scott paid by cheque £540, taking advantage of a £5 discount for prompt payment; on the same date £40 cash was taken out of the bank.
5 On 5 July salaries were paid with a cheque for £440.

Figure 22 shows how these items would be written up in a three-column cash book. It should be noted that the 'cash' and 'bank' columns each represent an account in the ledger, while the discount column does not.

A useful control over the records of bank transactions kept by the business is to make a comparison with the data in the bank statement. In order to make this comparison it is normally necessary to prepare a *bank reconciliation statement*, because it rarely happens that the balance in the records of the business agrees with the balance on the bank statement. The bank reconciliation explains the differences between the two balances, which can arise for the following reasons:

1 There may be errors in the way in which the cash book has been written up; prior to compiling the bank reconciliation these errors will be corrected.
2 There may be items which the business will only become aware of when the bank statement is received, such as bank charges, bank interest,

Figure 22 *Example of a three-column cash book*

Date	Particulars	Fo	Discount	Cash	Bank	Date	Particulars	Fo	Discount	Cash	Bank
1.7.85	Balance b/d			50		1.7.85	Balance b/d				1,150
2.7.85	Sales	79			2,400	3.7.85	Cleaning	21		28	
4.7.85	W. Scott	84	5		540	3.7.85	J. Austin	5	10		990
4.7.85	Bank	C		40		4.7.85	Cash	C			40
						5.7.85	Salaries	77			440
						5.7.85	Balance c/d			62	320
			5	90	2,940				10	90	
6.7.85	Balance b/d			62	320						2,940

Balances carried down on these two accounts

No balance struck on discount column because this is not an account

'C' stands for 'contra'

dishonoured cheques, and payments by standing order or direct debit. These will be entered in the cash book before compiling the bank reconciliation.

3 There may be errors in the preparation of the bank statement. These will be brought to the attention of the bank, and the first stage in the presentation of the bank reconciliation statement will be to show the balance on the face of the statement and then an adjustment to correct any errors.

4 Amounts paid into the bank and shown in the cash book may not yet have appeared on the bank statement at the date under consideration. The second stage of the bank reconciliation will be to show the bank statement balance adjusted, for these items. These items described as *uncleared bankings*, will be verified when traced on a subsequent bank statement.

5 Cheques drawn by the business and shown in the cash book may not yet have appeared on the bank statement at the date under consideration. The third stage of the bank reconciliation statement will be to show an adjustment for these items. For the purposes of verification these *outstanding cheques* will be traced to a subsequent bank statement.

The adjusted balance on the bank reconciliation statement should then be the same as the balance in the cash book. Example 4 illustrates the kind of differences that can arise:

Example 4

The accountant at Slowserve Ltd has just received

the bank statement covering the month of October. The bank statement shows a balance in hand of £3,250 at the end of the month while the cash book shows a balance of £5,331. A comparison of the cash book and bank statement reveals:

(a) A payment by cheque of £89 has been entered in the cash book as £98.
(b) A payment by cheque £60 has been shown in the cash book as a cash receipt in error.
(c) A cheque for £510 received from a debtor and entered in the cash book as a receipt has been returned by the bank and marked 'refer to drawer'; no entry to reflect the return of the cheque has been made in the cash book.
(d) Bank charges of £120 have not been recorded in the cash book.
(e) The bank has charged interest charges of £300 to Slowserve Ltd on a loan which in fact relates to another company. This error has been drawn to the attention of the bank who have agreed to correct the error.
(f) A payment into the bank of £2,400 on 30 October is not shown in the October bank statement; later examination of the November bank statement shows this item cleared by the bank on 2 November.
(g) Cheques for payment totalling £1,360 recorded in the October cash book were not presented to the bank until November.

The bank reconciliation statement is shown in Figure 23. Note that item 2, the cheque entered on the wrong side, has to be deducted as 2 x £60 to represent correction of the erroneous debit and insertion of the required credit, each of £60.

The imprest system

This is a system of control for the petty cash. The cashier is entrusted with an initial fixed sum. Periodically there is paid into petty cash an amount equal to total disbursements, thus restoring petty cash to the original amount. Each disbursement should be evidenced by a *voucher*, which should be made available to the official responsible for signing the cheque to replace the expended cash. Thus at any time a count of the petty cash should find cash with vouchers to the amount of the cash *float*.

Figure 23 *Example of a bank reconciliation statement*

Bank reconciliation

		£
Balance per bank statement		3,250
Correction of bank error (e)		300
Corrected balance		3,550
Add:		
Uncleared bankings (f)		2,400
		5,950
Less:		
o/s cheques (g)		1,360
Balance per corrected cash book		4,590

Cash book corrections

	£	£
Balance b/fwd		5,331
Add:		
(a) Adjustment re cheque wrongly entered		9
		5,340
Less:		
(b) Correction of cheque entered on wrong side	120	
(c) Returned cheque	510	
(d) Bank charges	120	
		750
Corrected balance		4,590

Control accounts

So far we have envisaged the ledger as a single collection of accounts. In practice it is common to split the ledger into sections. One example of such a split would be a *sales ledger*, containing the accounts of all customers, a *purchases ledger*, containing the accounts of all suppliers, and an *impersonal ledger* containing all other accounts. Sometimes the sales or purchase ledgers will be further subdivided.

Where the ledger is split in this way it is normal practice to maintain what are called *control accounts* or *total accounts* in respect of the sales ledger and the purchase ledger. These control accounts will contain the totals of each kind of transaction which affects the sales or purchase ledgers. The books of prime entry will be designed to make this practical; for example cash book will include separate analysis columns for payments to suppliers and receipts from customers so that the total amount can be posted in the control account. The uses of control accounts are:

1 They can reveal errors in the ledger, although it does not necessarily reveal all errors because in some cases both the control account and the ledger need adjustment.
2 They can help in the location of error where the trial balance does not balance, since the search for error can be concentrated on the appropriate part of the ledger.
3 Management can gain access to the total debtor and creditor amounts at any time without the need to extract a full list of ledger balances.
4 Where the control account is prepared by a responsible official independent of the preparation of the ledger a useful internal control mechanism is provided.

The preparation of a control account can be illustrated by working through Example 5, taken from an examination paper set by a professional accounting body:

Example 5

The following figures are taken from the books of Mortimer Ltd for the month of March:

	£
Sales ledger balances at 1 March – debit	30,693
– credit	317
Purchase ledger balances at 1 March – debit	172
– credit	27,322
Credit sales	37,197
Cash sales	19,743
Credit purchases	22,144
Receipts from credit customers	33,221
Payments to trade creditors	29,446
Discounts received	1,629
Discounts allowed	1,743
Interest charged to debtors	20
Returns inwards	655
Returns outwards	443
Bad debts written off	590
Sales ledger debits cancelled against purchase ledger	120
Debtors cheques dishonoured	332
Sales ledger balance at 31 March – credit	497
Purchase ledger balance at 31 March – debit	232

You are required to prepare the following accounts for the month of March, using such of the above figures as you consider necessary:

1 Sales ledger control account, and;
2 Purchase ledger control account.

(Society of Company and Commercial Accountants P1, November 1981)

The solution to Example 5 is presented in Figure 24. The following points are noted:

1 The sales ledger may include a small number of credit balances and the purchase ledger a small number of debit balances because of such factors as overpayments made in error, payments in advance, and returns of good already paid for. The control account can only identify a net balance.
2 Bad debts are considered in detail in Chapter 7 below. When it is assumed that a debtor will not pay, it is normal practice to write off the amount owing as a 'bad debt'.
3 It sometimes happens that a business is both a supplier to, and a customer of another business, so that the same business might appear with an account in the sales ledger and an account in the purchase ledger. In such a case it is common to make a 'contra' entry so that the smaller balance is set off against the larger, leaving only a net amount to be paid or received.

When correcting errors in a control account or a related ledger it is important to bear in mind that one or the other lies outside the scope of the double entry system as such, so that corrections will not necessarily be reflected in a corresponding entry on the other side of the accounting equation.

A further control which can be used in respect of

Mortimer Limited

(a) **Sales ledger control account**

1 March	Balance b/d	30,693	1 March	Balance b/d	317
	Sales	37,197		Bank	33,221
	Interest	20		Discount	1,743
				Returns	655
	Bank	332		Bad debts	590
				Contra	120
31 March	Balance c/d	497	31 March	Balance c/d	32,093
		68,739			68,739
1 April	Balance b/d	32,093	1 April	Balance b/d	497

(b) **Purchase ledger control account**

1 March	Balance b/d	172	1 March	Balance b/d	27,322
	Bank	29,446		Purchases	22,144
	Discount	1,629	31 March	Balance c/d	232
	Returns	443			
	Contra	120			
31 March	Balance c/d	17,888			
		49,698			49,698
1 April	Balance b/d	232	1 April	Balance b/d	17,888

Figure 24

the purchase ledger is to reconcile the balance on each account with the related supplier's statement. This exercise, similar in character to the bank reconciliation considered above, serves two purposes:

1 It serves as a control on the accuracy and honesty with which the purchase ledger is operated.
2 It helps to identify items which have been received in the accounting period but may have been recorded as purchased in a different accounting period, or vice versa. This is commonly used by auditors as a 'cut-off' test.

Suspense accounts

The two main functions of a suspense account are:
1 As an account for any item the nature of which is unclear at the time of posting. When the nature of the item is clarified it is then transferred to the appropriate account.
2 As an account to which any difference on the trial balance is posted pending discovery of the reasons for the difference. When the errors are discovered the balance is transferred to the appropriate accounts.

When correcting errors it is necessary to understand how the book-keeping system works in order to work out what correction is needed. If we consider Example 6:

Example 6

On extracting the trial balance of Slowserve Ltd as at 31 December 1985 a difference of £2,065 was found; in order to achieve a balance a suspense account has been opened with a credit balance.

An investigation of the books has revealed:

(a) A purchase invoice from Fastfood Ltd for £1,500 has been inadvertently posted from the purchase day book to the debit of Fastfood's account in the purchase ledger.
(b) A page in the purchase day book showing total food purchases of £1,050 was posted to the food purchase account as £1,005.

(c) A petty cash balance of £50 was omitted from the trial balance.
(d) A sale on credit terms of £110 was debited in the sales ledger to J. Burrow, when the sale was in fact to J.Burrough.
(e) Bank interest charges of £840 were correctly entered in the cash book when the bank reconciliation statement was prepared but the other side of the double entry has not been recorded.

It is common for examiners to require students to prepare both journal entries and a suspense account for the correction of errors. The journal entries for Example 6 are shown in Figure 25 and the suspense account in Figure 26 considering each error:

(a) Where an item has been posted to the debit instead of the credit side of the account the adjustment to be made will be double the amount of the item, to remove the erroneous £1,500 debit and then to introduce the required £1,500 credit.
(b) Since the individual purchase invoices will have been posted correctly to the purchase ledger, it is only necessary to correct the entry in the food purchases account.
(c) An omitted balance is inserted into the trial balance by transfer from the suspense account.
(d) This error does not affect the suspense account but must still be corrected.
(e) A simple case of rectifying the omission of a posting of one side of an entry.

Figure 25

Date		*Particulars*	*Fo*	*Dr*	*Cr*
31.12.85	(a)	Suspense account		3,000	
		Fastfood Limited			3,000
		Correction of items £1,500 debited instead of credited to Fastfood Limited			
31.12.85	(b)	Food purchases		45	
		Suspense account			45
		Correction of error in cast of purchase ledger			
31.12.85	(c)	Petty cash		50	
		Suspense account			50
		Petty cash balance omitted from trial balance			
31.12.85	(d)	J. Burrough		110	
		J. Burrough			110
		Correction of posting of sales invoice to wrong account			
31.12.85	(e)	Interest charges		840	
		Suspense account			840
		Correction of omission to post this item from cash book			

Figure 26 *Use of the suspense account*

Suspense account

31.12.85	Fastfood Limited	3,000	31.12.85	Balance b/d	2,065
			31.12.85	Food purchases	45
			31.12.85	Petty cash	50
			31.12.85	Interest charges	840
		3,000			3,000

Conclusion

In this chapter we have considered some of the detail of the operations of the data control system, and have seen that an understanding of the workings of the data collection system is important to the correction of errors. In later chapters we will see that examiners often present questions which link an understanding of suspense accounts to preparation of the financial statements, and in Chapter 9 we will see that an understanding of control accounts is often essential to the preparation of accounts from incomplete records.

Questions

1 Prepare a bank reconciliation for the Dover Company at May 31 of the current year, using the following information:

(a) Balance per cash account, May 31, £3,105.15
(b) Balance per bank statement, May 31, £3,150.25
(c) Deposits not reflected on bank statement, £454.00
(d) Outstanding cheques, May 31, £634.10
(e) Service charge on bank statement, not recorded in books, £5
(f) Error by bank – cheque of Rover Company charged on Dover Company's bank statement, £150
(g) Cheque for advertising expense, £460, incorrectly recorded as £480 in books.

(Heriot-Watt University, 1982)

2 As the accountant with Smithers Ltd you are asked to deal with the following problems:

The summarized cash-book as at 30 November 1982 is as follows:

Opening balance b/d	£ 2,130	Payments	£92,640
Receipts	£89,400		
Closing balance c/d	£ 1,110		
	£92,640		£92,640

The closing balance does not agree with the figure of £5,454 overdrawn appearing on the bank statement at the same date. On investigation you discover that:

(a) The opening balance in the cash-book should have been carried down as £2,310
(b) The bank has charged interest of £29 on 15 November 1982 but this has not been entered in the cash-book.
(c) Cheques totalling £12,730 were paid to suppliers on 28 November 1982. On 30 November 1982 only £9,430 of these had been presented for payment.
(d) A cheque for £60 has been entered in the cash-book as a receipt.
(e) Standing orders for £300 for insurance premiums had been paid by the bank on 21 November 1982 but no entry had been made in the cash-book.
(f) A cheque for £45 has been returned by the bank marked 'Refer to drawer' but has not been adjusted in the cash-book.
(g) On 29 November 1982 cheques from customers amounting to £7,300 were deposited in the bank but were not credited by the bank until 2 December 1982.
(h) On 14 November 1982 a customer sent a cheque for £970 in payment of an invoice for £1,000. The only entry in the cash-book is for £1,000.

Required:

(a) Show the necessary adjustments to be made in the cash-book and prepare a bank reconciliation statement as at 30 November 1982.
(b) Briefly describe two other areas in which checks are frequently made to prove the accuracy of the recording process.

(University of Stirling, 1982)

3 Balances and transactions affecting a company's control accounts for the month of May 1982 are listed below:

	£
Balances at 1 May 1982:	
Sales ledger	9,123 (debit)
	211 (credit)
Purchases ledger	4,490 (credit)
	88 (debit)

Transactions during May 1982:

Purchases on credit	18,135
Allowances from suppliers	629
Receipts from customers by cheque	27,370
Sales on credit	36,755
Discounts received	1,105
Payments to creditors by cheque	15,413
Contra settlements	3,046
Allowances to customers	1,720
Bills of exchange receivable	6,506
Customers' cheques dishonoured	489
Cash receipts from credit customers	4,201
Refunds to customers for overpayment of accounts	53
Discounts allowed	732

Balances at 31 May 1982:

Sales ledger	136 (credit)
Purchases ledger	67 (debit)

Required

(a) Explain the purposes for which control accounts are prepared.
(b) Post the sales ledger and purchases ledger control accounts for the month of May 1982 and derive the respective debit and credit closing balances on 31 May 1982.

(ACA Level 1, December 1982)

4 The trial balance of Hannay Ltd as at 31 January 1986 failed to balance when first extracted, and was posted to a suspense account. However, when the following errors had been discovered and dealt with the balance on the suspense account was cleared:

(a) A sales invoice to E. Leithen was entered correctly in the sales day book as £42 but was incorrectly recorded in E. Leithen's account as £24.
(b) A credit balance of £120 on the 'sundry income' account had been omitted from the trial balance.
(c) A sales invoice to Blenkiron PLC for £23 was entered in the sales day book as £32.
(d) A purchase invoice from P. Black for £52 had been entered in the purchase day book as coming from D. Black, and been posted to D. Black's account in the purchase ledger.
(e) The analysis column in the purchase day book for motor expenses had been added up as £4,790, but should have been added as £3,890.
(f) A cash refund of £40 road tax had been correctly entered in the cash-book but entered on the debit side of the motor expenses account.

You are required:

(a) To show the journal entries to correct these errors.
(b) To show the suspense account.

4

INTRODUCTION TO THE PREPARATION AND PRINCIPLES OF ACCOUNTS

Objectives

In Chapters 2 and 3 we have examined the double entry book-keeping system. In Chapter 5 to 9 we look in detail at the way in which we account for various types of asset and liability and report these in the final accounts. The objective of this chapter is to introduce the various types of adjustment made in preparing the accounts and to outline some of the conventions which underlie the preparation of accounts. Specifically this chapter:

1 Discusses the various types of post trial balance adjustment, and in particular covers 'accruals' and 'prepayments' in some detail.
2 Considers how to handle post trial balance adjustments under examination conditions.
3 Looks at some accounting conventions, and at the limitations of traditional accounting information.

Nature and purpose of post trial balance adjustments

Figure 18 summarizes the stages in preparing a set of accounts and shows that at the trial balance stage the balances on the accounts reflect:

1 The balances brought down at the beginning of the accounting period
2 The movements of resources during the year which have been evidenced by transactions.

At this stage we have seen that a number of adjustments have to be made in order to identify all the movements of resources during the year which have not been evidenced by transactions and summarized in the books of prime entry. The major reasons for requiring adjustments are:

Stock

The need to make an adjustment to the year-end trial balance in respect of stock has already been explained in Chapter 2 above, while the accounting problems that can arise in relation to stock are considered in detail in Chapter 7.

Depreciation

Depreciation is the process whereby the cost of fixed assets is allocated between the accounting periods in which the fixed assets are consumed. This topic is discussed in detail in Chapter 6 below. The accounting entry made for depreciation will be:

Dr P & L (depreciation)
Cr Fixed asset

In practice the credit is often made to a 'Provision for depreciation' account, which is in turn deducted from the cost of the fixed asset on the face of the balance sheet, rather than directly to the fixed asset account.

Debtors

At the end of the year the business may find that certain debtors are unlikely to pay, so that they should be written off as 'bad debts', or a 'provision' should be made against them. This topic is considered in detail in Chapter 7 below.

Accruals and prepayments

When services are supplied to the business, it frequently happens that the period during which the service is rendered spans the balance sheet date. In such a case it is necessary to allocate the cost of the service between the accounting periods to which it relates. The converse can arise in relation to services rendered.

When at the end of a year a business has received the benefit of services for which no invoice is recorded in the accounts until the following year, the cost of the service is recorded as an *accrued expense*, being added to the expense shown in the profit and loss account and recorded as a current liability in the balance sheet. In the following year the amount of the accrual will then be deducted from the total expense for the year. The way in which this adjustment is reflected in the double entry system can be illustrated with Example 7 'Porthos', being shown in Figure 27 and explained as follows:

1 Cash expended in the year will be shown in the expense account following the routine entry:

Dr Electricity	1275	
Cr Cash		1275

2 At the year end there is a further amount owing in relation to electricity consumed during November and December 1985. The bill covering this period also covers the month of January 1986, so that the 1985 portion of the bill can be estimated as:

$$\frac{2}{3} \times £450 = £300$$

This amount is carried down as a liability on the electricity account.

3 After inserting the balance to be carried down in the electricity account, the balance left on the account is then transferred to profit and loss. We can see that, as a result of the entries made, the expense shown in the profit and loss account will include both the electricity paid for during 1985 and the electricity consumed during the last two months of the year but not paid for until 1986.

4 During 1986 cash paid is recorded with the routine entry:

Dr Electricity	1,496	
Cr Cash		1,496

of this £1,496, an amount of £300 related to 1985. The 1985 accrual of £300 has been brought down as a credit balance in 1986, so that the balance on the electricity account at this point in time of £1,196 (1,496 – 300) represents payments during 1986 in respect of electricity supplied during 1986, excluding the £300 paid in 1986 relating to 1985.

5 At the end of 1986 it is necessary to compute once again the accrued expense, being:

$$\frac{2}{3} \times £570 = £380$$

This £380 is carried down as a liability on the electricity account.

6 The balance remaining on the electricity account in 1986 is then transferred to the 1986 profit and loss account.

Example 7

Porthos commenced business on 1 January 1985. In the year to 31 December 1985 he paid electricity bills amounting to £1,275. On 18 February 1986 he

Figure 27

Electricity			
(a) 1985 Cash	1,275	(c) 31.12.85 P & L	1,575
(b) 31.12.85 Bal c/d	300		
	1,575		1,575
(d) 1986 Cash	1,496	(b) 1.12.86 Bal b/d	300
(e) 31.12.86 Bal c/d	380	(f) 31.12.86 P & L	1,576
	1,876		1,876
		(e) 1.1.87 Bal b/d	380

received an electricity bill for £450 which covered the period 1 November 1985 to 31 January 1986.

In the year to 31 December 1986 he paid electricity bills (including the one received on 18 February 1986) amounting to £1,496, and on 20 February 1987 received a bill covering the quarter from 1 November 1986 to 31 January 1987 amounting to £570.

Example 8 extends the example Porthos to three other possible situations, illustrated in Figure 28. Briefly considering each of these:

1 The insurance position is an example of where a service has been paid for in advance. This *prepaid expense* is deducted from the expenses for the year and carried down as a current asset in the balance sheet.
2 The rent received in advance is an example of *prepaid income*, carried down as a current liability to reflect the fact that the service in respect of which cash has been received is still 'owing'. The converse situation, where income has been earned but not received, would be termed *accrued income*.
3 The road haulage example shows how an accrual can arise not in relation to a service split between accounting periods but simply because an amount paid in one accounting period in fact relates to another.

Figure 28

Insurance

1985 Cash	420	31.12.85 Bal c/d	40
		31.12.85 P & L	380
	420		420
1.1.86 Bal b/d	40	31.12.85 Bal c/d	50
1986 Cash	570	31.12.85 P & L	560
	610		610
1.1.87 Bal b/d	50		

Rent receivable

31.12.85 Bal c/d	500	1.7.85 Cash	1,000
31.12.85 P & L	500		
	1,000		1,000
31.12.86 Bal c/d	500	1.1.86 Bal b/d	500
31.12.86 P & L	1,000	1.1.86 Cash	1,000
	1,500		1,500
		1.1.87 Bal b/d	500

Distribution costs

1985 Cash	1,240	31.12.85 P & L	1,300
31.12.85 Bal c/d	60		
	1,300		1,300
1986 Cash	1,390	1.1.86 Bal b/d	60
		31.12.86 P & L	1,330
	1,390		1,390

Example 8

Porthos, introduced in the example above, also included the following transactions in his accounts during the first two years of trading.

1 During 1985 he paid insurance costs of £420, including an amount of £160 covering property insurance for the period 1 April 1985 to 31 March 1986. During 1986 insurance costs paid were £570, including property insurance for 1 April 1986 to 31 March 1987 of £200.
2 Porthos rented out part of his premises to Joel, commencing on 1 July 1985 when Joel paid one year's rent of £1,000 in advance. On 1 July 1986 Joel again paid £1,000 as one year's rent in advance.
3 Porthos paid a road haulage firm in cash £1,240 for delivering his products in 1985. In February 1986 it was discovered that Porthos had been undercharged £60 for a delivery made in 1985, and payment of this amount was included in the cash paid for road haulage in 1986 of £1,390.

In practice the identification of accruals and prepayments is normally made easier by the fact that accounts are prepared some time after the year end date. Where an invoice in respect of a service has not been received when the accounts are prepared an estimate of the necessary accrual must be made.

Accruals and prepayments are shown in the

balance sheet as current liabilities and current assets respectively, normally immediately under trade creditors and trade debtors. Sometimes accruals are shown as part of trade creditors and prepayments as part of trade debtors.

Appropriations

When the profit for the year is computed it may be necessary, depending on the form of business entity, to work out how the profit is to be shared amongst those with an interest in the business. This is considered in detail in Chapter 5 below.

Correction of error

One common form of post trial balance adjustment arises when it is necessary to correct errors made in the accounting system during the year. This topic is covered in detail in Chapter 3 above.

Handling the adjustments

We have already seen that at the end of an accounting period the trial balance will summarize the balances brought down at the beginning of the year and the transactions which have occurred during the year. Having extracted the trial balance it will then be necessary to make the various adjustments we have considered above in order to prepare the profit and loss account and balance sheet.

Examination questions are normally presented in the form of a trial balance followed by a list of matters which require adjustment. Under examination conditions, where time is short and the number of adjustments to be made is normally small, the technique normally used is as follows:

1 Look through the list of matters requiring adjustment and make a mark against each item in the trial balance affected by any adjustment.
2 Work through each item in the trial balance, transferring it directly to the face of the profit and loss account or balance sheet if it does not require adjustment. Any item which does require adjustment should be transferred to a working schedule.
3 Work through the items requiring adjustment, incorporating each in the appropriate working schedule. At this stage it is important to remember that each adjustment to the trial balance must follow the basic double entry principle of applying to each side of the balance sheet equation.
4 Transfer the data from the working to the face of the answer, total the profit and loss account, then total the balance sheet.

There are a variety of ways of presenting workings. The two must common are:

1 Show any necessary workings on the face of the answer, in brackets next to the related item.
2 Show the item to be adjusted in a 'T account', and complete the adjustments in double entry format.

The first method is very much quicker, but the second method is easier to think through. In practice it is common to combine the two approaches, showing simple adjustments on the face of the answer.

Example 9 shows a simple case of how an examination question might be formulated.

Example 9

At 31 December 1985, Athos, who was in business as a retailer of wines and spirits, extracted the following trial balance:

	£	£
Stock 1 January 1985	21,000	
Purchases	117,000	
Sales		150,000
Wages	14,000	
Rent	2,000	
Rates	1,500	
Insurance	780	
Motor expenses	1,220	
Fixtures and fittings	25,200	
Motor van	2,100	
Debtors	5,300	
Creditors		8,900
Bank	1,150	

Drawings	8,400	
Capital		40,750
	199,650	199,650

The following information is to be taken into account:

1 Stock at 31 December 1985 was £22,500.
2 Rates include £300 paid in advance; an amount of £120 in respect of 1985 insurance costs was not paid until 1986.
3 Fixtures and fittings are to be depreciated by £2,500 and the motor van is to be depreciated by £700.

The profit and loss account for Athos is formulated in Figure 29 and the balance sheet in Figure 30. The steps in preparing this answer, working steadily through the question, are:

1 Head the profit and loss account, showing the name of the subject and relevant dates. In attempting examination questions students often neglect these simple points of presentation.
2 Enter opening stock on the face of the profit and loss account (P & L) as part of cost of sales.
3 Similarly enter purchases as part of cost of sales.
4 Enter sales on the face of the P & L.
5 Enter wages on the face of the P & L.
6 Enter rent on the face of the P & L.
7 Using the simple workings method, open brackets alongside 'Rates' in the P & L and record the £1,500 from the trial balance.
8 Similarly show the insurance figure in brackets in the P & L
9 Motor expenses can be entered directly in the P & L.
10 Fixtures and fittings can be shown in brackets on the face of the balance sheet to await adjustments. Note that normally in examination questions fixed asset entries are normally so complex as to warrant use of a 'T account' working.
11 Similarly the motor van can be entered in brackets on the face of the balance sheet.
12 Debtors can be entered directly on the face of the balance sheet.
13 Enter creditors on the face of the balance sheet.
14 The bank is entered on the face of the balance sheet.
15 Drawings can be shown on the face of the balance sheet.

Figure 29

(1) Athos — Profit and Loss Account for the year ended 31 December 1985

		£	£
(4)	Sales		150,000
less:			
(2)	Stock 1.1.85	21,000	
(3)	Purchases	117,000	
		138,000	
(17)	less: Stock 31.12.85	22,500	
	Cost of sales		115,500
Gross profit			34,500
less:			
(5)	Wages	14,000	
(6)	Rent	2,000	
(7) & (18)	Rates (1500 - 300)	1,200	
(8) & (19)	Insurance (780 + 120)	900	
(9)	Motor expenses	1,220	
(20)	Depreciation - Fixtures	2,500	
(20)	- Van	700	22,520
Net profit			11,980

16 The opening capital is shown on the face of the balance sheet.

17 Having completed the transfer of all trial balance items to the face of the answer, the first item to be adjusted is the closing stock. This is shown as a deduction from cost of sales in the P & L and as a current asset in the balance sheet.

18 Rates prepaid are shown as a deduction from the P & L expense and as a current asset in the balance sheet.

19 Insurance accrued is shown as an addition to the expense in the P & L and as a current liability in the balance sheet.

20 Depreciation is shown as an expense on the face of the profit and loss account and as a deduction from fixed assets in the balance sheet.

21 Total all workings, then total the profit and loss account, inserting the profit or loss on the face of the balance sheet, then total the balance sheet.

Figure 30

(1) Athos – Balance Sheet as at 31 December 1985

		£	£
Fixed assets			
(10) & (20)	Fixtures and fittings (25,200 - 2,500)		22,700
(11) & (20)	Motor van (2,100 – 700)		1,400
			24,100
Current assets			
(17)	Stock	22,500	
(12)	Debtors	5,300	
(18)	Prepayments	300	
(14)	Bank	1,150	
		29,250	
Current liabilities			
(13)	Creditors	8,900	
(19)	Accruals	120	
		9,020	
Net current assets			20,230
			44,330
Capital:			40,750
(16)	At 1.1.85		11,980
(21)	Profit for the year		52,730
(15)	Drawings		8,400
			44,330

In practice adjustments are often more complex than in examinations, and a fuller form of working schedule is required in preparing the accounts. A common form of working schedule used in the *extended trial balance*. An example is presented in Figure 31 covering our example 'Athos'. The schedule consists of five pairs of columns:

1 The first pair of columns shows the trial balance extracted from the ledger.
2 The second pair of columns shows the adjustments to be made to the ledger.
3 The third pair of columns shows accruals and prepayments. These are normally presented in the order shown in Figure 31 so that the accruals represent the debits to be made to the various accounts and the prepayments represent the credits; the double entry is completed by showing the total prepayments as a debit item in the balance sheet and the total accruals as a credit item.
4 The fourth pair of columns shows the columns added across line by line relating to the profit and loss items.
5 The fifth column shows the balance sheet items, including profit for the year.

It should be enphasized that this system is far too cumbersome and time-consuming for examination purpose.

Accounting conventions

By 'accounting conventions' we mean the broad assumptions which underlie the way in which accounts are prepared and presented. Accountants use a range of terms to describe conventions, such as 'concepts', 'postulates', 'principles', 'imperatives', 'assumptions' or even 'standard' (used in a different sense to 'accounting standard' as discussed in Chapter 1 above).

Some authors have tried to distinguish between types of convention, using a different term for each type but it is fair to say that no generally accepted terminology has emerged.

Over 200 accounting conventions can be identified. In the UK both the Companies Act 1981 and

Figure 31 *Example of an extended trial balance*

	Trial balance		*Journal*		*Accruals*	*Prepay-ments*	*Profit and loss*		*Balance sheet*	
	Dr	*Cr*	*Dr*	*Cr*			*Dr*	*Cr*	*Dr*	*Cr*
Stock 1.1.85	21,000						21,000	22,500	22,500	
Purchases	117,000						117,000			
Sales		150,000						150,000		
Wages	14,000						14,000			
Rent	2,000						2,000			
Rates	1,500					300	1,200			
Insurance	780				120		900			
Motor expenses	1,220						1,220			
Fixtures & fittings	25,200			2,500					22,700	
Motor van	2,100			700					1,400	
Debtors	5,300								5,300	
Creditors		8,900								8,900
Bank	1,150								1,150	
Drawings	8,400								8,400	
Capital		40,750								40,750
Depreciation			3,200		120	300	3,200			
Prepayments/ Accruals									300	120
Net profit							11,980			11,980
	199,650	199,650					172,500	172,500	61,750	61,750

SSAP2 'Disclosure of Accounting Policies', identify a small number of basic conventions, as does IAS1 'Disclosure of Accounting Policies', but there has been no official listing in the UK of all the major conventions.

Some of the major accounting conventions can be identified as follows:

Business entity

The accounts deal with the affairs of the business and exclude the personal affairs of the proprietor. Thus the business is treated as an 'entity' in its own right, even though in the case of a sole trader or partnership the business has no legal identity independent of the proprietors.

Prudence

The prudence convention, also referred to as 'conservatism' is defined in SSAP2 as being that:

> revenues and profits are not anticipated, but are recognised in the Profit and Loss account only when realised in the form either of cash or of other assets the cash realisation of which can be assessed with reasonable certainty; provision is made for all known liabilities (expenses and losses) whether the amount of these is known with certainty or is a best estimate in the light of the information available.

This definition is perhaps a little cumbersome. The prudence convention is basically concerned with the question of *income recognition*. Gains are only recognized when *realized*, that is when a transaction has established a firm legal entitlement to receive those gains in cash; losses, on the other hand, are brought into the accounts as soon as they are anticipated.

Going concern

SSAP2 defines this convention:

> the enterprise will continue in operational existence for the foreseeable future. This means in particular that the profit and loss account and balance sheet assume no intention or necessity to liquidate or curtail significantly the scale of operation.

This convention should not be taken as claiming that the business will continue in perpetuity. The significance of the convention is that many assets would have little value if they were not used in the business, and even the marketable assets of the business might not raise substantial sums in a 'forced sale'. Normal accounting procedures are, therefore, based on the going-concern assumption. However if the circumstances of a business were such as to indicate imminent termination then it might be appropriate to prepare the accounts on a 'break-up' basis, making full provision for anticipated losses on a forced sale of the assets.

Accruals

SSAP2 defines the accruals convention:

> revenue and costs are accrued (that is recognised as they are earned or incurred, not as money is received or paid), matched with one another so far as their relationship can be established, or justifiably assumed, and dealt with in the profit and loss account of the period to which they relate.

This is also sometimes called the 'matching' convention. The practical problem of applying this convention arises in deciding when it is 'justifiable' to assume that expenditure can be related to future income.

Consistency

SSAP2 defines the consistency concept:

> there is consistency of accounting treatment of like items within each accounting period and from one accounting period to the next.

This convention can be regarded as serving two purposes:

1. It promotes comparability of one year's accounts with another.
2. It promotes objectivity, in that the management of a business are not free to choose between a variety of approaches to similar items depending on the result they wish to portray.

Note that our definition of consistency says nothing about the achievement of comparability between different businesses, although clearly this is a desirable objective which is being pursued by the Accounting Standards Committee.

Money measurement

When the various resources of the business are reported, it is necessary to have a common unit of measurement. The unit of measurement used is the *monetary unit*. This can cause confusion because it means that money has two types of significance in the accounts, both as a unit of measurement and as a resource of the business in the form of bank and cash balances. Another problem is that in times of inflation the significance of the monetary unit changes over the years, a point considered in detail in Chapter 11 on Inflation Accounting below.

Historical cost

The historical cost convention holds that the actual cost, evidenced by an arm's length transaction, is the amount at which an asset should be recorded in the accounts. Depreciation of an asset does not go against this convention in that it represents the consumption of part of the cost of an asset in a year.

Objectivity

This convention is based on the view that accounts should not be influenced by any personal bias on the part of those who present them. Those who present accounts have the opportunity to affect the amounts reported in two ways:

1 By the accounting methods chosen. The 'consistency' requirement attempts to reduce the opportunity to reflect bias in this way, as does the accounting standards programme.
2 By the way in which estimates are made. To a large extent this cannot be controlled by accounting rules and depends on the personal integrity of management.

Materiality

This convention requires that all items which are sufficiently material to affect evaluations or decisions should be disclosed, and that conversely costs should not be incurred in providing an unnecessarily detailed analysis.

Substance over form

The principle here is that the substance and financial reality of transactions should govern their treatment in the accounts rather than legal form. An example is that the legal form of a hire-purchase agreement is that the asset concerned is acquired by the hire-purchase company and rented out to the user of the asset, who has the right to acquire the asset at the end of the contract for a nominal sum; in practice, hire purchase constitutes a way of buying an asset with a loan from the hire-purchase company which is repaid in instalments, and the accounting treatment adopted reflects this.

Periodicity

This convention states that accounts should be presented regularly and at fixed intervals. In practice this normally means that accounts are presented at intervals of one year. Identification of this convention helps us to recognize that many of the problems of accounting arise because of the need to allocate items of expenditure or income between accounting periods.

Dual aspect

This convention has effectively already been covered in introducing the double entry book-keeping system, being that the accounts should represent a complete account of where all the resources of the firm have been derived from and the form in which those resources are held.

The Companies Act 1981 states that five 'accounting principles' must be followed in presenting company accounts; going concern, consistency, prudence, accruals, and that in determining the aggregate amount of any item the amount of each individual asset or liability should be determined separately. Any departure from these five principles must be disclosed and explained.

SSAP2 identifies four 'fundamental accounting concepts' being prudence, accruals, consistency, and going concern, in the event of a conflict between 'prudence' and 'accruals' then prudence should be given more weight.

SSAP2 states that any departure from these four concepts must be specifically stated and explained in the accounts. Two other terms are introduced in

SSAP2. 'Accounting bases' are methods for applying accounting conventions; for example, depreciation is a method applying the accruals concept. 'Accounting policies' are the specific accounting methods adopted by companies, e.g. a company might choose to adopt any of the specific depreciation methods described in Chapter 6 below. SSAP2 requires that the accounting policies on all material items should be disclosed in the notes to the accounts.

IAS1 suggests similar requirements on the disclosure of accounting policies to those in SSAP2. IAS1 recognizes three 'fundamental accounting assumptions', being going concern, consistency, and accruals, and three further important considerations, being 'prudence', 'materiality' and 'substance over form'.

These accounting conventions should not be regarded as immutable; for example, in Chapter 11 below we will see discussed systems which have been seriously considered by accountants which involve abandoning either money measurement (CPP) or historical cost (CCA). Probably the greatest amount of controversy arises in conflicts between the 'prudence' convention and the 'accruals' convention. It should be noted that the prudence concept derives more from the 'stewardship' role of accounting rather than the decision making role.

Having considered the basic accounting system and the underlying conventions it is possible for us to observe what a set of accounts tells us, and what they do not claim to represent. The balance sheet shows us what assets have been purchased and where the finance to cover their purchase has been derived, while the profit and loss account shows us the extent to which resources generated by trading during the year exceed resources consumed. The accounts do *not* represent what the business is worth. We can identify two major reasons for this:

1 The historical cost convention results in assets being shown at their original cost, rather than at their current value. In the case of long-lived fixed assets, particularly land and buildings, the difference between original cost and current value can be very substantial.

2 The value of a business as a whole is likely to be different from the total value of the individual assets that have been purchased. This difference is called 'goodwill' and it can arise for a variety of reasons such as, trading connections and reputation with customers, employee skills and loyalty, and established links with suppliers. Sometimes goodwill may be negative (accountants do not use the term 'badwill' in this situation!). Goodwill is only quantified by a transaction when one business buys another; apart from this situation, goodwill is not recognized in the accounts.

Conclusion

We have seen that following the extraction of a trial balance a number of adjustments have to be made before the accounts can be completed. We have also considered the conventions that underlie the preparation of accounts.

Questions

1 Aramis has been in business for some years, preparing accounts with a 31 March year end.

At 1 April 1985 he had prepaid insurance costs of £175.
On 30 May 1985 he paid insurance on the premises for the year to 31 March 1986 of £572.
On 30 June 1985 he paid a business insurance premium of £820 covering the year to 30 June 1986.

Write up the insurance account in the books of Aramis for the year to 31 March 1986.

2 The trial balance of Planchet, a grocer, showed the following at 31 December 1985:

	£	£
Sales		60,000
Purchases	46,000	
Stock 1.1.85	2,800	
Telephone	310	
Motor expenses	450	

Wages	4,200	
Rates	1,260	
Debtors	2,120	
Creditors		3,040
Premises	21,000	
Motor van	2,000	
Bank		1,120
Drawings	7,100	
Capital		23,080
	87,240	87,240

At 31 December 1985:

(a) Stock was £3,700
(b) Prepaid expenses were:

Telephone	20
Rates	270

(c) Accrued expenses were:

Motor expenses	40
Wages	70

(d) £500 depreciation is to be provided on the van.

You are required to prepare the profit and loss account and balance sheet for the year ended 31 December 1985.

3 Outline and discuss the basic conventions and concepts that underlie accounting practice.

(University College of North Wales)

4 What do you consider to be the fundamental concepts of accounting? Discuss why you consider each to be necessary.

(Preston Polytechnic)

5 Explain the undernoted conventions:
Money measurement
Dual aspect
Going concern
Accrual
Conservatism

(Ulster Polytechnic)

6 Briefly describe the following concepts, in each case indicating areas in which non-adherence to them can have a material effect on the preparation of financial statements:

(a) The matching concept.
(b) The cost concept.
(c) The prudence concept.

(University of Stirling)

5

TYPES OF COMMERCIAL ENTITY AND THE PROPRIETORS' INTEREST

Objectives

The objective of this chapter is to explain how accountants treat the proprietors' interest in different types of business organization. In order to achieve this objective we will:

1 Look at the reasons why the treatment of the proprietors' interest will vary according to the type of business organization.
2 Consider the basic principles of partnerships.
3 Explain how to account for changes in the structure of a partnership.
4 Outline the accounting procedures used on the termination of a partnership.
5 Discuss the legal status of limited liability companies.
6 Detail the meaning of 'share capital' and 'reserves'.
7 Briefly consider the way in which businesses are taxed.
8 Contrast partnerships and limited companies.
9 Briefly consider the special position of non-trading concerns.

Significance of the proprietors' interest

We have already introduced the basic balance sheet equation:

Capital = Assets - Liabilities

By 'capital' is meant the proprietors' interest in the business, and in this chapter we will use the term 'proprietors' interest' because the term 'capital' is used in a variety of ways and can be confusing.

So far we have looked at the accounting equation in the context of a 'sole trader'. A *sole trader* is a private individual engaged in business on his own. Although by convention his accounts are prepared showing only the business assets and liabilities he is personally in total control of the business, and is personally liable to meet all the obligations of the business. Thus the sole trader is free to transfer resources between his private purse and his business operations whenever he pleases. A single capital account showing the origins of any increase or decrease during the year is a perfectly adequate mechanism for recording the proprietors' interest in the case of a sole trader.

However, as soon as more than one person becomes involved in the ownership of the business it becomes necessary to keep more detailed records. It is necessary to distinguish between the amount of the net worth of the business attributable to each proprietor, and also to distinguish between different types of right that investment in the business conveys. It is also necessary to record how the profit of the business is shared between the various proprietors. For this purpose it is normal to show the allocation of profit in a section at the foot of the profit and loss account known as the *appropriation account*.

The two most common ways of arranging joint ownership of a business are the partnership and the limited liability company.

Partnership: basic principles

The Partnership Act 1980 and the Limited Partnership Act 1907 contain the major legal provisions relating to partnerships. The Partnership Act 1890 defines a partnership as:

> The relation which subsists between persons carrying on a business in common with a view to profit.

A partnership does not have an individual legal identity of its own. Each partner is personally liable for all the liabilities and obligations of the partnership, except where all the conditions of the Limited Partnership Act 1907 are met. The main conditions are:

1 The partnership must include 'general partners', who each accept personal liability for all debts of the partnership, as well as limited partners.
2 Details of the limited partnership must be filed with the Registrar of Companies.
3 The limited partner must not take part in the management of the business.

In these circumstances those who join together in a partnership are placing a great deal of trust in each other. The law therefore places partnership agreements in the special category of agreements which are *uberrimae fidei*, meaning that the partners are bound to give each other all material information which might influence the agreement.

The number of partners in a partnership is limited to 20, except for solicitors, stockbrokers, accountants, and other groups approved by the Board of Trade.

The conduct of the affairs of a partnership is a matter for the partners to agree between themselves, and it is advisable for a formal written agreement to be made with expert legal advice. The law makes provision for certain assumptions to be made in the absence of specific agreement. The main points to be covered in an agreement are:

1 The contribution to be made by each partner to the resources of the firm, and the extent to which each partner's contribution is to be regarded as capital or as a loan.
2 Whether interest should be credited or charged in respect of money lent to or borrowed from the firm by individual partners. In the absence of such agreement, the law allows a partner 5 per cent interest on any amount lent to the firm in excess of the agreed amount of capital subscribed.
3 The way in which profits or losses are to be divided between the partners. In the absence of agreement the law provides for an equal sharing of profits or losses.
4 Any limit on drawings to be made by partners.
5 Procedures for making policy decisions relating to the partnership, particularly on the admission of new partners.
6 The system of accounting, and whether there is to be an independent audit. The law provides that the partnership books should be kept at the central place of business, with every partner having a right of access.
7 Procedures in the event of retirement of a partner or dissolution of the partnership.

The way in which the partners share profits is a matter for agreement between themselves. The following points may be taken into account:

1 It is a normal to charge interest on loan accounts. As we have seen, in the absence of specific agreement to the contrary the Partnership Act 1890 allows for 5 per cent interest on loans. Loan interest is treated as an expense, not as an appropriation.
2 Sometimes interest is also allowed on capital accounts. This may seem particularly appropriate where there is a substantial difference between the amounts of capital put in by each partner. Interest on capital is an appropriation of profit, not an expense.
3 Interest may also be allowed or charged on the partners' current account balances.
4 Each partner may be allowed a fixed amount out of profits. Such an amount is often referred to as 'salary', and may be regarded as covering the value to the firm of the work performed by the partner; however, it is important to note that such amounts should be treated as an appropriation of profit, not as an expense.
5 After allowing for all the above items the

residual profit (or loss) will be shared between the partners in the profit sharing ratio.

6 Sometimes it is agreed that one or more of the partners shall, for a period of time, enjoy a minimum amount by way of profit share. Such an arrangement is particularly common when an employee is admitted to a partnership. If there is a shortfall of profit the additional amount is normally made up by the other partners in profit-sharing ratio, but sometimes it might be agreed that the shortfall should only be borne by certain partners.

Example 10 shows how a profit-sharing agreement between partners may be drafted, while Figure 32 shows the computation of each partner's profit share. Taking each stage:

1 In this example interest is only allowed on the loan account.
2 Note that salaries are an appropriation of profit. Sometimes salaries paid to partners are shown in the books of the partnership together with wages and salaries paid to employees, in such a case partners' salaries must be added back to net profit and then included in the computation of the appropriation of profit.
3 Residual profit is shared in profit-shared ratio.
4 A transfer of profit from Grantly to Arabin in order to give Arabin the agreed minimum profit.

Example 10

On 1 January 1985 Grantly, Harding and Arabin entered into a partnership agreement. Capital subscribed by each partner was:

Grantly	£20,000
Harding	£15,000
Arabin	£5,000

In addition Grantly lent the partnership £10,000

It was agreed that the loan should carry interest of 8 per cent, that Harding and Arabin should each receive a salary of £4,000, and that the remaining profit should be split in the ratio Grantly 50 per cent, Harding 30 per cent and Arabin 20 per cent. As an inducement to Arabin to join the partnership Grantly promised Arabin a minimum profit share of £7,500, to be made up by Grantly if necessary. In the year to 31 December 1985 the profit before interest and partners' salaries was £23,800.

During the year to 31 December 1985 drawings by partners were:

Grantly	£2,800
Harding	£6,200
Arabin	£6,100

Figure 32

	£	£
Profit per the accounts		23,800
less:		
Interest – Grantly		800
Profit to be appropriated		23,000
less – Salaries		
Harding	4,000	
Arabin	4,000	
		8,000
Residual profit		15,000
Shared:		
Grantly	7,500	
Harding	4,500	
Arabin	3,000	
		15,000

Profit appropriated:

	Salary	*Residue*	*Transfer*	*Total*
Grantly		7,500	(500)	7,000
Harding	4,000	4,500		8,500
Arabin	4,000	3,000	500	7,500
				23,000

Note that loan interest of £800 is treated as an expense, not as an appropriation.

It is common to record partners' accounts under three headings:

1 Loan accounts, being amounts lent to the business.
2 Capital accounts, recording capital subscribed by partners.
3 Current accounts, being a record of the partners' day-to-day dealings with the firm; drawings and profit shares would normally be dealt with through the current account.

Figure 33

Capital accounts

Date	Details	G	H	A	Date	Details	G	H	A
31.12.85	Bal c/d	20,000	15,000	5,000	1.1.85	Cash	20,000	15,000	5,000
					1.1.86	Bal b/d	20,000	15,000	5,000

Loan account – Grantly

Date	Details	Amount	Date	Details	Amount
31.12.85	Bal c/d	10,000	1.1.85	Cash	10,000
			1.1.86	Bal c/d	10,000

Current accounts

Date	Details	G	H	A	Date	Details	G	H	A
1985	Cash	2,800	6,200	6,100	31.12.85	P & L – Appropriation	7,000	8,500	7,500
31.12.85	Bal c/d	5,000	2,300	1,400	31.12.85	P & L Loan interest	800		
		7,800	8,500	7,500			7,800	8,500	7,500
					1.1.86	Bal b/d	5,000	2,300	1,400

Figure 33 shows how the accounts might be recorded in the case of Example 10. The 'columnar' format whereby the accounts for each partner are shown in adjacent columns is commonly used, particularly under examination conditions.

Partnership: accounting for changes

We have seen that the accounts record the interest of each partner in the firm, and that the share in the profit or loss of the firm allocated to each partner is computed by reference to the profit and loss account of each year. Thus the accounts are used as the basis for expressing the economic relationship between partners. However we have also seen that the accounts do not represent the economic value of the firm, and have identified the two main reasons for this as being:

1 The market value of the assets of the business may be substantially different form that recorded in the accounts.

2 The 'inherent goodwill' of the business is not normally recorded in the accounts, and in any case its value is difficult to define and fluctuates on a day-to-day basis.

If a partnership continued from commencement to cessation with the same partners and the same profit-sharing ratio then there would be no difficulty. On cessation of business the assets and the trading connection would be sold, thus identifying the differences between the economic value and the book value of the firm, and any surplus or deficit would be shared between the partners in profit-sharing ratio. However if, for any reason, there is a change in the profit-sharing ratio, then a problem arises.

If no adjustment is made then any increase or decrease in the value of assets *earned* before the date of the change in profit-sharing ratio but *realized* after the date of the change will be shared between partners in the new profit-sharing ratio, although it would seem only fair that such gains or losses should be shared in the old profit-sharing ratio.

Example 11 gives a simple instance of how such a situation might arise. Figure 34 shows how follow ing normal accounting practice Slope and Slide each take a gain of £17,500, but if we split the gain into two parts (pre and post the date of change in ratio) Slope has a gain of £20,000 and Slide gains £15,000.

Example 11

On 1 January 1975 Slope and Slide entered into partnership, subscribing capital as follows:

Slope	£30,000
Slide	£15,000

The entire £45,000 was invested in a block of holiday flats, which Slide was to manage. They agreed that each year profit and all other gains should be split, Slope two-thirds, Slide one-third. On 1 January 1980 the profit-sharing arrangement was changed, the new profit-sharing ratio being Slope one half, Slide one half. On 31 December 1985 the flats were sold for £80,000.

The partnership had no assets or liabilities, other than the flats, at any time. Each year the income from the flats had been exactly equal to expenses. At 1 January 1980 the flats were valued at £60,000.

There are two ways of tackling this problem:

1 By revaluing the assets of the business at each date when there is a change in profit-sharing ratios. For this purpose a revaluation account is used and in respect of each revalued asset entry is made:

   Dr Asset account / Cr Revaluation account } Amount of revaluation surplus

   or vice versa for revaluation deficits.

   The balance on the revaluation account is then transferred to the partners' capital accounts in profit-sharing ratio.

   Figure 35 shows how this system might apply to Example 11.

2 Where the partners do not want to incorporate a revaluation in the accounts an alternative approach is to compute the total revaluation surplus or deficit, taking this to the partners' capital accounts in the old profit-sharing ratio

Figure 34

In 1985 the gain on the flats is:

	£	£
Sale price		80,000
less: Cost		45,000
Surplus		35,000
Shared:		
Slope	17,500	
Slide	17,500	
		35,000

However the gain might be regarded as earned in two stages:

Pre 1.1.80

	£	£
Revalued amount		60,000
Less: Cost		45,000
Surplus		15,000
Shared:		
Slope	10,000	
Slide	5,000	
		15,000

Post 1.1.80

Sale proceeds		80,000
less: Value 1.1.80		60,000
Surplus		20,000
Shared:		
Slope	10,000	
Slide	10,000	20,000
Total gain – Slope		20,000
Slide		15,000
		35,000

and then removing it in the new profit-sharing ratio. In Example 11 the entry would be:

Dr Slope	7,500	
Slide	7,500	
Cr Slope		10,000
Slide		5,000
	15,000	15,000

Being revaluation surplus of £15,000 credited to

Figure 35

Capital accounts

		Slope	Slide			Slope	Slide
31.12.80	Bal c/d	40,000	20,000	1.1.75	Cash	30,000	15,000
				1.1.80	Revaluation	10,000	5,000
		40,000	20,000			40,000	20,000
31.12.85	Bal c/d	50,000	30,000	1.1.85	Bal b/d	40,000	20,000
				31.12.85	P & L on disposal	10,000	10,000
		50,000	30,000			50,000	30,000
				1.1.86	Bal b/d	50,000	30,000

Revaluation

1.1.80	Slope	10,000	1.1.80	Flats	15,000
	Slide	5,000			
		15,000			15,000

Flats

1.1.75	Cash	45,000	31.12.75	Bal c/d	45,000
1.1.80	Bal b/d	45,000	31.12.80	Bal c/d	60,000
1.1.80	Revaluation	15,000			
		60,000			60,000
1.1.85	Bal b/d	60,000	31.12.85	Disposal	60,000

P & L on disposal

31.12.85	Flats	60,000	31.12.85	Cash	80,000
31.12.85	Profit shared:				
	Slope	10,000			
	Slide	10,000			
		80,000			80,000

partners in the old ratio of 2:1 and debited in the new ratio of 1:1.

Figure 36 shows how this approach would be recorded. Note that after realization of the asset each approach produces the same result.

In principle the revaluation of goodwill has the same effect as any other asset revaluation. However in practice businessmen are often reluctant to record goodwill in the accounts because of its nebulous character, and it is not uncommon to find that tangible assets are revalued in accordance with method 1 above, while goodwill is treated in accordance with method 2.

Valuation of goodwill necessarily involves considerable problems of estimation. In order to avoid arguments, it is common for a partnership agreement to include provisions on how goodwill is to be computed. Methods used include:

1 Expressing goodwill as a multiple of turnover.
2 Assessing goodwill as a multiple of profits.
3 Computing goodwill as a multiple of the excess

Figure 36

Capital accounts

	Slope	Slide		Slope	Slide
1.1.80 Revaluation – new ratios	7,500	7,500	1.1.75 Cash	30,000	15,000
31.12.80 Bal c/d	32,500	12,500	1.1.80 Revaluation – old ratios	10,000	5,000
	40,000	20,000		40,000	20,000
31.12.85 Bal c/d	50,000	30,000	1.1.85 Bal b/d	32,500	12,500
			31.12.85 P & L on disposal	17,500	17,500
	50,000	30,000		50,000	30,000
			1.1.86 Bal c/d	50,000	30,000

Flats

1.1.75 Cash	45,000	31.12.75 Bal c/d	45,000
1.1.85 Bal b/d	45,000	31.12.80 Disposal	45,000

P & L on disposal

31.12.85 Flats	45,000	31.12.85 Cash	80,000
31.12.85 Profit shared: Slope	17,500		
Slide	17,500		
	80,000		80,000

of profit actually achieved over the yield which might be expected from the tangible assets employed in the business.

In each case the accounting figures used might be derived from the most recent accounts or from the average of several years' accounts.

Partnership: retirement and dissolution

Legally whenever the composition of a partnership changes the old partnership ceases and a new partnership commences. In practice it is normal to treat the partnership as a continuing entity for accounting purposes.

When a partner retires the assets and goodwill will be valued, and the accounting procedures as described above for a change in profit-sharing ratio will be followed. The balances on the retiring partner's various accounts will then be transferred to a single account which will represent the total amount due to that partner. The amount due may be paid over in cash or may be met in part by the transfer of some of the assets at an agreed valuation. Sometimes part of the amount owing may be left in the firm as a loan.

The retirement of a partner can place a severe strain on the cash resources of a partnership, and often the partners will plan ahead to accumulate the necessary cash resources for an agreed retirement date. Often some form of life insurance policy is arranged for this purpose.

On dissolution of a partnership the assets of the firm must be applied in the following order:

1 In paying all amounts owing to persons who are not partners.
2 In repaying partners' loan accounts.
3 In paying to each partner amounts due on capital and current acounts.

On dissolution of a partnership a 'realization account' is opened, which effectively summarizes

Figure 37

Realization account

31.3.82	Fixed assets		14,130	31.3.82	Pref. shares		3,000
31.3.82	Stock		8,400	31.3.82	Ord. shares		18,000
31.3.82	Debtors		13,770	31.3.82	Cash		12,690
31.3.82	Capital – A	1,140		31.3.82	Capital (car)		4,320
	V	570					
			1,710				
			38,010				38,010

Bank

31.3.82	Bal b/d		2,290	31.3.82	Creditors		7,500
31.3.82	Realization		12,690	31.3.82	Capital – V	7,306	
					A	174	7,480
			14,980				14,980

Capital accounts

		Ardiles	Villa			Ardiles	Villa
31.3.82	Pref. shares		1,000	31.3.82	Bal b/d	16,000	6,000
31.3.82	Realization (cars)	1,870	2,450	31.3.82	Current accounts	4,036	3,054
31.3.82	Ord. shares	12,000	6,000		Realization	1,140	570
31.3.84	Bank	7,306	174				
		21,176	9,624			21,176	9,624

all gains or losses on realization. The account is operated as follows:

1 All assets are transferred to the debit of the realization account, except for cash and bank balances (which in effect are already 'realized').
2 The sale proceeds of all assets are credited to the realization account. Thus the balance on the realization account now represents the gain or loss on disposal of all assets.
3 Pay all liabilities. Any difference between the amounts paid and the amounts shown in the accounts is taken to the realization account.
4 The balance on the realization account is now equal to the total gain or loss on realization. This is transferred to the partners' capital accounts in profit-sharing ratio.
5 The balance on partners' current accounts are transferred to their capital accounts. Any debit balance on a capital account is transferred against any loan account in respect of the same partner, then loans are repaid.
6 If, after the above, any partner has a debit balance on capital account this should be paid into the business. If a partner defaults on payment then, following the rule laid down in the case of *Garner* v *Murray*, this loss is divided between the other partners in the ratio of the capital they have in the firm, not profit-sharing ratio, unless there is a specific agreement to the contrary.
7 At this stage the bank and cash balances should equal the balances on the capital accounts. Thus when these amounts are paid over to the partners the accounts can be closed.

Sometimes the purchase consideration for some of the assets is realized in a form other than cash, which is then passed on to the partners. When such consideration is received the entry made will be:

Dr Asset account (for type of asset received) } Value of
Cr Realization account } consideration

and when the asset is passed on:

Dr Partner } Value of consideration
Cr Asset account } passed on

Example 12 is taken from an old examination paper. Figure 37 shows how this problem would be tackled.

Example 12

The following balance sheet was prepared for the partnership of Ardiles and Villa, who shared profits in the ratio of 2:1, as at 31 March 1982:

	£	£		£	£
Capital accounts			Fixed assets		14,130
Ardiles		16,000	Current assets		
Villa	6,000	22,000	Stock	8,400	
			Debtors	13,770	
			Bank	2,290	24,460
Current accounts					
Ardiles	4,036				
Villa	3,054	7,090			
Loan account					
Ardiles		2,000			
Creditors		7,500			
		38,590			38,590

Included in the fixed assets were two cars, having book values of £1,800 and £2,500.

Burkinshaw Ltd made an offer to buy the stock and fixed assets, other than the cars, of the partnership for £21,000, and the partners, wishing to retire from business, accepted. The consideration was satisfied by allotting to the partners 3,000 preference shares and 18,000 ordinary shares in the company.

The debtors were settled for £12,690, and the creditors paid off in full.

The partners agreed the closing distribution as follows:

1 Ardiles to take one car for £1,870, and Villa the other for £2,450;
2 Ardiles to take preference shares to the value of his loan, the balance to Villa;
3 the ordinary shares to be allocated according to their profit-sharing ratio; and
4 the balance to be settled in cash.

You are required to prepare:

1 the realization account;
2 the bank account, and
3 the partners' capital accounts.

(Society of Company and Commercial Accountants, May 1982)

One circumstance in which a partnership may be dissolved is when the partners decide to 'convert' to a limited company. Legally this constitutes cessation of the partnership and commencement of a new company, so that a new set of books of account are required. Thus the normal dissolution accounting procedures are applied, the shares issued by the new company being treated as purchase consideration received and passed on to the partners.

Limited companies: legal position

The most common way of forming a company is by registering a limited company under the provisions of the Companies Act 1948 to 1981. Two types of limited company can be registered.

1 ***Public companies***
To qualify as a public company a company must have a share capital of £50,000, must comply with certain formalities in the registration documents, and must end its name with the expression 'public limited company' (often abbreviated to PLC). A public company is allowed to offer its securities to the public.

2 ***Private companies***
A private company is any company which does not qualify as a public company. A private company is not allowed to offer securities to the public, and therefore is effectively barred from raising finance through the stock market.

However in a number of other ways the law allows private companies a substantially greater degree of freedom than public companies. Every private company must end its name with the word 'Limited', (often abbreviated to Ltd).

A company is an artificial legal personality, which can sue and be sued in its own right. A company must have at least two 'members'. All public companies, and most private companies, issue shares, and each shareholder is a 'member' of the company. The liability of each shareholder is limited to the amount which has to be paid for shares, so that once shares have been fully paid for shareholders have no further personal liability even if the company is unable to pay its debts. A small number of private companies have no shareholders, instead being limited by *guarantee*, so that each member guarantees to contribute a certain amount to the company if called upon to do so; companies limited by guarantee are normally only formed for non-commercial purposes.

A company is managed by a *board of directors*, who are elected by and answerable to the members. Thus the ownership and management of a company are separated. Often in practice the shareholders also serve as directors, particularly in small companies. The way in which the company is to operate will be laid down in two documents:

1 The *memorandum of association* is the document which forms the constitution of a company, stating its objects and powers.
2 The *articles of association* lay down the rules to be followed in running the company. They define the rights of members and the position of the directors.

While in certain matters company law prescribes certain requirements which must be included in the memorandum and articles of association, there remains some flexibility in the way in which a company chooses to organize itself. The Companies Act 1948 includes a specimen set of articles of association in *Table A*, and provides that the provisions of Table A shall apply in any case where a company does not adopt articles of its own. In practice it is common for companies to adopt Table A with certain specified amendments.

The privilege of limited liability is a very valuable one, and if not strictly controlled could obviously be subject to serious abuse. The law tries to control the operation of limited liability in three ways:

1 Specific rules prevent the directors from managing a company in an irresponsible way. Breach of these rules can render the directors subject to legal penalties, and in some cases may render the directors personally liable for the obligations of the company.
2 Each year a company has to file audited accounts with the registrar of companies. Thus those having dealings with the company have access to information on its financial position.
3 A company is only permitted to distribute realized profits to shareholders as dividends, so that amounts subscribed as share capital have to be retained in the company.

A small number of companies are registered with unlimited liability. These are not required to file accounts, and enjoy considerably more freedom in the way they conduct their business.

Limited companies: share capital and reserves

As we have already seen, most companies issue shares to their members. A share can be regarded as representing a bundle of rights, both in terms of an entitlement to benefits distributed by the company to its members and also in terms of voting rights in company meetings. The rights attaching to various categories of share will be laid down in the company's articles of association, but the two main broad categories of share are preference shares and ordinary shares.

Preference shares normally carry an entitlement to a fixed rate of dividend each year. Dividends of any kind can only be paid if the company has accumulated sufficient retained profits to cover the amount of the dividend. Preference shares may be *cumulative*, in which case if a dividend cannot be paid in one year the right to receive it will be carried forward until such time as there are sufficient realized profits to cover the dividend. *Non-cumulative* preference shares do not carry such a right, so that if a dividend is not paid in a year all rights to it are lost. It is normal for preference shares not to carry votes in general meeting, although they are likely to have a vote as a class of shares on any proposal to change class rights. Sometimes the articles grant preference shareholders voting rights in the event of the preference dividend not being paid.

Ordinary shares normally carry a right to participate in the residue of profit which remains after all other claims, including preference dividends, have been met. The directors propose a dividend to the annual general meeting, which ordinary shareholders may reduce but not increase. Ordinary shares normally carry equal votes in company meetings, including the right to vote on the appointment of directors.

Various other forms of share arise. Three possibilities are:

1 Ordinary shares split into voting and non-voting categories. This can arise when the proprietors of the business are willing to share the profits of the business but are reluctant to lose control.
2 Ordinary shares split into different classes, each class voting separately on the appointment of directors to represent them although on other matters the various classes of share vote together.
3 'Deferred' shares, enjoying a right to a large share of all profit in excess of a specified amount.

For each class of share a *par value* (sometimes known as *nominal* value) is specified. This can be of any amount, e.g. 25p per share, £1 per share, £5 per share. This par value is significant for the following reasons:

1 Dividends are normally expressed as a percentage of the par value of shares.
2 A company is not allowed to issue new shares at a price less than the par value.
3 A shareholder can identify the proportion of a class of share owned by them by computing the proportion:

$$\frac{\text{Nominal value of shares owned}}{\text{Nominal value of shares in issue}}$$

Thus a shareholder owning ordinary shares with a nominal value of £1,000 in a company with issued ordinary shares with a nominal value of £5,000 owns 20 per cent ($\frac{1,000}{5,000}$) of the ordinary shares.

When shares are issued for an amount equal to the par value the accounting entry will be:

Dr Cash Cr Share capital	Par value of shares issued

However shares may be issued for an amount in excess of the par value, in which case the accounting entry will be:

Dr Cash	Proceeds of share issue
Cr Share capital	Par value of shares issued
Cr Share premium	Excess over par value

The *share premium account* is a type of *capital reserve* which is considered in detail below.

It is important to note that the par value of a share does not purport to represent the market value of shares at any point in time; it is purely a legal device serving the specific purpose identified above. There is some controversy over the concept of par value. Critics point out that some countries, e.g. the USA, manage perfectly well with shares of no par value, and that the term is misleading to the layman who may not appreciate that in this context the term 'value' is being used in a way that differs totally from everyday usage.

The total of the shareholders' interest in a company consists of the share capital and the *reserves*. 'Reserve' is a technical term used by accountants to describe any part of the proprietors' interest in a limited company other than the par value of issued shares. The term can cause confusion for two reasons:

1 In some English-speaking countries the term 'reserve' is used to describe what in the UK would be called a 'provision'. In the UK a reserve is part of the proprietors' interest while a provision is a liability.
2 In everyday language the term 'reserve' implies a horde of resources held back to meet some eventuality. By contrast the term is used by

accountants simply to describe where the resources of the company have been derived from; the assets owned are shown on the other side of the balance sheet.

Thus it is essential to apppreciate that the way in which accountants use the word 'reserve' has a special technical meaning totally different from normal usage.

Reserves are divided into two categories:

1 *Revenue reserves* represent retained realized profits. This is the only part of the shareholders' interest which may be distributed as dividends.
2 *Capital reserves* represent all reserves other than retained realized profits.

Figure 38 illustrates the way in which the proprietors' interest of a company is made up. Note the term 'equity' which is often used to describe the ordinary shareholders' interest in a company.

Figure 38 *Shareholders' funds in a limited company*

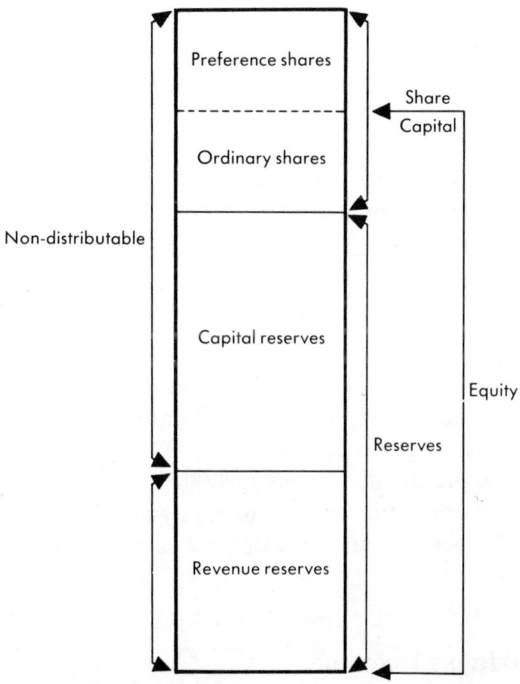

Capital reserves can arise for a number of reasons. Three of the most common are:

1 ***Share premium account***
We have already seen that this reserve arises when shares are issued at a price in excess of par value. This amount can not be distributed as dividends, and may only be used to write off preliminary expenses, expenses of issuing shares or debentures, and the premium on redemption of shares or debentures. It may also be used to cover a bonus issue, discussed in detail below.

2 ***Capital redemption reserve***
In certain strictly controlled conditions a company may redeem some of its own shares. When this happens either the redemption must be financed by a new issue of shares or an account covering the redemption of the shares must be transferred from revenue reserves to a capital redemption reserve; this reserve can only be used in the same way as a share premium account. Thus in either case the total non-distributable capital of the company is not reduced.

3 ***Revaluation reserve***
When an asset is revalued any gain cannot be regarded as a *realized* surplus, and therefore must be credited to a revaluation reserve.

Revenue reserves in total represent the retained realized profits of the company. The simplest way of accounting for retained profits is to have a single 'retained profits' account, but in some cases it has been customary for companies to express their intentions in relation to realized profits by transferring a portion to specially named reserves. A common practice, particularly in examinations, is for a transfer to be made each year from the appropriation account to a *general reserve*; in making such a transfer the directors are making it clear that they do not intend to distribute these profits, but are not binding themselves to retain these profits indefinitely.

It sometimes happens that a company chooses to make a *bonus issue* whereby a free issue of new shares is made to existing shareholders in proportion to their shareholdings; the par value of the shares issued is covered by a transfer from one of the reserve accounts. The transfer may be made from capital or revenue reserves, but in the absence of information to the contrary we would expect capital reserves to be consumed first. The issue does not change the proportion of the class of share owned by each shareholder, but if the dividend continues at the same rate will increase the amount of dividend received because of the increase in the nominal value of shares issued. When a bonus issue is made by a transfer out of revenue reserves the effect is to increase the non-distributable capital of the company, and this may increase the confidence of creditors.

We have already seen that the return paid to shareholders is given in the form of 'dividends'. Often a company will pay two dividends during a year, an *interim* dividend declared by the directors during the year and a *final* dividend proposed after the year end when the accounts have been prepared, and paid after confirmation by the shareholders at the annual general meeting.

A simple example of the way in which the make-up of shareholders' funds may change during a year is presented in Example 13, and the double entry book-keeping for this example is presented in Figure 39. The following entries are made in the year:

(a) The issue of 20,000 shares of 50p at a premium of 30p is accounted for:

Dr Cash	16,000	
Cr Ordinary shares		10,000
Cr Share premium		6,000

(b) The interim dividend of 5 per cent is expressed as a percentage of nominal value £110,000 so that 5% × 10,000 = 5,500:

Dr P & L appropriation	5,500	
Cr Cash		5,500

(c) A 1 for 4 bonus issue is assumed to be taken from share premium:

Dr Share premium	27,500	
Cr Ordinary shares		27,500

(d) Only the appropriation section of the profit and loss account is shown.

(e) The proposed dividend is based on the total issue share capital, including bonus shares, i.e. 10% × 137,500 = 13,750. Since the dividend has not yet been paid it is shown as a liability:

Dr P & L	13,750	
Cr Proposed dividend (current liability)		13,750

And the transfer to general reserve:

Dr P & L	12,000	
Cr General reserve		12,000

Example 13

Wortle Ltd included the following balances relating to shareholders funds at 1 January 1985:

	£
Ordinary shares – 200,000 shares @ 50p	100,000
Share premium account	30,000
Revaluation reserve	18,000
General reserve	40,000
Retained profit	9,000
	197,000

During the year 31 December 1985 the following transactions took place:

(a) On 1 February 1985 20,000 ordinary shares were issued at a price of 80p each.
(b) On 30 August 1985 an interim dividend of 5 per cent was paid.
(c) On 30 November 1985 a 1 for 4 bonus issue was made, ranking for dividend immediately.
(d) In the year to 31 December 1985 the net profit before dividends was £34,000
(e) The directors decided to pay a final dividend of 10 per cent and to transfer £12,000 to general reserve.

Business taxation

The detail of how the UK taxation system operates falls outside the scope of this book. However a very simple introduction to a few major aspects of the

Figure 39

Ordinary shares of 50p			
31.12.85 Bal c/d	137,500	1.1.85 Bal b/d	100,000
		1.2.85 (a) Cash	10,000
		30.11.85 (c) Share premuim	27,500
	137,500		137,500
		1.1.86 Bal b/d	137,500

Share premium			
30.11.85 (c) Ord. shares	27,500	1.1.85 Bal b/d	30,000
31.12.85 Bal c/d	8,500	1.2.85 (a) Cash	6,000
	36,000		36,000
		1.1.86 Bal b/d	8,500

General reserve			
31.12.85 Bal c/d	52,000	1.1.85 Bal b/d	40,000
		31.12.85 P & L	12,000
	52,000		52,000
		1.1.86 Bal b/d	52,000

Retained profit			
31.12.85 Bal c/d	11,750	1.1.85 Bal b/d	9,000
		31.12.85 P & L	2,750
	11,750		11,750
		1.1.86 Bal b/d	11,750

Profit and loss (appropriation section only)			
30.8.85 (a) Cash-interim dividend	5,500	31.12.85 (d) Net profit b/d	34,000
31.12.85 (e) Proposed dividend	13,750		
31.12.85 (e) General reserve	12,000		
31.12.85 Retained profit	2,750		
	34,000		34,000

tax system is desirable from the point of view of understanding the way in which the tax position is reported in the accounts.

Taxes can be split into two broad categories:

1 Indirect taxes are levied on the supply of goods and services. Examples include Value Added Tax (VAT), excise duties, and rates.

2 Direct taxes are levied directly on the individual. These can be split into taxes on revenue, such as income tax and corporation tax, and taxes on capital, such as capital gains tax and capital transfer tax.

Indirect taxes affect partnerships and companies in the same way. The business will normally be involved in collecting tax on goods and services supplied to customers and paying this over to the customs and excise; the business will also normally be able to reclaim input value added tax on purchases made for business purposes.

Sole traders are liable to pay income tax on their business profits, while each partner will similarly pay tax on his share of the business profits of a partnership. Payments of income tax are not regarded as a business expense but as a personal expense of the proprietor, and if paid with a cheque drawn on the business bank account will be regarded as drawings. Currently the basic rate of income tax is 30 per cent rising to 60 per cent on higher income levels.

A limited company pays *corporation tax* on business profits, and it is currently planned to set the corporation tax rate at 30 per cent for small companies and 35 per cent for other companies from the mid-1980s onwards. In addition, shareholders are liable to income tax on their income received from the company. This system would result in shareholders being taxed twice on company profits, once when corporation tax is paid and again when profits are distributed as dividends; to avoid this the UK operates what is known as the imputation system.

Under the imputation system a company is required to pay an amount of *Advance Corporation Tax* (ACT) whenever a dividend is paid. The amount of ACT is computed as

$$\frac{\text{Basic income tax rate}}{100 - \text{Basic income tax rate}} \times \text{Dividend paid}$$

Currently the multiplier would be:

$$\frac{30}{100 - 30} = \frac{3}{7}$$

Subject to certain restrictions, the company can deduct the amount of ACT paid from the corporation tax payable on the profit for the year in which the dividend is paid, so that the total corporation tax paid by the company will normally be the same whatever the level of dividend.

The individual shareholder is treated for tax purposes as having received an income of the cash amount of the dividend plus the amount of related ACT, while the ACT can be set off against the shareholder's total tax liability. Thus a shareholder who pays basic rate tax has no further tax to pay on a dividend received, a shareholder whose total income takes him into higher rate tax bands only has to pay tax at the difference between the basic rate and the higher rate, while a shareholder whose income is not liable even to basic rate tax can claim a refund of the ACT from the Inland Revenue.

The proprietor of a business normally has to pay capital gains tax on the gain on sale of a capital asset; this rule applies equally to sole traders, partnerships, and limited companies. In addition a shareholder has to pay capital gains tax on any increase in the value of shares; this can effectively mean that capital gains on an asset owned by a company are taxed twice.

Comparison between partnerships and limited companies

The following points might be made in comparing partnerships and limited companies:

1 ***Legal entity***
A company is an artificial legal personality, independent of its members. A partnership has no separate legal identity from its members.

2 ***Numbers***
Apart from certain professional activities, partnerships are limited to a maximum of 20 members. A company has a minimum membership of two with no maximum.

3 ***Management***
A company's members delegate all powers of management to the directors. Normally all members of a partnership except for limited partners play a part in the management of the partnership.

4 ***Liability***
All partners, other than limited partners, bear full personal liability for all the obligations of the firm. In a limited company the personal liability of members is limited to any amounts owing in respect of share capital subscribed for.

5 ***Access to accounts***
In a limited company each member receives a copy of the annual accounts, but has no right of access to the detailed books of account. In a partnership each partner has a right to inspect the firm's books of account.

6 ***Publication of accounts***
A limited company is required to file a copy of the annual accounts with the registrar of companies. A partnership is under no such obligation.

7 ***Drawings***
In the case of a limited company, dividends are declared by the Directors, and must not exceed realized profits. In a partnership drawings are a matter for private agreement between the partners.

8 ***Taxation on income***
Each partner is liable to income tax on his share of the partnership profits. A limited company is liable to corporation tax, part of which (ACT) can be set off against the shareholder's personal income tax liability on dividends received.

9 ***Capital Gains Tax***
Each partner is liable to tax on his share of capital gains. A company is liable to tax on any capital gain, and in addition the individual shareholder is liable to tax on any capital gain on his shares.

10 ***Transferability***
A partner's interest in a partnership can only be transferred by agreement with all the partners. A member's interest in a limited company can be transferred by selling the shares, subject to the conditions laid down in the articles of association.

Non-trading concerns

Non-trading concerns embrace organizations such as sports clubs, social clubs, and political associations, which carry on their objectives with some common aim other than the making of profit. The net worth of such an organization will be known by some such term as *Accumulated Fund* or *General Fund*, so that:

Accumulated fund = assets − liabilities

The financial activities of the year will be reported in an *Income and Expenditure Account* rather than a profit and loss account.

Sometimes funds are raised for a specific purpose, in which case the amount raised from this source might be shown as a separate item in the balance sheet, or might be added on to the general fund on the face of the balance sheet rather than being shown as part of the income and expenditure account for the year.

Conclusion

We have seen that various forms of business organization have different legal positions and require different approaches to accounting for the way in which the proprietors' interest is built up. It is important to remember that in all cases the fundamental principles of the accounting equation apply.

Questions

1 For a partnership, what are the advantages and disadvantages of converting into a limited company?

(Society of Company and Commercial Accountants, November 1982)

2 Martin, Robertson and Stoneham were partners, sharing profits in the proportions of 40 per cent, 35 per cent and 25 per cent respectively. The partnership agreement provided that each partner was to receive interest at the rate of 5 per cent per annum on capital and advances, and that Martin and Robertson were to receive salaries of £500 per annum each. The trial balance of the partnership books at 30 June 1982 before making these adjustments, was as under:

	£	£
Bank	4,200	
Martin – Capital		12,000
Robertson – Capital		10,000
Stoneham – Capital		6,000
Martin – Advance		2,000
Martin – Current account	800	
Robertson – Current account	700	
Expenses	1,750	
Freehold property	10,200	
Plant	3,560	
Purchases	18,730	
Sales		24,160
Stock 1 July 1981	10,000	
Sundry creditors		3,700
Sundry debtors	6,720	
Wages	1,200	
	£57,860	£57,860

The inventory of stock on hand at 30 June 1982 amounted to £12,400. The partnership was dissolved as at 30 June 1982.

The freehold property was sold for £9,000 and a quarter of the stock for £3,000. Martin took over the balance of the stock at £9,000, the book debts at £6,000, and the plant at £3,000.

Required:

(a) Prepare a trading, profit and loss and appropriation account for the year ending 30 June 1982 and a balance sheet as at that date.

(b) Give the ledger accounts to close the books of the partnership.

(Heriot Watt University)

3

Kenmar Limited

Income statement for the year ended 30.9.82

	£	£	£
Sales			80,000
Opening stock	14,000		
Purchases	44,000		
	58,000		
Less: Closing stock	(15,000)		(43,000)
Gross profit			37,000
Wages and salaries		18,300	
Insurance		1,800	
General expenses		1,000	
Debenture interest		800	
Depreciation		4,400	
Provision for doubtful debts		(150)	
			(26,150)
Net profit			£10,850
Unappropriated profit 1.10.81			2,000
Net profit for year			10,850
			12,850
Interim dividend paid: Preference shares	600		
Proposed final dividend: Preference shares	600		
Proposed final dividend: Ordinary shares	1,000		
	2,200		
Transfer to general reserve	8,000		(10,200)
Unappropiated profit 30.9.82			2,650

Kenmar Limited

Balance sheet as at 30 September 1983

Fixed assets	*Cost*	*Dep.*	*£*
Land and buildings	56,000	—	56,000
Fixtures and fittings	22,000	14,400	7,600
	78,000	14,400	63,600
Current assets			
Stock		15,000	
Debtors	13,000		
Less: Provision	650	12,350	
Prepayments		100	
Cash		900	
		28,350	
Less: current liabilities			
Creditors	6,000		
Accruals	700		
Prop. dividends	1,600		
Bank overdraft	6,000	(14,300)	14,050
			£77,650
Share capital			
£1 Ordinary shares			20,000
6% £1 Preference shares			20,000
			40,000
Reserves			
Share premium account		1,000	
General reserve		18,000	
Unappropriated profits		2,650	21,650
Long-term loans			
5% Debentures			16,000
			£77,650

Required:

Answer the following questions clearly and concisely referring to the income statement and balance sheet of Kenmar Ltd where appropriate.

(a) Why are debenture interest and dividends not shown in the same section of the income statement?
(b) What is the purpose of transferring profits to the general reserve?
(c) Which of the reserves shown in Kenmar Ltd's balance sheet are revenue reserves and which are capital reserves?
(d) How did the share premium account arise?
(e) What, in principle, is the difference between revenue and capital reserves?
(f) What is the 'working capital' of the company and what is its importance?
(g) What is the net worth of Kenmar Ltd at the balance sheet date? Why is it unlikely to be its 'real' worth?
(h) What is the net asset value of each £1 ordinary share? Why would you expect it to be greater than par?
(i) Is the company a public limited company or a private company? State your reasons.

(Kingston Polytechnic)

4 Birch, Rose and Larch were in partnership sharing profits and losses: Birch one-half and Rose one-third, Larch one-sixth.

The draft balance sheet as at 31 March 1982 was as follows:

Fixed assets			
Freehold premises			6,000
Plant and equipment			9,400
			15,400
Current assets			
Stock		4,600	
Debtors	6,200		
Less: Provision for bad debts	600		
		5,600	
Cash at bank		8,060	
		18,260	

	£	£
Current liabilities		
Creditors	10,300	
		7,960
		£23,360
Capital accounts		
Birch		12,000
Rose		6,000
Larch		3,000
		21,000
Current accounts		
Birch	960	
Rose	840	
Larch	560	
		2,360
		£23,360

Birch retired on 31 March 1982. Rose and Larch admitted Elm into partnership with profits on 1 April 1982 and losses to be shared: Rose one-half, Larch one-quarter, Elm one-quarter.

It was agreed that, at 31 March 1982, the current market value of the freehold premises was £12,000 and the plant and equipment £7,900.

The partnership agreement provided that on the retirement of a partner, goodwill was to be valued at an amount equal to the weighted average annual profits of the previous three years. These profits were:

Year ended:	31 March 1980	£6,520
	31 March 1981	£8,420
	31 March 1982	£7,210

No account for goodwill was to be maintained in the books. It was agreed that Birch was to be paid £5,000 of the balance on his capital account and that the remaining balance should remain on loan to the partnership.

Elm introduced as capital, cash of £4,000 and plant and equipment worth £1,000.

You are required to prepare:

(a) the revaluation account, showing the surplus on revaluation;
(b) the partners' capital accounts;
(c) the balance sheet of Rose, Larch and Elm as at 1 April 1982.

(Sunderland Polytechnic)

5 Bee, Cee and Dee have been holding preliminary discussions with a view to forming a partnership to buy and sell antiques.

The position has now been reached where the prospective partners have agreed the basic arrangements under which the partnership will operate.

Bee will contribute £40,000 as capital and, up to £10,000 as a long-term loan to the partnership, if needed. He has extensive other business interests and will not therefore be taking an active part in the running of the business.

Cee is unable to bring in more than £2,000 as capital initially, but because he has an expert knowledge of the antique trade, will act as the manager of the business on a full-time basis.

Dee is willing to contribute £10,000 as capital. He will also assist in running the business as the need arises. In particular, he is prepared to attend auctions anywhere within the United Kingdom in order to acquire trading stock which he will transport back to the firm's premises in his van. On occasions he may also help Cee to restore the articles prior to sale to the public.

At their next meeting, the three prospective partners intend to decide upon the financial arrangements for sharing out the profits (or losses) made by the firm and have approached you for advice.

Required:

Prepare a set of explanatory notes, under suitable headings, of the considerations which the prospective partners should take into account in arriving at their decisions at the next meeting.

(ACCA Level 1, June 1982)

6

LONG-TERM ASSETS

Objective

The objective of this chapter is to consider the problems of accounting for assets held by a business on a long-term basis. Specifically the chapter considers:

1 The meaning of the term 'fixed asset'.
2 The problems in defining the cost of fixed assets.
3 Methods of computing depreciation.
4 Accounting for depreciation in the double entry system.
5 The link between depreciation and asset replacement.
6 Accounting for fixed asset disposals.
7 Accounting for revaluations and changes in estimates of asset lives.
8 Required disclosures.
9 Accounting for investments.
10 The special problems of intangible assets.

There are various requirements in company law, particularly the Companies Act 1981, to which we will refer. Another significant source of authority is SSAP12, 'Accounting for Depreciation'.

Fixed assets

The Companies Act 1981 defines as fixed assets those assets which 'are intended for use on a continuing basis in the company's activities'. (Sch.I, para. 75).

There are two key elements which are central to this definition:

1 Length of use. Normally we would expect an asset classified as 'fixed' to have a life of at least one year.
2 Purpose. A fixed asset is one acquired with the intention that it should be used in the business. For example a motor car acquired by a wholesaler for use by a commercial traveller visiting customers would be a fixed asset, whereas if the same car were acquired by a garage for resale it would be part of the current asset, stock.

In addition there is in practice a third consideration. It is not normal to treat items of small value as fixed assets, even if they meet the other two criteria identified above.

The Companies Act 1981 identifies three main categories of fixed asset:

1 ***Intangible assets***
These are rights or other economic benefits which are not physical in nature. Examples are patents, trade marks, and goodwill. The accounting treatment of intangible assets is considered in detail below.

2 ***Tangible assets***
These are items owned by the business with a physical existence. Examples are land, buildings, plant, machinery, fixtures, fittings, and motor vehicles.

3 ***Investments***
These are investments in other business held for the long term and are considered in detail below.

The terminology used in the Companies Act 1981

gives a somewhat broader definition to the term 'fixed asset' than that which has traditionally been used by accountants. Many accountants have tended to restrict the term 'fixed asset' to tangible assets, classifying intangible assets and investments as long-term items which are neither fixed nor current.

While records of each category of fixed asset are normally recorded in separate accounts, detailed records of each individual fixed asset are often recorded in a *fixed asset register*, which normally falls outside the double entry system.

Defining the cost of fixed assets

Accountants often describe expenditure on fixed assets as *capital* expenditure, as compared with *revenue* expenditure which is written off as an expense in the profit and loss account in the year incurred; when an item of expenditure is treated as part of the cost of a fixed asset it is often referred to as being *capitalized.* Clearly the decision as to whether to regard an item of expenditure as 'capital' or 'revenue' can have a significant effect on the reported profit for the year.

The cost of a fixed asset consists of both the purchase price and other directly attributable costs. Example of directly attributable costs include:

1 Costs of handling and delivering the asset to the business.
2 Costs of installing the fixed asset.
3 Professional fees incurred in the course of acquiring the asset, e.g. legal fees.

It may be necessary to exercise judgement in deciding which costs are directly attributable to acquisition of a new fixed asset.

One area of controversy relates to finance charges; some accountants argue that finance charges on money borrowed to finance the construction of a fixed asset up to the date when the asset is brought into use should be regarded as part of the cost of the fixed asset. In support of this view it is argued that in principle such costs can be regarded as part of the cost of bringing the asset into use.

On the other hand, it can be argued that it is not practical to link the expenditure on a fixed asset with any specific source of finance. In the UK capitalization of finance charges is rare.

Sometimes a business will construct a fixed asset for its own use. For example, a building contractor might construct a building to be used by the business itself. In this situation it is necessary to identify that part of the normal operating expenses of the business which relates to the construction of the fixed asset. However, if the total construction cost is greater than the market value of the asset constructed then only the market value would be capitalized as the cost of the asset, the excess amount being written off in the year incurred.

Another problem that can arise is that a group of assets are acquired together in a single purchase transaction. In this case it will be necessary to estimate what part of the total purchase price relates to each individual asset.

Expenditure on repairs and maintenance to fixed assets should be written off to profit and loss as an expense in the year incurred. In the past business often employed a 'provision for repairs account', making a charge to the profit and loss account each year in anticipation of major repairs expected to arise in the future, so as to set off the provision against the actual expense incurred in the year of the repair. Example 14 illustrates how such a system might operate. In practice it has become rare for such provision accounts to be used, but such an approach might still be taken by a business with a small number of fixed asset items subject to major overhaul expenses at intervals of several years.

Example 14

Barry Ltd prepare accounts with a 31 December year-end date. In 1983 the directors of Barry Ltd decided to open a provision for repairs account to cover a major overhaul of the company's plant expected to cost £300,000 in 1985. In 1985 the actual cost of the overhaul amounted to £280,000.

Provision for Repairs

31.12.83 Bal c/d	100,000	31.12.83 P & L	100,000

31.12.84	Bal c/d	200,000	1.01.84 Bal b/d	100,000
			31.12.84 P & L	100,000
		200,000		200,000
31.12.85	Repairs	200,000	1.01.85 Bal b/d	200,000

Repairs

1985	Cash	280,000	31.12.85 Provision	200,000
			31.12.85 P & L	80,000
		280,000		280,000

Profit and loss extracts

	1983	*1984*	*1985*
Repairs	100,000	100,000	80,000

There may sometimes be a practical problem in distinguishing between expenditure on maintenance and on the improvement of an asset. Expenditure on improvements should only be capitalized if it increases the future benefits of the asset above the level expected when the asset was acquired.

Depreciation: various methods

All tangible fixed assets, with the exception of freehold land, have a limited useful life. Thus it is necessary to allocate the expense of owning each tangible fixed asset between the accounting periods in which the asset is used by the business. The term 'depreciation' is used to describe the amount written off fixed assets and recorded as an expense in the profit and loss account. The process of depreciating fixed assets can be seen as an example of the 'accruals' concept, whereby expenditure is written off in the accounting period in which related income is recorded as earned. The term 'amortization' is sometimes used in place of 'depreciation'.

SSAP 12 defines depreciation as:

> The measure of the wearing out, consumption or other loss of value of a fixed asset whether arising from use, effluxion of time or obsolescence through technology and market changes.

By 'value' is meant the amount at which fixed assets are introduced into the accounts; it is important to note that depreciation is *not* a process of 'valuation'.

The specific causes for depreciation listed in SSAP 12 are:

1 ***Use***
In some cases usage will be the major reason for consumption of a fixed asset. For example, the value of a quarry will be consumed as a result of stone being removed from it. In the case of some other fixed assets gradual deterioration will be attributable to a mixture of usage and the passage of time; a motor car is an example of such an asset.

2 ***Effluxion of time***
In some cases the passage of time will be the major cause for the consumption of a fixed asset; for example, a leasehold property will lose its value over the period of the lease irrespective of the level of usage.

3 ***Obsolescence***
In some cases the value of an asset is lost because the asset becomes out of date, even though still in good working order. *Technology* may result in obsolescence because an alternative and preferable item is developed; in recent years computer systems have been particularly vulnerable to this. *Market changes* can be another cause; for example in the textile industry changes in fashion may cause certain specialist machinery to become obsolete.

A further possible cause for obsolescence not mentioned in SSAP 12 is that developments inside the business itself can render a fixed asset out of date. For example, a rapidly expanding firm may outgrow the capacity of its computer accounting system and be forced to replace it.

The total amount which has to be written off as depreciation in respect of a fixed asset will be the cost less the amount which the asset is expected to realize when it is disposed of. The amount which it is estimated the asset will realize is referred to as the 'scrap value' or 'residual value', and consists of the sale proceeds less costs of removal and disposal. Where the estimated residual value is small in relation to the cost, it is often ignored in computing the depreciation charge so that the whole cost of the asset is depreciated.

Depreciation methods fall into two broad categories, *time-based* and *usage-based*. There are three main time-based methods:

1 *Straight-line*

The straight-line method involves writing off an equal amount of depreciation in each year of the asset's life. The depreciation charge for each year will therefore be:

$$\frac{\text{Cost} - \text{scrap value}}{\text{Number of years life}}$$

On the basis of the information in Example 15 the depreciation charge in each year would be:

$$\frac{1000 - 100}{4} = £225$$

This is often expressed as the percentage of the original cost to be written off each year, in our example being:

$$\frac{225}{1{,}000} = 22.5\%$$

Where the scrap value of an asset is not taken into account in computing the amount of depreciation then the percentage of the cost of a fixed asset to be written off each year can be computed as:

$$\frac{1}{\text{Number of years' life}}$$

For Pendennis this will be:

$$\frac{1}{4} = 25\%$$

2 *Reducing balance*

The reducing balance method involves applying a percentage rate to the written down value of the asset each year. Thus the depreciation charge will be heavier in the early years. There is a formula for computing the rate to be used:

$$r = 1 - \sqrt[n]{\frac{s}{c}}$$

where:
r is rate to be used
n is number of years life
s is scrap value
c is cost.

In our example Pendennis the depreciation rate will be:

$$1 - \sqrt[4]{\frac{100}{1{,}000}} = 44\%$$

So that the depreciation provided on the glove-making machine will be:

1984	Cost	1,000
	Depreciation	440
1985	Written-down value b/d	560
	Depreciation @ 44%	246
1986	Written-down value b/d	314
	Depreciation @ 44%	138
1987	Written-down value b/d	176
	Depreciation @ 44%	77
	Scrap value	99

Note that because the depreciation rate calculation has been rounded to 44 per cent the scrap value at the end of four years is not exactly £100.

A reducing balance rate of depreciation can only be computed if some scrap value is assumed, and unless the assumed scrap value is a significant amount an absurd rate will be computed.

3 *Sum of years' digits (SYD)*

This is another method designed to provide progressively smaller amounts of depreciation over the asset's life. The depreciation for the year is computed as:

$$\frac{\text{Number of years remaining life}}{\text{Sum of digits}} \times (\text{Cost} - \text{scrap value})$$

The 'sum of digits' is the total of the numbers

representing years of life; for Pendennis this will be 1 + 2 + 3 + 4 = 10

Thus the SYD depreciation for our example Pendennis will be:

1984 $\frac{4}{10} \times 900 = 360$
1985 $\frac{3}{10} \times 900 = 270$
1986 $\frac{2}{10} \times 900 = 180$
1987 $\frac{1}{10} \times 900 = 90$

Usage-based methods of depreciation try to write off depreciation in each year in proportion to the amount of usage, so that the formula for usage-based depreciation will be:

$$\frac{\text{Usage in year}}{\text{Total expected usage}} \times (\text{Cost} - \text{scrap value})$$

Two commonly used measures of usage are:

(*a*) *Output*
This is sometimes called the *units of production method*. For Pendennis depreciation in 1984 would be:

$$\frac{150{,}000}{500{,}000} \times 900 = 270$$

(*b*) *Production hours*
Under the *production hours method* depreciation for Pendennis in 1984 would be:

$$\frac{5{,}800}{20{,}000} \times 900 = 261$$

Example 15

Pendennis prepares accounts with a 31 December year end. On 1 January 1984 he bought a glove-making machine for £1,000. The machine has a four-year life and a residual value of £100. The machine is expected to make 500,000 pairs of gloves in 20,000 running hours. In the year to 31 December 1984 the machine produced 150,000 pairs of gloves in 5,800 running hours.

A practical problem which arises in relation to the computation of depreciation on a time basis is that of what to do when assets are acquired or disposed of part way through a year. There are two approaches:

1 To provide a full year's depreciation in the year of acquisition and no depreciation in the year of disposal.
2 To provide depreciation in the years of acquisition and disposal for that part of the year in which the assets are in use.

In examinations it sometimes happens that the examiner does not specifically state which approach is to be taken; in that case it is normal to take approach 2 if specific dates of acquisition and disposal are given.

A further method sometimes used is the *revaluation method*, whereby a group of fixed assets are revalued at the end of each accounting period and any loss of value is written off as depreciation. As we have seen, in principle depreciation should only be regarded as representing losses in value due to certain specific causes. However, this method is sometimes used in relation to groups of fixed assets with a small individual value, where keeping detailed records of each asset would be burdensome; loose tools are a good example of such an asset.

In choosing between time-based and usage-based depreciation methods an important factor to consider is the basic cause for the asset depreciating. For example a leasehold property will normally be amortized on a time basis. Where depreciation is in practice attributable to a mixture of usage and time factors then the following points might be considered:

1 Availability of a measure of usage. Clearly a usage-based appraoch is only practical where some measure of usage is available.
2 Required effort to measure usage. For example, in a haulage firm with two lorries it would be practical to calculate the mileage covered by the lorries each year, whereas with 100 lorries the effort involved might seem unreasonable.
3 Integration with the cost accounting system. For example a manufacturer who wishes to keep detailed records of the cost of individual items or batches of production may find it convenient to

follow a usage-based depreciation approach, both because usage records are available and because this makes it easier to allocate the depreciation expense to items produced.

In choosing between the various time-based methods the following points would be considered:

1 The straight-line method is generally seen as being the simplest.
2 Advocates of reducing balance and sum of the years digits argue that these methods are particularly appropriate where an asset is subject to higher repair costs and periods out of service in the later years of use.

In choosing between various usage-based measures the following points might be considered:

1 The units of production method is often more convenient because normally a business will have data available on the quantity of units produced for stock control purposes.
2 The production hours method is technically more correct in relating depreciation to actual usage. By contrast, the depreciation charge under the production hours method will vary according to how efficiently the machine has been used.

Depreciation: the double entry system

In the double entry system it is normal practice to record a separate depreciation account in respect of each type of fixed asset owned by the business. Figure 40 shows how the depreciation on the glove-making machine in our example Pendennis, computed by the straight-line method, would be recorded over a four-year period. Each year the depreciation charge for the year is computed, and then debited to profit and loss and credited to the depreciation account. The balance carried down on the depreciation account will then consist of the total depreciation accumulated in relation to the asset.

Figure 40 *Recording depreciation in one depreciation account*

Depreciation on machinery					
31.12.84	Bal c/d	225	31.12.84	P & L	225
31.12.85	Bal c/d	450	1.1.85	Bal b/d	225
			31.12.85	P & L	225
		450			450
31.12.86	Bal c/d	675	1.1.86	Bal b/d	450
			31.12.86	P & L	225
		675			675
31.12.87	Bal c/d	900	1.1.87	Bal b/d	675
			31.12.87	P & L	225
		900			900
			1.1.88	Bal b/d	900

Balance sheet extracts

Plant	1984	1985	1986	1987
	£	£	£	£
Cost	1,000	1,000	1,000	1,000
Depreciation	225	450	675	900
Net	775	550	325	100

Figure 41 *Recording both cost and accumulated depreciation in one account*

Machinery

1.1.84	Bank	1,000	31.12.84	P & L – depreciation	225
31.12.84	Depreciation c/d	225	31.12.84	Cost c/d	1,000
		1,225			1,225
1.1.85	Cost b/d	1,000	1.1.85	Depreciation b/d	225
31.12.85	Depreciation c/d	450	31.12.85	P & L depreciation	225
			31.12.85	Cost c/d	1,000
		1,450			1,450
1.1.86	Cost b/d	1,000	1.1.86	Depreciation b/d	450
31.12.86	Depreciation c/d	675	31.12.86	P & L depreciation	225
			31.12.86	Cost c/d	1,000
		1,675			1,675
1.1.87	Cost b/d	1,000	1.1.87	Depreciation b/d	675
31.12.87	Depreciation c/d	900	31.12.87	P & L depreciation	225
			31.12.87	Cost c/d	1,000
		1,900			1,900
1.1.88	Cost b/d	1,000	1.1.88	Depreciation b/d	900

Figure 42 *Using both a depreciation account and a provision for depreciation account*

Provision for depreciation

31.12.84	Bal c/d	225	31.12.84	Depreciation	225
31.12.85	Bal c/d	450	1.1.85	Bal b/d	225
			31.12.85	Depreciation	225
		450			450
31.12.86	Bal c/d	675	1.1.86	Bal c/d	450
			31.12.86	Depreciation	225
		675			675
31.12.87	Bal c/d	900	1.1.87	Bal b/d	675
			31.12.87	Depreciation	225
		900			900
			1.1.88	Bal b/d	900

Depreciation

31.12.84	Provision for depr.	225	31.12.84	P & L	225
31.12.85	Provision for depr.	225	31.12.85	P & L	225
31.12.86	Provision for depr.	225	31.12.86	P & L	225
31.12.87	Provision for depr.	225	31.12.87	P & L	225

There are other methods of recording the data in the accounts:

1 Sometimes data on both the cost and the accumulated depreciation relating to a category of fixed asset is shown in one account, the balance of cost being carried down as a debit balance and the balance of depreciation as a credit balance. Figure 41 illustrates how this might be recorded for Pendennis.
2 Sometimes two accounts relating to depreciation are recorded. One called a 'depreciation account' is debited with the depreciation charges for the year, and the balance at the year end is transferred to profit and loss. The other is the 'provision for depreciation account' which is credited with the depreciation charge for the year, and on which the total depreciation accumulated is carried down as a credit balance. Figure 42 illustrates this system.

In the accounts it is normal to show both the cost and the accumulated depreciation relating to each category of fixed asset. The reasons for this can be illustrated if we consider the possible accounting information for two businesses, A and B:

Motor cars	*A*	*B*
	£000	*£000*
Cost	100	12
Depreciation	90	2
Net	10	10

If only the net amount were shown, both businesses would appear to be in a similar position. By disclosing the original cost and the accumulated depreciation two substantial benefits are gained:

1 The very different positions of the two businesses can be identified, we can see that business A has a large number of motor cars nearing the end of their useful life, while business B has a small number of motor cars which are recently acquired.
2 Computation of the depreciation charge necessarily involves estimates to be made. In our example we can see that the amount of £10,000 shown as an asset 'motor cars' is very much more dependent on the accuracy of estimates in business A than in business B. For example, a 10 per cent error in the estimate of accumulated depreciation could double or totally eliminate the motor-car asset shown in business A but would not be significant in business B.

The link between depreciation and replacement

As explained above, depreciation is a system for allocating the cost of a fixed asset to the accounting periods when it is consumed. The accumulated depreciation provision represents a deduction from the original cost of the asset necessary to show the written-down value. Thus there is no direct link between depreciation and the replacement of fixed assets.

An indirect link between depreciation and replacement exists in so far as one of the uses of the profit and loss account is as a guide to the amount which the proprietors of the business can prudently withdraw as drawings. By providing depreciation over the life of an asset we help to ensure that the original resources invested in the fixed asset are retained in the business. However, the resources retained are not necessarily held in a form which can be used for replacement, since they may be tied up in other fixed assets or in working capital.

It is important, therefore, that the provision of depreciation is *not* regarded as a mechanism enabling the business to ensure that funds are available for the replacement of fixed assets when required.

Disposals of fixed assets

When a fixed asset is disposed of it is necessary to remove the fixed asset from the balance sheet and to reflect the difference between the disposal proceeds and the written-down value of the fixed asset in the profit and loss account.

Example 16, Lyndon Ltd, shows a simple example of a disposal of a fixed asset. The first step which has to be taken is to find out the cost and the accumulated depreciation relating to the fixed asset disposed of. In practice this would be ascertained from the fixed asset register or, where this is not available, from the working papers relating to the preparation of previous years' accounts. In examination conditions, the cost of any asset disposed of will normally be given, but often the student is required to compute the accumulated depreciation; the workings note at the foot of Figure 43 shows how this might be computed for our example, Lyndon Ltd.

In the double entry system the following steps must be taken; these are illustrated in Figure 43.

(a) A fixed asset disposal account is opened, and the cost of the asset is transferred from the fixed asset account to the disposal account. The entry in our example will be:

Dr Disposal	6,400	
Cr Motor vehicles		6,400

(b) The accumulated depreciation on the asset is transferred from the depreciation account to the disposal account. The entry in our example will be:

Dr Depreciation	3,700	
Cr Disposal		3,700

The combined effect of entries (a) and (b) is to remove the fixed asset from the balance sheet and to record the written-down value of the asset in the disposal account.

(c) When the disposal proceeds are received these should be credited to the disposal account. In our example, assuming that the amount received was paid into the bank, the entry will be:

Dr Bank	2,850	
Cr Disposal		2,850

(d) The balance on the disposal account now reflects the difference between the disposal proceeds and the written down value of the assets disposed of. This can represent either a gain or a loss. In our example there has been a gain which is transferred to profit and loss by the entry:

Dr Disposal	150	
Cr Profit & Loss		150

(e) The year's depreciation charge must be computed on the basis of asset and accumulated depreciation figures which exclude the assets disposed of. In our example the charge will be:

$$25\% \times ((35{,}000 - 6{,}400) - (15{,}000 - 3{,}700)) = \underline{\underline{4{,}325}}$$

Example 16

Lyndon Ltd prepares accounts to 31 March each year. The balance sheet at 31 March 1985 showed in relation to motor vehicles:

	£
Cost	35,000
Depreciation	15,000
Net	20,000

On 1 April 1985 a motor van which had cost £6,400 on 31 December 1982 was sold for £2,850. The company's policy is to provide depreciation by the reducing balance method at the rate of 25 per cent, with a full year's depreciation in the year of acquisition and no depreciation in the year of disposal.

In the year to 31 March 1986 there were no further additions or disposals.

In the example presented above it has been assumed that the entries relating to the disposal have been entered at the date of disposal. In practice it often happens that the only entry made at the time of the disposal transaction is to record receipt of the disposal proceeds; both in examinations and in practice it is common for these to be credited to an inappropriate account, e.g. fixed assets, sales, or suspense. In such case it is necessary to transfer the credit entry to the disposal account, and to transfer the cost and accumulated depreciation to the disposal account at the year end.

It sometimes happens that a fixed asset is disposed of in a part exchanged deal for a new fixed asset rather than for cash. In such a case the normal accounting entry will be:

Figure 43

Disposal account							
(a)	1.4.85	Motor vehicle – Cost	6,400	(b)	1.4.85	Motor vehicle – depreciation	3,700
(d)	31.3.86	P & L	150	(c)	1.4.85	Bank	2,850
			6,550				6,550

Motor vehicles							
	1.4.85	Bal b/d	35,000	(a)	1.4.85	Disposal	6,400
					31.3.86	Bal c/d	28,600
			35,000				35,000
	1.4.86	Bal b/d	28,600				

Depreciation on motor vehicles							
(b)	1.4.85	Disposal	3,700		1.4.85	Bal b/d	15,000
	31.3.86	Bal c/d	15,625	(e)	31.3.86	P & L	4,325
			19,325				19,325
					1.4.86	Bal b/d	15,625

Workings – Accumulated depreciation on disposal

	Depreciation each year £	*Cumulative depreciation* £
Cost	6,400	
less: Depreciation year to 31.3.83	1,600	1,600
WDV at 1.4.83	4,800	
Depreciation year to 31.3.84	1,200	1,200
WDV at 1.4.84	3,600	
Depreciation year to 31.3.85	900	900
	2,700	3,700

Dr Fixed Assets	Cost of new asset
Cr Bank	Cash payment
Cr Disposal account	Trade in allowance

It sometimes happens, particularly in relation to motor cars, that an artificially high trade-in allowance is given which in fact constitutes a trade discount allowed on the new asset. In such a case the amount of the *excess* trade-in allowance should, in principle, be deducted from cost of the new asset recorded in the fixed asset account and from the trade-in allowance credited to the disposal account. Example 17 illustrates how this might be done.

Example 17

On 30 June 1985, Warrington traded in his car for a new model. The purchase invoice showed:

	£
Cost	5,000
Trade-in allowance	2,800
Cash due	2,200

On this basis the accounting entries would be:

Dr Motor vehicles	5,000	
Cr Cash		2,200
Cr Disposal		2,800

Let us suppose that, as an alternative to a part-exchange deal, Warrington had been offered a straight discount on the cost of the new car of £500. In principle the correct entries would be:

Dr Motor vehicles	4,500	
Cr Cash		2,200
Cr Disposal		2,300

In either case the same entries would still have to be made to eliminate the cost and accumulated depreciation on the vehicle sold from the accounts.

Revaluations and changes in estimate

It frequently happens that the managers of a business will wish to depart from historical cost priniciples by revaluing some of the fixed assets in the accounts. This is particularly common in the case of property, which can be held by the business for such a period of time as to make the original cost figure quite meaningless. In such a case the accounting entry required in principle is:

Dr Asset account }
Cr Proprietors } Amount of the revaluation surplus

In the case of a limited company it is important to note that the revaluation surplus does not constitute a realized profit and accordingly must be taken to a capital reserve; thus the entry would be:

Dr Asset account }
Cr Revaluation reserve } Amount of the revaluation surplus

It sometimes happens that during the life of an asset the management of the business change their mind as to the estimated life span or as to the depreciation method used. SSAP12 provides that in such a case the part of the cost of the asset not yet written off should be depreciated over the residue of life as now estimated by the new depreciation method, except that where the written-down amount exceeds current value the excess should be written off immediately.

Disclosure requirements

The Companies Act 1981 requires disclosure in respect of each category of fixed asset shown in the accounts of:

1 The cost brought forward, any valuation adjustment, additions, disposals, and cost carried forward.
2 The accumulated depreciation brought forward, the depreciation charge for the year, any provision removed because of an asset disposal, any other adjustment to depreciation, and the balance carried forward.

Example 18 shows how a note to the accounts might be drafted so as to convey this information.

SSAP12 requires disclosure of the accounting policy adopted in relation to depreciation, specifying the depreciation methods used and the useful lives or depreciation rates assumed in relation to each major category of fixed asset. Example 18 shows how such a note might be presented.

Example 18

Depreciation disclosure – tangible fixed assets

	Freehold land & buildings	*Plant*	*Total*
Cost	£	£	£
At January 1 1985	120,000	180,000	300,000
Additions	35,000	60,000	95,000
Disposals	—	(50,000)	(50,000)
At December 31 1985	155,000	190,000	345,000
Depreciation			
At January 1 1985	—	54,000	54,000
Provided during year	—	38,000	38,000
Disposals	—	(20,000)	(20,000)
At December 31 1985	—	72,000	72,000
Net book amount December 31 1985	155,000	118,000	273,000
Net book amount January 1 1985	120,000	126,000	246,000

Accounting policies - extract

Depreciation

Fixed assets are depreciated over their estimated useful lives. No depreciation is provided on freehold land and buildings. Other fixed assets are depreciated by the straight-line method at the following rates:

Plant 10%

Investments

An investment in another business can take the form either of owning part of the equity of the business, with the right to a share in the profits, or of making a loan to the business, with the right to receive a fixed rate of interest. Sometimes the investment in a business will combine both forms. The most common type of business in which to invest is a limited company, and such investments can be considered under three headings:

1 ***Subsidiary companies***
These are companies in which the investing company owns a controlling interest.

2 ***Associated companies***
These are defined by SSAP1, 'Accounting for Associated Companies'. Broadly speaking, the definition covers investments which are long-term, carry significant influence on the affairs of the investee, and are substantial (generally taken as 20 per cent or more). The Companies Act 1981 uses the term 'related company' to cover much the same situation.

3 ***Others***
Other investments involve a lesser degree of influence over the affairs of the investee.

The Companies Act 1981 requires that each type of investment be separately identified in the balance sheet. The distinction is also important because it is normal practice to take proposed dividends receivable from subsidiary and associated companies into the profit and loss account of the investor at the date when they are proposed, whereas dividends from other investments are only credited to profit and loss when actually received.

Where a company has subsidiaries, it is required to present *group accounts* in addition to its own accounts. Group accounts are normally presented in the form of *consolidated accounts*, which report the affairs of the company and its subsidiaries as though they were a single entity, and in addition include the investing company's share of the profit of the associate. The preparation of group accounts is a topic which falls outside the scope of this text.

Depending on their nature and the purpose for which they are held investments may be classified either as a long-term asset or as a current asset; as we have seen the former would be counted as a fixed asset in terms of the Companies Act 1981.

The Companies Acts require disclosure of the market value of listed investments and the directors' estimate of the value of other investments, these valuations are not normally introduced into the accounts in place of the historical cost amounts unless there has been a diminution in value which is expected to be permanent.

Intangible assets

We have already defined intangible assets as rights or other economic benefits which are not physical in nature. As a broad principle it can be said that accountants are generally reluctant to record such items as assets in the balance sheet because of their nebulous character. The accounting treatment of intangible assets can be considered under three broad headings:

1 ***Development costs***
Development costs are expenses incurred in developing a new or improved product for commercial exploitation. The Companies Act 1981 states that such costs should only be capitalized in 'special circumstances'. SSAP13, 'Accounting for Research and Development', allows companies to choose between a policy of writing off all development expenditure as it is incurred and a policy of capitalizing development

expenditure which can be expected with confidence to be recovered from the profits generated from the related project. Where development expenditure is capitalized it should be written off over the period of the related project on a prudent basis.

2 ***Legal rights***
A business may incur costs in acquiring valuable legal rights. Examples include patent rights, trade marks, and franchise agreements. Where such rights can reasonably be expected to generate future profits then it is normal to capitalize the costs, if material, and amortize the cost over the useful life of the legal rights.

3 ***Goodwill***
Goodwill is the difference between the value of a business as a whole and the total value of its individual identifiable assets. At any point in time every business has what might be termed 'inherent goodwill', but goodwill is only identified by a transaction when a business is bought as a whole. Accountants have argued at length on the appropriate treatment for such 'purchased goodwill' and three main approaches have emerged:

(a) Write off purchased goodwill when it is acquired, on the grounds that such an item is too nebulous to be prudently reported as an asset.
(b) Carry the purchase goodwill in the accounts indefinitely, unless circumstances suggest that the value of goodwill has been lost. The argument for this approach is that as long as the business acquired continues the related goodwill may also be regarded as in existence.
(c) Capitalize purchase goodwill, and amortize it over its economic life. This approach treats purchase goodwill like other fixed assets.

The Companies Act 1981 requires individual companies to amortize any capitalized goodwill within the useful economic life, but does not extend this requirement to the group accounts.

Conclusion

Fixed assets are those assets held for use in the activities of the business on a long-term basis. Depreciation is the system whereby the cost of fixed assets is allocated to the accounting periods which benefit from their use. Judgements which have a significant impact on the amounts reported in the accounts have to be made, particularly in the following areas:

1 Deciding which items should be regarded as fixed assets.
2 Defining the cost of fixed assets.
3 Choosing depreciation methods to be used.
4 Estimating asset lives.

Thus the accounting policies chosen in relation to fixed assets and depreciation can have a material effect on the accounts.

Questions

1 The depreciation process is often given, by people who should know better, certain magical qualities; that it is a valuation exercise and that it will help the firm replace the asset when the time comes. Lewis and Gilespie (1976).

Discuss two misconceptions of the depreciation process and explain its role in financial accounting.

(Trent Polytechnic)

2 On 1 January 1978, a manufacturing business bought three machines at a cost of £30,000 each. The business normally provided depreciation at 20 per cent per year on the reducing balance basis. On 1 January 1981, a further machine was acquired at a cost of £35,000. On 30 June 1981, and on 31 October, two machines originally acquired on 1 January 1978 were sold for £10,000, and £12,000. A full year's depreciation is charged in the year of purchase of any assets, but none is charged in the year of disposal.

(a) You are required to prepare:
(i) The following accounts for the year ending 31 December 1981:

Machinery account
Provision for depreciation (machinery) account
Asset disposal account.

(ii) The Balance Sheet Extract at 31 December 1981.

(b) The manufacturer, observing the data given in the asset disposal account and noting the cost of the new machine owing to inflation, ruled that 'in future we must increase the depreciation rate because we underestimated the amount of cash needed to replace the asset.' Comment on this statement.

(Huddersfield Polytechnic)

3 A business has the following fixed assets at 31 December 1980:

Freehold land & buildings - cost		25,000
Plant & machinery - cost	12,800	
Depreciation to date	6,200	6,600
Motor vehicles - cost	10,450	
Depreciation to date	6,100	4,350
Fixtures and fittings at valuation		1,800
		£37,750

Depreciation policies are as follows:

Freehold land and buildings: none considered necessary

Plant and machinery: 10 per cent p.a. straight line
Motor vehicles: 30 per cent p.a. reducing balance
each giving a full year's depreciation in the year of purchase and none in the year of disposal.

Fixtures and fittings: annual valuation by the directors

During the year to 31 December 1981 the following transactions took place.

(a) Plant and machinery costing £4,000 were purchased.

(b) A machine (purchased on 1 October 1974 for £3,000) was sold for scrap for £200.

(c) A motor vehicle, which had been purchased on 1 March 1978 for £4,000, was part-exchanged on 30 June 1981 for a new vehicle costing £6,000. The balance, paid in cash, amounted to £4,500.

(d) Fixtures and fittings were purchased for £600.

At 31 December 1981 the fixtures and fittings were estimated to have a value of £2,050.

You are required:

(i) To show how these facts are reflected in the relevant ledger accounts of the business, and

(ii) To give relevant extracts from the Profit and Loss Account for the year ended 31 December 1981 and the Balance Sheet at that date.

(Wolverhampton Polytechnic)

4 The balance sheet of Black Ltd as at 30 June 1981 shows motor vehicles as follows:

	£
Motor vehicles at cost	61,850
Less depreciation	32,426
	£29,424

Vehicles are depreciated on the straight line basis over a five year life. Depreciation is charged pro rata to time in the year of acquisition but no charge is made in the year of disposal. The disposal account is written up on the last day of each year.

During 1981–2 the following vehicle transactions took place:

30 September, purchased delivery van £8,600.
31 October, purchased sales manager's car £10,800.
28 February, purchased lorry £4,000. The lorry was second-hand and originally cost £9,600.

Sales of vehicles:
31 October, car, £300, cost £2,800 when purchased on 1 July 1977.
31 December, tractor, £540, cost £2,400 when purchased on 30 November 1978.
31 March, van, £420 cost £1,900 when purchased on 1 April 1979.

You are required to write up the following accounts for the year ended 30 June 1982:

(a) Motor Vehicles Account.

(b) Provision for Depreciation of Motor Vehicles Account.

(c) Disposal of Motor Vehicles Account.
(d) Show the relevant entries in the Balance Sheet at 30 June 1982.

(Preston Polytechnic)

5 You have been given the task, by one of the partners of the firm of accountants for which you work, of assisting in the preparation of a trend statement for a client.

The client's business has been in existence for four years. Figures for the three previous years are known but those for the fourth year need to be calculated. Unfortunately, the supporting workings for the previous years' figures cannot be found and the client's own ledger accounts and workings are not available. One item in particular, plant, is causing difficulty and the following figures have been given to you:

	12 Months ended 31 March			
	1979	*1980*	*1981*	*1982*
	£	£	£	£
A Plant at cost	80,000	80,000	90,000	?
B Accumulated depreciation	(16,000)	(28,000)	(36,720)	?
C Net (written down value)	64,000	51,200	53,280	?

The only other information available is that disposals have taken place at the beginning of the financial years concerned.

	Date of Disposal	*Original acquisition*	*Original cost*	*Sales proceeds*
	12 months ended 31 March		£	£
First disposal	1981	1979	15,000	8,000
Second disposal	1982	1979	30,000	21,000

Plant sold was replaced on the same day by new plant. The cost of the plant which replaced the first disposal is not known but the replacement for the second disposal is known to have cost £50,000.

Required:

(a) Identify the method of providing for depreciation on plant employed by the client, stating how you have arrived at your conclusion.
(b) Reconstruct a working schedule to support the figures shown at line *B* for each of the years ended 31 March 1979, 1980 and 1981. Extend your workings to cover year ended 31 March 1982.
(c) Produce the figures that should be included in the blank spaces on the trend statement at lines *A*, *B* and *C* for year ended 31 March 1982.
(d) Calculate the profit or loss arising on each of the two disposals.

(ACCA Level 1 - June 1982)

7

CURRENT ASSETS

Objectives

The broad objective of this chapter is to define current assets and to look in detail at two types of current assets, stock and debtors. Specific objectives are:

1 To define and consider the significance of current assets.
2 To consider the nature and significance of stock and work in progress.
3 To describe the way in which stock held is recorded and controlled.
4 To look at the rules governing the valuation of stock.
5 To examine the problem of allocating costs to stock.
6 To discuss the special problems of accounting for long-term contract work in progress.
7 To describe the procedures adopted to account for trade debtors and bad debts.

Definition of current

There are two approaches to the classification of assets as *current*:

1 The classification can be regarded as being intended to give an indication of *liquidity*, i.e. the availability of cash resources to meet the financial obligations of the business on a day-to-day basis. For this purpose a current asset would generally be regarded as one expected to be realized in the form of cash within one year.
2 The classification can be regarded as being intended to identify those resources which are constantly circulating in the course of the business. For this purpose a current asset would be regarded as one which is expected eventually to be realized in cash within the normal operating cycle of the business.

In practice the convention that has emerged is that the accounts show as current both those assets that are expected to be realized within one year and those assets which are within the normal operating cycle of the business.

The major categories of current asset are:

1 Stocks and work in progress.
2 Trade debtors.
3 Prepayments, considered in detail in Chapter 4 above.
4 Investments held for the short term considered in detail in Chapter 6 above.
5 Bank and cash balances. The control of these has been considered in Chapter 3.

The convention as to the definition of a current asset which has emerged does mean that there can sometimes be incompatibility between the two purposes for which current assets are identified. For example where a business enters into a long-term building contract a period substantially in excess of one year may pass between commencing and completing the work, but since the work falls within the normal operating cycle work in progress will be regarded as a current asset.

Stock and work in progress: nature and significance

The computation of the closing stock figure has a significant effect on the profit for the year and on the total assets shown in the balance sheet. There are a number of problems, both in practice and in principle, in the process of ascertaining the value of stock. These include:

1 The problem of how to ascertain the physical amount of each type of stock held.
2 The issue of the basis on which stock should be valued. Within the historical cost convention stock will normally be valued at cost but there may be situations where, following the prudence concept, some lower value will be appropriate.
3 Where similar items have been acquired at different prices it may be necessary to decide which price should be regarded as the cost of the stock of those items still held.
4 Where the business has performed work on stock, particularly any form of manufacturing process, it will be necessary to decide exactly which expenses form part of the cost of stock.
5 Where costs are incurred in work on a long-term contract then strict adherence to the prudence concept, whereby profit is only recognized in the accounts at the end of the contract, may result in serious distortion of the reported profit. Accordingly the question arises as to whether some element of profit earned should be recognized during the course of such contracts.

The Companies Act 1981 includes some guidance on stock valuation. The subject has been considered in detail in the UK in an accounting standard, SSAP9. There are also two International Accounting Standards, IAS2 and IAS11, relating to stock and work in progress. These sources of authority have helped to reduce, but by no means eliminate, the variety of practice in the valuation of stock.

SSAP9 offers the following definition:

> Stocks and work in progress comprise:
> (a) goods or other assets purchased for resale;
> (b) consumable stores;
> (c) raw materials and components purchased for incorporation into products for sale;
> (d) products and services in intermediate stages of completion;
> (e) finished goods.

Although the principles of valuation are the same for each type of stock, the problems of valuation vary between types. For example the range of costs attributable to goods manufactured by the business is very much greater, and therefore complex, than in the case of goods purchased for resale.

Identification of stock quantities

There are two approaches to the problem of identifying and recording quantities of stock held:

1 *Continuous stock recording*, described in the US as *perpetual inventory*. With this approach a system of recording identifies all items of stock received and issued, so that the balance of stock held at any point in time can be identified. Such a system is sometimes integrated with the accounting system, so that a cost of sales account is maintained in the ledger; sometimes the stock recording system is independent of the double entry book-keeping system so that it is only when a profit and loss account is prepared that the cost of sales can be identified, based on the stock figure extracted from the stock recording system.
2 *Periodic stock counts*, described in the US as *periodic inventory*. With this approach the stock figure is ascertained by making a physical count of the stock held at the point in time for which information on stock is required.

Continuous stock-record systems can be very useful to management for the following purposes:

1 As part of a system to control the use of stock and ensure it is properly used for the company's benefit.
2 As part of the system for identifying the point in time when it is necessary to reorder stock.
3 Management are able to identify the level of stock at any point in time, a particularly useful

facility when interim accounts are prepared during a year.
4 The causes of consumption of stock can be identified. Where there is no continuous stock recording system it is normally assumed that all consumption of goods is attributable to cost of sales.

The main factor which prevents many businesses, particularly small ones, from using continuous stock records is the expense of operating such a system.

It is generally accepted by accountants that where a continuous stock-record system is in operation the record should be tested by making a count of each type of stock item at least once a year. This can be done either by a system of *continuous stocktaking*, whereby a count is made of a few items each day in the year, or by *annual stocktaking*, whereby a count of all items is made at the same time. The benefits of continuous stocktaking are:

1 It avoids the need for a total close-down of business activity while a complete count is made.
2 Any irregularities or changes in procedure on the part of those responsible for the custody of stock are revealed more rapidly.
3 In some cases the volume of stock may be such as to make a complete count in one day impossible.
4 In a large business it is possible to employ staff specifically as stocktakers, so that a greater degree of skill in performing the job is built up.

The benefits of annual stocktaking are:

1 Where the stock count is performed on the accounting date then all corrections made will serve to ensure the accuracy of the stock figure shown in the accounts; indeed, where continuous stocktaking regularly reveals material differences it may be essential to make a year-end stock count to ensure the accuracy of the accounts.
2 It may be substantially less costly than a continuous stocktaking system.

At the end of each accounting period it is necessary to ensure that all stock owned by the business is recorded in the accounts, even if the stock is not actually on the premises; for example, when goods are sent out to customers on a sale-or-return basis then if a sale has not been confirmed the goods must be included in stock. Conversely when stock is counted at the year end it is important to exclude any stock held on the business premises which is not in fact the property of the business.

Valuation of stock

Once the physical quantity of stock has been ascertained, it is necessary to determine the monetary amount at which stock should be shown in the accounts. The principle laid down in SSAP9 is that stock and work in progress, except for long-term contract work in progress which is considered in detail below, should be stated at:

> The total of the lower of cost and net realizable value of the separate items of stock and work in progress or of groups of similar items.

Net realizable value is the actual or estimated selling price of items, less all further costs to be incurred in relation to the items and all related selling costs. Normally we would expect the net realizable value of stock to be greater than cost, since the business is presumably based on the assumption that goods purchased will be sold at a profit. The 'lower of cost and net realizable value' rule is a good illustration of the application of the prudence concept; where net realizable value is greater than cost the profit will only be recognized when a sale is made, stock being recorded at cost, but where net realizable value is less than cost the expected loss is recognized in the accounts immediately by reducing the stock to net realizable value. Prior to the issue of SSAP9 some companies used to value stock at the lowest of cost, net realizable value, and replacement cost. SSAP9 specifically rejects this approach, on the grounds that if the replacement cost of stock falls the only loss suffered by the company arises if, and to the extent that, the net realizable value falls; thus to reduce the stock to a lower replacement cost figure reduces profit in the current period by an amount which does not represent an actual loss and increases the reported profit in the period of sale by an equal amount.

In computing the amount of stock it is important to compare the cost and net realizable value of individual items or groups of items, not the total of cost and the total of net realizable value. Thus the stock valuation of a small shop might be computed as:

	Cost	*Net realizable value (NRV)*	*Lower of cost and NRV*
	£	£	£
Books	1,200	1,800	1,200
Stationery	400	600	400
Calendars	700	200	200
	2,300	2,600	1,800

Stock will be shown at £1,800, even though total net realizable value of £2,600 exceeds total cost of £2,300; this is because it would be wrong to set off the loss of £500 incurred in buying calendars against a future profit which we expect to earn by selling books and stationery.

SSAP9 defines 'cost' as the expenditure incurred in the normal course of business in bringing the product of service to its present location or condition. This includes:

1 The 'cost of purchase', being the purchase price and associated costs such as import duties and import costs.
2 The 'cost of conversion', being costs incurred in working on the product. These include a proportion of the labour and overhead costs incurred in the course of production.

The computation of costs of conversion necessarily involves the exercise of judgement in deciding the method to be used in allocating costs to individual units of production; this process is known as 'overhead absorption' and is the subject of extensive literature on cost accounting. The process is particularly complex when a number of different types of product are the output of a single production process.

Allocation of cost

A situation which frequently arises is that a business will buy batches of identical stock items at different prices at different points in time. Under the historical cost convention the problem that then arises is in deciding which purchase cost should be related to goods that have been sold and which purchase costs should be related to goods retained in stock. This problem can be particularly significant in times of inflation.

It is not normally practical to identify which purchase batch an item of stock which has been sold actually came from. Even if such identification were practicable, it would generally not be desirable to use this as a basis for matching costs with income in the accounts. This is because the managers of a business which deals in non-perishable goods would be able to manipulate the reported profit figure by selecting high purchase cost batches for sale when they wish to depress the reported profit figure and by selecting low purchase cost batches for sale when they wish to increase the reported profit figure.

Example 19 shows a simple series of transactions which will be used to illustrate the main methods of allocating costs to stock.

Example 19

B. Vaughan started in business as a wholesaler of windsurfing boards on 1 January 1986. During the month of January he had the following transactions:

1 January	Bought 300 boards for £200 each
10 January	Bought 200 boards for £210 each
12 January	Sold 100 boards
17 January	Bought 200 boards for £213 each
21 January	Sold 250 boards
25 January	Bought 200 boards at £218 each

The Companies Act 1981 identifies three main methods of determining the cost of stock:

1 *First-in, first-out* (commonly abbreviated to FIFO). Under this method the cost of the earliest batch of stock received is treated as the

cost of goods sold until all that batch is consumed, then the cost of the next batch of stock received is used in turn. The cost of issues, and the cost of stock held after each transaction, for Example 19 is summarized in Figure 44. The FIFO method is easy to operate because the cost to be allocated to stock held can be ascertained at any time as the cost of the most recently acquired batches.

2 *Last-in, first out* (commonly abbreviated to LIFO). Under this method the cost of the latest batch received is treated as the cost of goods sold until that batch is consumed, then the cost of the previous batch is used in turn. The application of the LIFO method to Example 19 is illustrated in Figure 45. If the LIFO method is going to be used then it is necessary to maintain a detailed record of when goods come in and go out, because it is not possible to state at any point in time which batch costs relate to the stock held. Thus in our example the stock of goods held at 31 January includes the cost of the first and the fourth batches acquired while including only part of the second batch and excluding all the third batch. A crude way of applying the LIFO method is to assume that within each accounting period all purchases take place prior to all sales, and examiners often set questions in a form which compels students to make this assumption; this is sometimes called the *periodic flow* basis, while the method of identifying each individual batch going in and out is referred to as the *perpetual flow* basis.

3 *Weighted average cost* (commonly referred to as average cost and sometimes abbreviated to AVCO). This method adds each new batch of goods received to the existing cost of stock and whenever goods are disposed of treats the unit cost as the average cost of goods in stock at that point in time. Figure 46 gives an example of how this method would be applied. In order to use average cost it is necessary to have a continuous stock-recording system. Where such a system is in operation, average cost is actually the simplest system to use because each batch of goods disposed of is charged against profit at one unit cost; by contrast, we have seen in our example that with both FIFO and LIFO the disposal of goods on 21 January involved applying different unit costs to the one batch of goods disposed of.

The Companies Act 1981 also permits any other method similar to any of the methods mentioned above.

In times of rising prices FIFO charges earlier, and therefore lower, costs to the profit and loss account while allocating to closing stock the most recent, and therefore higher, costs. LIFO operates conversely. On the assumption that the most recent cost figures are likely to be more relevant to decision making, it is often argued that FIFO produces a more useful balance sheet figure and LIFO produces a more meaningful profit figure. Other points made on the relative merits of FIFO and LIFO are:

Figure 44 *Allocation of cost by first-in-first-out method*

Date	Goods in			Goods out			Balance	
	Quantity	Cost per unit £	Total cost £	Quantity	Cost per unit £	Total cost £	Quantity	Total cost £
1.1.86	300	200	60,000				300	60,000
10.1.86	200	210	42,000				500	102,000
12.1.86				100	200	20,000	400	82,000
17.1.86	200	213	42,600				600	124,600
21.1.86				200	200	40,000		
				50	210	10,500	350	74,100
25.1.86	200	218	43,600				550	117,700

Figure 45 *Allocation of cost by last-in-first-out method*

Date	Goods in Quantity	Goods in Cost per unit £	Goods in Total cost £	Goods out Quantity	Goods out Cost per unit £	Goods out Total cost £	Balance Quantity	Balance Total cost £
1.1.86	300	200	60,000				300	60,000
10.1.86	200	210	42,000				500	102,000
12.1.86				100	210	21,000	400	81,000
17.1.86	200	213	42,600				600	123,600
21.1.86				200	213	42,600		
				50	210	10,500	350	70,500
25.1.86	200	218	43,600				550	114,100

Figure 46 *Allocation of cost by average cost method*

Date	Goods in Quantity	Goods in Cost per unit £	Goods in Total cost £	Goods out Quantity	Goods out Cost per unit £	Goods out Total cost £	Balance Quantity	Balance Cost per unit £	Balance Total cost £
1.1.86	300	200	60,000				300	200	60,000
10.1.86	200	210	42,000				500	204	102,000
12.1.86				100	204	20,400	400	204	81,600
17.1.86	200	213	42,600				600	207	124,200
21.1.86				250	207	51,750	350	207	72,450
25.1.86	200	218	43,600				550	211	116,050

1 FIFO is more realistic, in that the way in which costs are allocated to stock reflects the way in which stock is in practice likely to be processed by the business.
2 FIFO is simpler to operate than LIFO.
3 LIFO can give a distorted picture if stock levels fall below the normal level so that outdated cost figures are drawn into the profit and loss account.
4 LIFO gives a very prudent balance sheet figure.

The weighted average method normally produces results somewhere between FIFO and LIFO. As we have seen, it has the merit of being simple to use when a continuous stock recording system is in use; on the other hand, the issue price used is artificial in that it is a price which the business may never actually have paid.

An important factor in determining the accounting policies chosen by business is tax law. In the UK the Inland Revenue does not accept the LIFO basis of valuation; this does not mean that a business may not use LIFO, but does mean that the Revenue will adjust the profit figure presented in a set of accounts prepared using LIFO to allow for a different basis of stock valuation. By contrast, in the USA the tax authorities do regard LIFO as an acceptable stock valuation basis. Thus in the USA LIFO is a widely used method. In the UK LIFO is rarely used in practice, except by companies with strong US connections.

SSAP9 specifically states that LIFO is not regarded as an acceptable method of stock valuation.

A method of stock valuation which falls outside the scope of historical cost accounting is *replacement cost*. Under this method both goods consumed and stock held are recorded in the accounts at replacement cost. This gives rise to a difference in the accounts between the actual cost at the time of purchase and the replacement cost; this difference, which in times of rising prices will be a surplus, is normally credited to a revaluation reserve and not regarded as part of profit. This system has the advantage of giving realistic figures in both the profit and loss account and in the balance sheet, but is rarely used in historical cost accounts. Replacement cost has a fundamental place in some inflation accounting systems, considered in detail in Chapter 11 below.

A small number of businesses use a *base stock* approach whereby part of the stock of the business, regarded as representing a level of stock held permanently, is valued at the original cost of acquisition, while additional amounts, which are regarded as subject to fluctuation, are valued by some other method.

A special problem is faced by businesses producing crops. Some businesses in this position value crops held at the end of an accounting period at the selling price eventually received, with a deduction for selling expenses. Although this method falls outside the normal accounting conventions, it is widely accepted because of the practical difficulty in defining the costs of such stock.

As has already been mentioned in Chapter 6 above, investments are similar to stock in being a 'fungible' asset, and the same cost allocation methods can be applied.

Long-term contracts

A long-term contract is, according to SSAP9, one entered into for the construction of a single substantial entity where performance of a substantial proportion of the work will extend over a period exceeding one year. It is argued that the normal stock valuation principles, taking the lower of cost and net realizable value, will not prove satisfactory in the case of long-term contract work in progress. There are two reasons for this:

1 Where a contract is profitable, then the work in progress will be shown in the accounts at cost until the contract is completed at which time all the profit will be recognized. Thus no profit will be recognized in the earlier years of the contract, even though a large proportion of the work may have been completed in those years.
2 Where a contract has been entered into on terms which are likely to result in a loss, we would expect the net realizable value of work in progress to be lower than cost. Following the prudence concept, it would seem appropriate to recognize the total expected loss on the contract in the accounts as soon as it is anticipated.

SSAP9 requires that long-term contract work in progress be shown at cost plus *attributable profit* less *foreseeable losses*. *Foreseeable losses* are the total losses expected to arise from the contract, while *attributable profit* is the part of the total expected profit which relates to the work on the contract already performed at the accounting date. It is common practice in long-term contract agreements to include provision for a portion of the total contract price to be paid at the completion of each stage of the contract; these *progress payments* should be deducted from long-term contract work in progress.

The computation of the amount of attributable profit necessarily involves the exercise of judgement. SSAP9 provides that attributable profit should be computed 'with prudence' and that no attributable profit should be taken into account unless the outcome of the contract can be foreseen 'with reasonable certainty'.

Debtors and bad debts

Any business which sells on credit terms will need to have a system for ensuring that amounts receivable are collected promptly from debtors; this is often described as the *credit control* system. From time to time a decision will be made that an amount owed by a debtor cannot be collected. Sometimes this arises because of the liquidation or bankruptcy of the debtor, while sometimes a decision is taken that the amount to be collected does not warrant the expense of pursuing the debtor further. When a decision is taken to write off a bad debt an accounting entry will be made:

Dr Bad debts
Cr Individual debtor

At the same time it will also be necessary to credit the debtor's control account with the amount of the bad debt written off. At the end of the accounting period the total balance on the bad debts account will be shown as an expense in the profit and loss account.

Occasionally it may happen that a debtor whose balance has been written off as bad unexpectedly pays the amount owing. The normal accounting entry in such a case would be:

Dr Bank
Cr Bad debts

Sometimes instead of crediting bad debts a special 'bad debts recovered' account might be used.

Example 20 shows a simple series of bad debt items, while Figure 47 shows how these would be reflected in the accounts. It should be noted that some entries in the bad debts account will arise during an accounting period as a result of reviews of the debtor position for credit control purposes, while some entries will arise after the first trial balance has been extracted. Thus in our example 'Lufton' the balance on the bad debts account will be £170 at the time of extraction of the first trial balance.

Example 20

Lufton is a plumber who prepares accounts with a year end 31 December. During the year on 31 July he wrote off a bad debt for £250 owed by Slope, and on 30 September unexpectedly received payment of £80 owed by Finn which had been written off as a bad debt five years ago. At the year end debtors shown in the trial balance amounted to £3,640, and on reviewing these Lufton decided that there was no hope of recovering an amount of £340 owed by Vavasor.

Figure 47

Bad debts

31. 7	Slope	250	30. 9	Bank	80
31.12	Vavasor	340	31.13	P & L	510
		590			590

Vavasor

31.12	b/d	340	31.12	Bad debts	340

Balance sheet extract

Debtors	3,300

The record of amounts owing by individual debtors provided by the debtors ledger is normally used for credit control purposes; accordingly, it is important that the only debts written off as bad are those where it is reasonably certain that there is no hope of recovery. However it is also important that only debts which are likely to be collected are shown in the balance sheet. Accordingly it is normal practice to make a *provision for bad debts* in respect of those debtors where there is some uncertainty as to how likely amounts due are to be collected. There are two ways of arriving at the amount of the provision for bad debts:

1 A *general provision* is computed as a proportion of total debtors. Sometimes debtors are 'age-listed', and a larger proportion of long outstanding debts is provided for.
2 A *specific provision* is arrived at by listing those individual debtor balances in respect of which a provision is considered necessary.

In the UK specific provisions are accepted as an expense for tax purposes by the Inland Revenue whereas general provisions are not; for this reason many businesses prefer a specific provision approach.

Normally the amount of the provision for bad debts is computed at the end of each accounting period, and is then not adjusted again until the end of the next accounting period. Example 21 gives a simple example of a series of accounting periods. Figure 48 shows one method for treating the bad debt provision in the accounting period, whereby a separate provision for bad debts account is recorded in the ledger and the difference between the opening and closing provision each year is taken to the profit and loss account. It should be noted that an increase in the provision leads to an expense being shown in the profit and loss account, while a reduction in the provision leads to a credit in the profit and loss account. Normally the adjustment to the bad debt provision is combined with the bad debt write-off in the profit and loss account to give one figure.

Figure 49 shows an alternative way of recording the bad debt position in the ledger, combining the bad debt account and the provision for bad debts account. This method produces the same combined profit and loss figure as the method shown in Figure 49.

Figure 48

Bad debts					
1983	Debtors	790	31.3.83	P & L	790
1984	Debtors	880	31.3.84	P & L	880
1985	Debtors	1,020	31.3.85	P & L	1,020
1986	Debtors	1,150	31.3.86	P & L	1,150
1987	Debtors	1,290	31.3.87	P & L	1,290

Provision for bad debts					
31.3.84	Bal c/d	200	31.1.83	P & L	200
31.3.84	Bal c/d	570	1.4.83	Bal b/d	200
			31.3.84	P & L	370
		570			570
31.3.85	Bal c/d	150	1.4.84	Bal b/d	570
31.3.85	P & L	420			
		570			570
31.3.86	Bal c/d	470	1.4.85	Bal b/d	150
			31.3.86	P & L	320
		470			470
31.3.87	Bal c/d	680	1.4.86	Bal b/d	470
			31.3.87	P & L	210
		680			680
			1.4.87	Bal b/d	680

Whichever method is used, the provision for bad debts is shown in the balance sheet as a deduction from debtors, not as a separate liability.

Example 21

Coningsby is a grocer, who commenced trade on 1 April 1982 and prepares accounts with a year end date of 31 March. In the five years to 31 March 1987 he shows:

	Bad debts written off in year	*Provision at year end*
	£	£
1983	790	200
1984	880	570
1985	1,020	150
1986	1,150	470
1987	1,290	680

In examinations bad debt problems are normally presented as part of a question on the preparation of accounts. In such a case the question will normally present the first trial balance extracted,

Figure 49

Bad debts					
1983	Debtors	790	31.3.83	P & L	990
31.3.83	Bal c/d	200			
		990			990
1984	Debtors	880	1.4.83	Bal b/d	200
31.3.84	Bal c/d	570	31.3.84	P & L	1,250
		1,450			1,450
1985	Debtors	1,020	1.4.84	Bal b/d	570
31.3.85	Bal c/d	150	31.3.85	P & L	600
		1,170			1,170
1986	Debtors	1,150	1.4.85	Bal b/d	150
31.3.86	Bal c/d	470	31.3.86	P & L	1,470
		1,620			1,620
1987	Debtors	1,290	1.4.86	Bal b/d	470
31.3.87	Bal c/d	680	31.3.87	P & L	1,500
		1,970			1,970
			1.4.87	Bal b/d	680

showing a debit balance of bad debts written off in the year and a credit balance on the provision for bad debts account representing the balance brought forward at the beginning of the year. The adjustments which normally have to be made are:

1 Any further bad debts identified at the year end must be written off.
2 Any change in the bad debt provision has to be introduced into the accounts, with the change in the provision recorded in the profit and loss account.

Conclusion

In this chapter we have considered the nature of current assets, and have looked specifically at:

1 The problems of accounting for stock and work in progress.
2 Accounting for bad debts.

Questions

1 (a) How is it possible at any moment in time to ascertain stock without a physical stocktaking?
(b) What are the advantages of continuous stocktaking over annual stocktaking?

(Ulster Polytechnic)

2 An evaluation of a physical stock count on 30 April 1982 in respect of the financial year ending on that date at Cranfleet Commodities has produced a figure of £187,033.

The firm's book-keeper has approached you, as the accountant, for assistance in dealing with the following matters to enable him to arrive at a final figure of closing stock for inclusion in the annual accounts:

(a) 320 components included at their original cost of £11 each can now be bought in for only £6 each due to over production by the manufacturer. This drop in price is expected to be only temporary and the price rise is expected to exceed its original figure within 12 months. Cranfleet Commodities intends to continue selling the existing stock at the present price of £15 each.
(b) It has been discovered that certain items which had cost £5,657 have been damaged. It will cost £804 to repair them after which they can be sold for £6,321.
(c) On one stock sheet a sub-total of £9,105 has been carried forward as £1,095.
(d) 480 units which cost £1.50 each have been extended at £15.00 each.
(e) The firm has sent goods with a selling price of £1,500 (being cost plus 25 per cent) to a customer on a sale or return basis. At 30 April 1982, the customer had not signified acceptance, but the goods have not been returned, and consequently had not been included in the physical stock count.
(f) Included in stock were goods bought on credit for £4,679 from Byfleet Enterprises. At 30 April 1982, Cranfleet Commodities had not paid this account.
(g) Byfleet Enterprises has also sent some free samples (for advertising purposes only). These have been included in stock at their catalogue price of £152.

Required:

Taking account of such of the above facts as are relevant, calculate a closing stock figure for inclusion in the 1982 annual accounts of Cranfleet Commodities, giving reasons for the action you have taken in each individual case.

(ACCA Level 1 December 1982)

3 Container Construction Ltd (CCL) commenced trading on 1 January 1981. The trial balance as at 31 December 1981 shows the following:

	£000 *Dr*	*£000* *Cr*
Sales — containers		2,100
Purchases of steel	1,200	
Share captial, 500,000 £1 shares		500
Plant and equipment	600	
Debtors	500	
Creditors		450

Factory wages	450	
Factory rent	225	
Factory electricity	70	
Administrative expenses	230	
Bank		225
	3,275	3,275

You are provided with the following additional information:

(a) For accounts purposes, stock as at the year end is valued at a cost of £360,000.
(b) Factory plant and equipment is to be depreciated at a rate of 15 per cent per annum on a straight-line basis.
(c) CCL pays factory rental of £45,000 per quarter in advance. The rental for the first quarter of 1982 was paid on 30 December 1981
(d) At the year end the factory manager estimates that £20,000 of electricity has been used but not yet billed.
(e) The directors of CCL wish to make a bad debt provision of 5 per cent of year-end trade debtors.
(f) The directors propose a final dividend of 15p per share, payable in February 1982.

Required:

(a) Prepare an historic cost profit and loss account for CCL for the year ending 31 December 1981 and a balance sheet as at that date.
(b) Throughout the year CCL has sold containers for £3,000 each. The cost of steel has been steady at £1,200 for sufficient steel to make one container. As at the year end two thirds of the steel stock has been converted into completed containers and the remainder is untouched. What difference would it make to CCL's profit for the year if it were to value its stock in accordance with SSAP9?

(University of Wales Aberystwyth)

4 On 1 January 1979 Sam Martin began trading as a coal merchant. He invested £11,000 in the business by purchasing a lorry, which cost him £10,000 and by providing £1,000 for working capital. He ceased trading on 31 December 1982 when he sold the lorry for £2,000, the scrap value he assumed for it on 1 January 1979. His purchase and sales of coal were as follows:

Year	*Number of cwts purchased*	*Purchase price per cwt £s*	*Number of cwts sold*	*Sale price per cwt*
1979	10,000	1.0	8,000	2.0
1980	12,000	1.4	10,000	2.2
1981	14,000	1.6	12,000	2.3
1982	4,000	1.8	10,000	2.4

The other expenses of the business amounted to £3,000 a year. Sam Martin neither gave nor received credit.

Required:

(a) Calculate the profit or loss for Sam Martin for each of the four years on the basis
  (i) That the lorry is depreciated by the reducing balance method and stock is valued by the FIFO method.
  (ii) That the lorry is depreciated by the straight-line method and stock is valued by the LIFO method.
(b) Comment on your results.

(University College Cardiff)

5 At December 31 of the current year, the Edelweiss Company had a balance of £91,500 in its trade debtors account and a credit balance of £500 in the provision for bad debts account. The company has aged its accounts as follows:

Current	£80,000
30–90 days past due	6,000
91–180 days past due	4,000
Over 6 months past due	1,500
	£91,500

In the past, the company has experienced losses as follows: 1 per cent of current balances, 5 per cent of balances 30–90 days past due, 10 per cent of balances 91–180 days past due, and 40 per cent of balances over six months past due. The company bases its bad debts provision on the aging analysis.

Required:

(a) Prepare the adjusting journal entry to record the bad debts provision for the year.
(b) Show how trade debtors and provision for bad debts would appear in the December 31 balance sheet.

8

SOURCES OF FINANCE

Objectives

This chapter has two broad objectives:

1 To give an introduction to the various sources of finance shown in a business balance sheet, explaining their significance and how they are accounted for.
2 To introduce the major factors taken into account in deciding how to raise finance for the establishment, running, and expansion, of a business.

Specifically we consider

1 The ways in which new shares can be issued.
2 Retained profits as a source of finance.
3 Forms of long-term borrowing.
4 Types of short-term borrowing.
5 The nature of the tax liabilities shown in the balance sheet.
6 Sources of finance which do not appear in the balance sheet.
7 The effect of the financial structure on fluctuations in profit (gearing).
8 The relationship between the trading structure and the financial structure.
9 The factors taken into account in choosing between sources of finance.

Raising funds from share issues

One of the sources from which a new company will derive funds will be from the issue of shares in the business. If additional finance is required during a company's life an issue of new shares is one way of raising finance that might be considered. In this respect a private company, which is not permitted to issue any form of security to the public, is at a severe disadvantage compared to a public company. A public company will normally only be able to benefit from the legal permission to issue securities to the public if it is *listed* on the Stock Exchange. To become a listed company requires approval from the Council of the Stock Exchange, which is only granted if a range of regulations are complied with. These regulations have three broad objectives:

1 To ensure that the company publishes a full range of information enabling investors to make a fair judgement on its position.
2 To ensure that there are sufficient shares in issue, spread over a sufficiently wide number of shareholders, to create a viable market.
3 To ensure a reasonable level of ethical conduct by the directors.

Compliance with the requirements which have to be met to obtain a listing is very expensive, so that access to the Stock Exchange as a source of finance is limited to companies of a substantial size. A somewhat cheaper form of access to the Stock Exchange has recently been created in the form of the 'Unlisted Securities Market', but the costs are still substantial.

Once a company is listed its shares can be freely traded on the Stock Exchange, the market through which both institutional and private investors buy and sell investments. The benefits to the proprietors of a company in seeking a listing include:

1 Shareholders have the opportunity to sell some of the shares they own. In particular, it often happens that the founders of a successful company wish to realize part of the value of their shareholdings in cash.
2 The company has the opportunity to raise new finance from the issue of new shares or loan stock; not only does the listing give access to the general public, but institutional investors are likely to find shares in listed companies more attractive.
3 A market valuation of the shares is established. Shareholders can find this useful in their dealings with the Inland Revenue on capital gains tax and capital transfer tax.
4 An expanding company may wish to make a takeover bid for another company; a Stock Exchange listing means that an offer to issue new shares in exchange for the shares of the company to be taken over will be more attractive.
5 A Stock Exchange listing facilitates the setting up of an employee share scheme, both for tax purposes and because employees will obtain a marketable benefit.

Having obtained a Stock Exchange listing there are a number of ways in which a company can issue shares to the public:

1 ***Public issue by prospectus***
This is a way of advertising sales to the general public through a document called the *prospectus*, which contains detailed information on the company's history and is widely advertised. In making such an issue the company will be advised by an *issuing house*, normally a merchant bank. Normally an arrangement is made with a firm of *underwriters*, who for a fee undertake to buy any shares not taken up by the public. There are substantial costs involved in such an issue.

2 ***Offer by tender***
In this case an offer is made of shares, and the public are invited to name the price they are willing to pay. The shares are then issued at what is called the *striking price*, to those investors who tendered at or above the price. This involves issuing a prospectus, but avoids underwriting costs.

3 ***Offer for sale***
In this case the company issues shares to the issuing house, who in turn offer the shares for sale to the general public.

4 ***Rights issue***
In the case of a rights issue the company offer shares to existing shareholders, in proportion to their shareholdings. The price is normally set below the current market price, as an incentive to shareholders to take up their rights or sell them to other investors.

5 ***Placing***
In a placing shares issued are 'placed' with investors by an advisor to the company, most commonly a merchant bank. Since a placing does not use the market mechanism it is not conditional on the company being listed.

An issue of preference shares has similar effects on the financial position of the company to a debenture issue, and is considered under the heading 'long-term borrowing' below. An issue of ordinary shares to new investors has two forms of cost to existing shareholders:

1 The profits of the company have to be shared amongst a greater number of shareholders. Thus shareholders will only benefit from finance being raised from new shareholders if the return to be earned on the total funds in the new business exceeds the rate of return that can be earned on existing funds.
2 Existing shareholders will have to share their control of the company with the new shareholders. This may be a disincentive to the issue of shares, particularly in a family-controlled company.

Retained profits

The most common source of funds for business expansion is the retention of profits earned in the business. This is linked to the issue of *dividend policy*, deciding what proportion of profits earned should be paid out by way of dividend.

In principle the retention of profits inside the company can only be justified if it is possible for the company to earn a higher return on the retained profits than the shareholders could earn for themselves outside the company. A company which distributes a low proportion of profit as dividend will be expected to be able to increase the level of profit in future years as a result of the increased resources held by the company, and so be able to increase the level of dividend. Thus there are two broad approaches which a company can take to dividend payments:

1 Maintain dividends at a fairly constant level which absorbs most of the profit earned.
2 Distribute a dividend which represents a modest proportion of profit earned but which increases year by year.

Investors will then be able to choose between a higher level of current dividends and a better prospect of growth in future dividends; the choice made will depend upon the individual investor.

A third approach to dividend policy is to pay out a steady percentage of profit by way of dividend, so that in less profitable years the dividend level actually falls. This may be attractive to the company, which will benefit because the level of cash outflows will fall when profit falls, but is unattractive to shareholders who generally prefer to be able to rely on a steady flow of dividends.

Long-term borrowing

A listed company can raise long-term loans by the same methods as are involved in an issue of shares, as considered above. Any company, or other form of business entity, is free to raise long-term loans by private arrangement or through one of the financial institutions.

The term 'debenture' is commonly used in relation to long-term loans. The legal definition of a debenture is simply 'a document which creates or acknowledges a debt due from a company.'

Any form of borrowing must fall within the limits of the company's borrowing powers, which will be defined in the company's articles of association. The borrowing powers will normally be defined as a multiple of share capital and reserves.

In practice a debenture is normally *secured* on assets of the company by a *charge* which means that in the event of the company being liquidated the proceeds from the sale of those assets will be applied to paying the amount due to the debenture holder; if the sale proceeds are less than the amount owing then the debenture holders will rank with the unsecured creditors in respect of the shortfall. There are two types of charge on assets:

1 ***Fixed charge***
A fixed charge is a mortgage on specific assets, under which the company loses the power to sell the assets charged without the permission of the mortgagee.

2 ***Floating charge***
A floating charge is a charge on a class of assets which in the ordinary course of business change from time to time; stock is a good example. The company is free to trade in the asset unless some act, e.g. a default on interest payments, 'crystallizes' the charge which then applies to the assets covered held at that time.

A debenture is often issued under the terms of a 'debenture trust deed', which lays down the conditions with which the company has to comply and appoints trustees to enforce these conditions. The conditions often include limitations on the company's total borrowing powers, not necessarily on the same terms as shown in the articles of association, breach of which may render the company liable to repay the debentures.

The interest rate on a debenture is expressed as a percentage of the face value of the debenture. The debenture is not necessarily issued at its face value, and it is common to issue debentures at a discount. Where a debenture is issued at a discount the stated interest rate will apply to the face value of the debenture; to calculate the interest rate we need to know whether the debenture is perpetual or redeemable:

1 *Perpetual debentures*
A perpetual debenture is one which does not bind the company to any repayment date, and can therefore be left outstanding in perpetuity. The cost of such a debenture is:

$$\frac{\text{Interest charge}}{\text{Amount of cash raised from debenture issue}}$$

Example 22 shows how the cost of a perpetual debenture issued by Brattle Ltd would be computed.

2 *Redeemable debentures*
A redeemable debenture is one which the company is bound to redeem within a specified period, normally at face value. The cost of such a debenture falls in two parts:

(a) The interest paid each year.
(b) The difference between the discounted amount at which the debenture was issued and the face value at which the debenture is redeemed.

There is no formula for computing the total finance cost as a percentage of the sum borrowed; Example 22 shows that in the example Brattle Ltd the cost is 10 per cent and this could have been computed by trying a number of percentage rates on a trial-and-error basis.

Example 22

On 31 December 1985 Brattle Ltd issued £10,000 of 5 per cent debentures for a consideration of £8,756.

If the debentures are perpetual then the cost will be:

$$\frac{500}{8,756} = 5.7\%$$

If the debentures are redeemable at par in three years' time then the cost will be 10 per cent as follows:

Y/e 31.12.86	
Cash borrowed	8,756
10% finance cost	876
	9,632
Less: Interest paid	500
Y/e 31.12.87 Amount b/fwd	9,132
10% finance cost	913
	10,045
Less: Interest paid	500
Y/e 31.12.88 Amount b/fwd	9,545
10% finance cost	955
	10,500
Less: Interest paid	500
Repayment at 31.12.88	10,000

Where a debenture is issued at a discount the nominal value must be shown as a liability, the cash received is recorded in the bank account, and the amount of the discount is shown as a debit balance. The amount of the discount should be transferred to the profit and loss account over the period of the loan, in principle so as to give an even percentage finance cost. Thus for our example Brattle Ltd the discount written off each year would be:

1986	876 – 500	=	376
1987	913 – 500	=	413
1988	955 – 500	=	455
			1,244

In practice an equal write-off each year would be more common. Figure 50 shows the double entry for our example Brattle Ltd.

Convertible loan stocks are a special form of debenture which carry the right to convert into shares (normally ordinary shares) on a specified date or dates at specified prices; normally the conversion price would be set at a point somewhere above the market price of shares at the time of issue. Effectively the holders of convertible loan stock are being given an option to subscribe for shares in the future as an inducement to subscribe for the loan. From the point of view of the company the objective of issuing convertible loan stock is to secure borrowings at a more favourable finance cost than would otherwise be available. The disadvantages are:

1 If the share price does not perform as well as expected, when the conversion date comes the loan stockholders are unlikely to convert and it will be necessary to find alternative finance to meet any obligation to redeem the loan.
2 If the share price performs better than expected then the ordinary shareholders will suffer dilution of the equity or less favourable terms than might have been achieved by a market issue at the conversion date.

The accounting procedures in relation to convertible loan stock are the same as for other debentures unless conversion takes place. When conversion takes place the double entry is:

Dr Loan stock	Nominal value of stock converted
Cr Share capital	Nominal value of shares issued
Cr Share premium	Difference between the two items above

Short-term borrowing

The bank overdraft is a common form of short-

Figure 50

5% Debentures

31.12.85	Bal c/d	10,000	31.12.85	Cash	8,756	
				Discount	1,244	10,000
31.12.86	Bal c/d	10,000	1.1.86	Bal b/d		10,000
31.12.87	Bal c/d	10,000	1.1.87	Bal b/d		10,000
31.12.88	Cash	10,000	1.1.88	Bal b/d		10,000

Discount on debentures

31.12.85	Debentures	1,244	31.12.85	Bal c/d	1,244
1.1.86	Bal b/d	1,244	31.12.86	P & L	376
			31.12.86	Bal c/d	868
		1,244			1,244
1.1.87	Bal b/d	868	31.12.87	P & L	413
			31.12.87	Bal c/d	455
		868			868
1.1.88	Bal b/d	455	31.12.88	P & L	455

Profit and loss expense:

	1986	*1987*	*1988*
Interest	500	500	500
Discount	376	413	455
	876	913	955

Note It may seem strange that the finance cost increases each year when apparently no increased sum has been borrowed. The reason for this is that the discount portion of the finance cost is not paid until the redemption date, and therefore increases the amount borrowed each year.

term borrowing. It is important that any overdrawing on the bank account is agreed with the bank in advance, and kept within the limits agreed by the bank. There are two reasons for this:

1 An unauthorized overdrawing is likely to make the bank suspicious of the customer's reliability, and may lead to difficulties in agreeing a facility with the bank.
2 The bank may choose not to honour cheques overdrawn beyond an agreed limit, and a dishonoured cheque can do grave harm to the reputation of the business.

An overdraft will carry interest charges on the balance outstanding from day to day. In addition, there is likely to be a commitment charge in respect of the agreed overdraft limit. Where the requirement for finance fluctuates during the year this may be an attractive source of finance because only the amount needed at any point in time need be borrowed. The interest rate on a bank overdraft will be expressed as a certain addition to the bank's base rate; thus the interest rate on an overdraft fluctuates, in effect, with market rates of interest.

When a business expects the market rate of interest to fall a commitment to long-term borrowing may seem unattractive, because the company is committed to paying high rates of interest in future years. In these circumstances a bank overdraft might be arranged as a short-term measure, pending a fall in interest rates when a long-term loan would be negotiated.

The disadvantage of a bank overdraft is that the bank has no long-term commitment to extend the overdraft facility, so that repayment can be demanded at short notice. Thus this is a relatively high-risk source of finance, although in practice banks are often willing to extend overdraft facilities over a number of years.

Thus a bank overdraft can be seen as a particularly appropriate source of finance:

1 To cover a short-term financial need.
2 To cover fluctuating needs for finance.
3 To provide finance in a period of high interest rates pending negotiation of a long-term loan when interest rates fall.

Trade credit is another form of short-term borrowing, which a company might deliberately exploit as a source of finance. The delaying of payments to trade creditors may seem an attractive source of finance since, once the cash discounts allowed for rapid payment have been foregone, there is no apparent interest cost. Excessive reliance on trade credit can, however, have the following disadvantages:

1 The business loses goodwill with suppliers, and may suffer in terms of the quality of service received.
2 When payment periods taken become excessive suppliers may refuse to supply further goods except against immediate cash payment.
3 Small newly launched businesses are particularly vulnerable to delays in payment by their customers. Thus they may be reluctant to approach any business with a reputation for slow payment with their goods. Consequently a business which acquires such a reputation may lose access to the most innovative products on the market.
4 Slow payment affects the reputation of a business, and may therefore actually damage its ability to sell goods.

Thus the costs of delaying payment to suppliers are intangible but can be substantial; such delays also carry the risk of trade credit being cut off.

An interesting legal device which can be used to obtain short-term finance is the *bill of exchange*. A bill of exchange is a document whereby the *drawer* addresses an order to a *drawee* to pay a sum of money to a payee at a future date. For example when goods are supplied the supplier can draw a bill of exchange for the cost on the customer, who may be granted a date at some time in the future to pay; the drawee *accepts* the bill by signing it and returning it to the drawer. The advantage of this system is that the drawer can *discount* the bill, normally with a bank, who thereby acquire the right to collect the sum due. The amount paid for a bill will reflect the finance cost of waiting to collect the money and the handling costs; normally a bill is discounted 'with resource', so that if the drawee fails to pay on the due date the drawer is liable to pay. Bills of exchange are commonly used to settle international transactions.

Taxation

We have already briefly introduced the taxation system in Chapter 5. In practice the Inland Revenue allows a period of time after the year end for companies to pay tax which can vary between 9 months and 21 months; thus a company with a gap in excess of 12 months will show two tax liabilities, one current liability in respect of the previous year and one long-term liability in respect of the accounting year which is being reported on.

The tax system in some cases gives companies allowances against taxable income which are potentially subject to reversal in future years. Thus a company may find it necessary to show a long-term liability for 'deferred taxation' in the accounts, being an estimate of the tax which is liable to become payable when the allowances which have been given in the past are reversed and thereby 'clawed back'.

Off balance sheet finance

The term 'off balance sheet finance' is used to describe an arrangement entered into which obtains the benefit of finance without that finance appearing as a loan in the balance sheet.

In recent years a growing form of 'off balance sheet finance' has been the leasing of fixed assets. Under a lease agreement the business enters into an arrangement with a leasing company who own the desired fixed asset and lease it at an agreed rental to the business; unlike a hire-purchase agreement, the business has no right to acquire the asset at the end of the lease period. Leases can be divided into two categories:

1 *Finance leases*, whereby the lease covers virtually the whole of the expected asset life.
2 *Operating leases*, whereby the leasing company leases out the asset on such terms that it can be expected to be leased out to more than one party over its life.

A finance lease is effectively a device for acquiring the use of fixed assets with outside finance on terms which in legal form do not constitute the acquisition of the asset or the incurring of a liability. SSAP21, issued recently, follows the 'substance over form' convention by requiring companies to disclose in respect of finance leases the value of the leased assets and the total effective amount owing as leased obligations. If companies comply with SSAP21, therefore, we can expect finance leases to cease to be an 'off balance sheet' form of finance. However in the United States experience has shown that many companies avoid the provisions of an accounting standard similar to SSAP21 by drafting lease agreements which technically fall outside the definition of a finance lease; thus it may well be that leasing will continue to be a concealed form of finance in the UK. Where the requirements of SSAP21 are not followed the existence of leasing agreements may be deduced from the accounts in two ways:

1 By any increase in plant hire charges, disclosed in conformity with the Companies Acts.
2 By the disposal of fixed assets shown in the accounts without any apparent replacement.

The other common form of 'off balance sheet finance' can arise from the factoring of debtors. Debt factoring services are offered by a range of financial institutions, and can cover any combination of the following services:

1 Invoice discounting, whereby the factor acquires the right to the amount due from the debtor. The most common form of agreement is that the factor advances a large part of the cash due (commonly 80 per cent), and the business pays interest to the factor on the advance until the debt is received, when the advance is repaid.
2 Debt collection, whereby the factor also collects the debts, often running the sales ledger function on behalf of the business as well.
3 Bad debt insurance, whereby the factor agrees to accept the bad debt risk in respect of specified customers.

Gearing

An important factor to be considered in deciding on how to go about raising new finance is the impact on the *gearing* position. The term gearing (in the USA referred to as leverage) is used to refer to the relationship between the amount invested in the business by the proprietors and the amount borrowed by the business; a business with a high proportion of borrowings is said to be 'high geared' and a business with a low proportion of borrowing is said to be 'low geared'.

Example 23 shows a simplified case of two companies which have very different financial structures. Of the two, Gilmore which derives 20 per cent of its resources from borrowing is relatively low geared compared to Fenwick, which with 60 per cent of its resources derived from borrowing is relatively high geared. From this example we can see the two effects of gearing on the business:

1 ***Capital risk***
The higher the level of gearing, the higher the risk that the business will be unable to repay borrowings in full. Comparing our two examples, Gilmore will be able to repay the debentures in full unless it loses in excess of 80 per cent of total assets, whereas Fenwick will be unable to repay debentures in full if it loses more than 40 per cent of total assets.

2 ***Income fluctuation***
Example 23 suggests three possible levels of profit earned on total assets, while Figure 51 shows the profit available for dividend on each share. If the profit on total assets is £100,000 the profit available for dividend per share is the same; this is because the return earned on total assets of 10 per cent $\left(\frac{100,000}{1,000,000}\right)$ is equal to the rate of interest on the debentures. However if the profit on total assets falls by 20 per cent to £80,000 then the profit available for dividend falls by 25 per cent for the low-geared Gilmore but by 50 per cent for the high-geared Fenwick. Conversely an increase in the profit on total assets of 20 per cent from £100,000 to £120,000, would result in an increase in the profit available for dividend per share of 25 per cent for the lower-geared company and 50 per cent for the higher-geared company. The reason for this is that the interest entitlement of the debenture holders is fixed, while the shareholders are entitled to the residue of profit after interest has been paid. Thus any fluctuation in profit before interest will have a greater proportional effect on the residual profit available to shareholders, and the higher the level of gearing the greater this effect will be.

Example 23

Two companies, Gilmore Ltd and Fenwick Ltd, are engaged in similar activities. Their balance sheets show:

	Gilmore *£000*	*Fenwick* *£000*
Ordinary share capital – ordinary share of £1	800	400
10% debentures	200	600
	1,000	1,000
Total assets	1,000	1,000

Both companies have a policy of paying out all profits as dividends. What will be the dividend paid on each share if profit before interest charges is:

1 £100,000?
2 £ 80,000?
3 £120,000?

(Assume no taxation)

The benefit of gearing to ordinary shareholders is that if a project yields a return on funds employed greater than the interest paid on related borrowings then the excess profit is enjoyed by the shareholders without the investment of any additional funds on their part. However, as we have seen, increased gearing carries a higher degree of risk.

In an analysis of a company's gearing position preference shares are normally treated as similar to

Figure 51

Gilmore	*(1)*	*(2)*	*(3)*
Profit for the year	100	80	120
Interest (10% × 200)	20	20	20
Profit available for shareholders	80	60	100
Dividend per share	$\frac{80}{800}$ = 10p	$\frac{60}{800}$ = 7.5p	$\frac{100}{800}$ = 12.5p
Fluctuation in dividend per share compared to (a)	-	-25%	+25%

Fenwick			
Profit for the year	100	80	120
Interest (10% × 600)	60	60	60
Profit available for shareholders	40	20	60
Dividend per share	$\frac{40}{400}$ = 10p	$\frac{20}{400}$ = 5p	$\frac{60}{400}$ = 15p
Fluctuation in dividend per share compared to (a)	-	-50%	+50%

fixed interest borrowing. However it should be noted that in law preference shares are a form of share capital, with two important consequences:

1 In a liquidation all liabilities must be met before any portion of capital is returned to preference shareholders.
2 Preference dividends can only be paid out of retained profits.

A further important point is that loan interest is treated as an expense for tax purposes. Preference dividends, by contrast, are not treated as an expense and accordingly are not deducted from profit in computing the income liable to tax.

Trading structure

When considering the financial structure of the firm it is important to bear in mind the trading structure of the business as well, because of the impact of what is coming to be known as *operational gearing*.

Operational gearing arises because the costs of a firm can be regarded as falling in two categories:

1 *Variable costs* being those costs which vary with the level of sales. Examples include raw material costs, energy costs incurred in the course of production, etc.
2 *Fixed costs* being those costs which are of a fixed amount whatever the level of sales, e.g. rent of the factory, administrative salaries.

Of course the distinction is somewhat artificial – for example, wages might be fixed to the extent that there is a firm commitment to pay employees their basic wage, but in practice might be variable because additional production involves overtime payments. But in practice management accountants have techniques for identifying variable and fixed costs.

Example 24 shows two types of split between fixed and variable costs, while Figure 52 demonstrates how this can affect fluctuations in profit. Marrable Ltd, with higher variable costs and lower fixed costs, shows a fluctuation of 40 per cent in profit when sales fluctuate by 20 per cent. By contrast Lowther Ltd, with higher fixed and lower variable costs, shows a fluctuation in profit of 80 per cent when sales fluctuate by 20 per cent. The higher the relative significance of fixed costs, the higher the level of operational gearing.

Figure 52

Marrable Ltd

		(1)		(2)		(3)
Sales		100		80		120
Less:						
Variable costs	60		48		72	
Fixed costs	20		20		20	
		80		68		92
Net profit		20		12		28
Profit (decrease)/increase		—		(40%)		40%

Lowther Ltd

		(1)		(2)		(3)
Sales		100		80		120
Less:						
Variable costs	20		16		24	
Fixed costs	60		60		60	
		80		76		84
Net profit		20		4		36
Profit (decrease)/increase		—		(80%)		80%

Example 24

Two companies have the following relationship between fixed and variable costs:

	Marrable Ltd	**Lowther Ltd**
Fixed costs per year	£20,000	£60,000
Variable costs as a % of sales	60%	20%

Compute profit for the year:

1 On sales of £100,000.
2 If sales fall by 20 per cent.
3 If sales rise by 20 per cent.

The operational gearing is relevant to the decisions made by management on how to meet the financial requirements of the business because of the question of *risk*. The higher the level of operational gearing, the lower the level of financial gearing will be desired because of the risk it carries.

When considering the financial requirements posed by a new project it is often worth considering, when trying to find adequate financial resources, whether it is possible to reduce the level of finance required by a change in the method of trading. For example:

1 It may be possible to avoid the cost of new machinery by subcontracting production work.
2 A customer placing an unusually large order may be prepared to agree to accept the order in several parts, paying on account as each batch is received.
3 A business with strong seasonal demands for working capital might diversify into a line of business giving cash flow at other times of year.

Controlling the financial structure

In deciding how to finance a new project the following points are amongst those to be considered:

Time span

The length of time for which finance is needed will be an important factor in choosing the type of finance to be raised. Thus a short-term cash requirement would not be met with long-term finance. Although a long-term requirement for finance might be met by a series of short-term arrangements such an approach carries an unsatisfactory degree of risk, although this might be mitigated where the asset to be acquired is easily realized in case of need.

Gearing

The level of gearing the company chooses to maintain is an important consideration in choosing sources of finance. On the one hand the management of the company will wish the proprietors to enjoy the benefit of investing in projects which yield a higher rate of return than the finance costs of related borrowed funds; on the other hand the higher the level of gearing the higher the level of risk.

Type of business entity

The form of legal entity chosen for carrying on business will have an influence on what forms of finance are available. Listed companies are in the special situation of having access to the capital markets. A large unlisted company may actually choose to raise new finance by means of a share issue in order to justify seeking listing and so obtaining the benefits of being listed.

Personal liability

One factor which may influence the proprietors of a business in borrowing new finance is the degree of personal liability they incur. In the case of private companies where the principal shareholders are also directors it is common for institutional lenders to require a personal guarantee from the directors as a condition in advancing any loan.

Security

The opportunity to raise loans may be influenced by the availability of suitable assets which can be charged as security. Thus it will be easier to borrow money to buy a building than to finance an advertising campaign.

Sum to be raised

The size of the sum to be raised is a factor influencing the method of raising finance. There are substantial transaction costs involved in raising long-term finance, particularly through the Stock Exchange, and these are only justified when substantial sums are to be raised.

Costs

Clearly the costs of each type of source of finance must be considered. It is important to be conscious of the intangible costs of such sources of finance as extending the period of trade credit taken, when comparing them with sources of finance where the costs are more straightforward.

Trading risk

In deciding on the level of gearing which is acceptable the degree of fluctuation to which trading profit is subject will be borne in mind. Thus an investment in a property which is to be rented out is likely to yield a more consistent and predictable return than an investment in plant to be hired out on a short-term basis.

Importance of control

The willingness of the existing shareholders to lose part of their influence over the control of the company will be an important factor when deciding whether to raise new equity from outsiders.

Legal restrictions

There may be special legal restrictions preventing the business from raising certain types of finance. For example, a company which is at the limit of its borrowing powers might choose to lease fixed assets as an alternative to buying the assets with a long-term loan.

Social factors

The broad term 'social factors' is used to raise the point that it may be possible to raise finance on rather more favourable terms than those available on a normal commercial basis for projects which are seen to have benefits to society as a whole. This may take the form of grants and low interest loans from central or local government, support by private charitable organizations, or simply a more favourable hearing from a bank wishing to project a sympathetic image.

Conclusion

There are a wide range of factors which determine the sources of finance to which a business has access and which influence the appropriate finance mix for each business.

Questions

1 When the amount of ordinary capital is small in relation to preference capital and long-term loans the capital structure is said to be highly geared and the effect of this is that the equity capital is acutely responsive to fluctuations in profits.

You are required to:

(a) Comment on the above statement with the aid of a suitable illustrations.
(b) Report on the capital and income gearing of Sam PLC as shown below:

Sam PLC capital structure (all issued) at 31 December 1985

	£
Ordinary share capital (£1 shares)	100,000
Undistributed profits	200,000
10% Preference share capital (£1 shares)	100,000
12% Debentures	160,000

The profits before interest and taxation are in the region of £100,000 per annum.

2 (a) 'The Capital Structure of a company is said to be a system of risks and costs because both are associated with each source of finance used.'

Discuss this statement in the context of the sources of finance which may comprise the capital structure and the effects of capital gearing.

(b) The following alternative capital structures are planned by the BABS Public Limited Company.

Structure	(1)	(2)
Ordinary shares £1 each	100,000	40,000
8% Debentures £100 each	—	50,000
10% Preference shares £1 each	—	10,000
	£100,000	£100,000

From the above data compute the earnings per ordinary share when:
(i) profits are £40,000
(ii) profits are £10,000

(Assume Corporation Tax is 50 per cent)
Which capital structure would you recommend?

(Huddersfield Polytechnic)

3 Discuss the sources of finance a firm might use in financing a new project involving £5 million of capital equipment and £1 million of working capital. What factors should a firm take into account in selecting finance for such a project?

(Trent Polytechnic)

9

PRESENTATION OF THE ACCOUNTS

Objectives

The basic objective of this chapter is to consider the issues that arise in the presentation of accounts, particularly the published accounts of limited companies. Specifically considered are:

1. A brief review of the factors that govern presentation.
2. Presentation of the balance sheet, and the relative merits of vertical and horizontal formats.
3. Presentation of the published profit and loss account.
4. Reports accompanying the published accounts of limited companies.
5. The presentation of the detailed profit and loss account by manufacturing businesses.
6. The preparation of accounts from incomplete records.
7. Presentation of the accounts of non-profit-making organizations.

Factors governing presentation

We have already considered, in Chapter 1 above, the various sources of authority that govern the presentation of published accounts. Sole traders and partnerships are not governed by any such regulations, but to some extent their accounting practices are influenced by the example set in relation to companies. Two factors, apart from regulations, have a powerful influence on the way in which accounts are used:

1. ***Tradition***
   Certain practices in the presentation of accounts are established by tradition. For example, the custom of showing assets in reverse order of liquidity, known as 'marshalling' the assets, has become established by tradition rather than by any type of regulation.

2. ***User needs***
   An awareness of the way in which users are going to analyse accounts has an influence on the form of presentation. For example in Chapter 13 below, we will see that an analysis of the relationship between current assets and current liabilities is important to users of accounts; this explains the practice of identifying current items separately in the balance sheet.

Presentation of the balance sheet

As we have already seen, the balance sheet of any business can be presented in two forms. Both of these forms are permitted for limited companies by the Companies Act 1981.

1. ***Horizontal format***
   The Companies Act 1981 reverses traditional UK practice, showing assets on the left hand side and capital and liabilities on the right hand side.

2. ***Vertical format***
   This is the form which lists fixed assets, then

current assets, deducts current liabilities from current assets to give net current assets, then deducts long-term loans to give net assets of the company. This is balanced by a listing of share capital and reserves. In the past long-term loans have often been shown as added to share capital and reserves rather than deducted from assets, and this practice may continue with unincorporated businesses. Figure 53 illustrates this format.

Figure 53 *Outline format of vertical balance sheet as per Companies Act 1981*

	£	£
Fixed assets		x
Current assets	x	
Less: current liabilities	x	
Net current assets		x
		x
Long term loans		(x)
		x
Share capital		x
Reserves		x
		x

Presentation of the published profit and loss accounts

The published profit and loss account of a limited company can be presented in two types of format, which are illustrated in Appendix A at the end of the book. The basic difference between the two is in the way in which costs are analysed.

1 ***By type of operation***
With this format costs are analysed according to the purpose for which they are incurred. For example a factory worker's wages will be part of cost of sales, the office manager's salary part of administrative costs, a salesman's salary part of distribution costs.

2 ***By type of expenditure***
With this format costs are analysed according to their nature. Thus all three of the wage costs we considered above would be shown together under the heading 'staff costs'.

Whichever format is adopted, the various items of expenditure can be summarized under a very small number of headings in the *published* profit and loss account. In practice a limited company will also produce a detailed trading profit and loss account for internal management use. It should also be noted that companies are required to produce certain detailed information on specified items of income and expenditure, as summarized in Appendix A.

Reports accompanying the accounts

Three reports normally accompany a set of published company accounts. These are the directors' report, the auditors' report, and the chairman's statement. Considering each of these:

The directors' report

The Companies Acts require that each set of accounts should be accompanied by a directors' report, which must include details of

1 The dividend recommended and the amounts to be transferred to reserves.
2 The principal activities of the business, and any significant change therein.
3 A fair review of the development of the business during the year and its position at the year end.
4 Details of transactions in the company's own shares.
5 Any material difference between the 'book value' at which land and buildings are shown in the accounts and their market value.
6 Significant changes in fixed assets.
7 Likely future developments in the company's position.
8 Activities in the area of research and development.
9 Important post balance sheet events.
10 Names of all directors during the year and since the year-end date with details of their

interest in shares or loan capital of the company at the end of the year and at the beginning of the year or, if it comes later, their date of appointment.

11 The amount of political and charitable donations if the total exceeds £200, and the recipient of any political donation in excess of £200.

The auditors' report

The auditors of a limited company are appointed by, and report to, the shareholders. As discussed in Chapter 1 above, it is necessary to become a member of one of the four chartered professional accounting bodies approved to perform audits in order to become an auditor. It is essential that the auditors be independent of the directors of the company, and there are a number of rules both in company law and in the ethical codes of the professional bodies which are designed to promote that independence.

The prime responsibility of the auditor is to form an opinion as to whether the accounts of the company give a true and fair view of its position. Figure 54 shows how an audit report might be presented. Note that

1 The report is addressed to the shareholders, *not* the directors.

2 Members of the professional accounting bodies are required to comply with approved auditing standards.

3 It is normal practice to state whether the accounts have been prepared under the historical cost convention or the current cost convention (discussed in Chapter 11 below).

4 The report must specifically state whether or not the auditor believes the accounts give a true and fair view and comply with the Companies Acts.

5 The date of the audit report is important, because it indicates the date up to which the auditors will have considered any post balance sheet events.

A 'clean' audit report is a brief and formal document. Its significance lies in the fact that it does *not* raise any doubts. Any user analysing the accounts would be likely to consider carefully any reservation, doubt, or disagreement expressed by the auditors.

Figure 54

Auditors' Report to the members of Fergus Ltd

We have audited the financial statements on pages 3 to 19 in accordance with approved auditing standards.

In our opinion the financial statements, which have been prepared under the historical cost convention as modified by the revaluation of land and buildings, give a true and fair view of the state of the company' s affairs at 31 December 1985 and of its profit and source and application of funds for the year then ended and comply with the Companies Acts 1948 to 1981.

Bean, Lean and Co.
Chartered Accountants
26 May 1986

The chairman's statement

A chairman's statement is normally included in the annual report of large companies. There are no legal requirements as to the contents of the statement, and it commonly includes general discussion of the company's position and prospects. Research has shown that users of accounts tend to pay particular attention to the chairman's statement, perhaps because it normally includes some predictions of future prospects.

Manufacturing accounts

Where a business manufactures goods for sale it is common practice to identify the cost of production in a *manufacturing account*. The cost of production is then transferred to the trading account, in the same way as the cost of goods bought in for resale.

Figure 55 illustrates how the income statement will be made up when a manufacturing account is presented. The three sections of the statement are shown separately, but in practice it is normal to head the whole statement 'Manufacturing Trading and Profit and Loss Account'. In the case of a company or partnership the appropriate account would follow the profit and loss account.

The manufacturing account is divided into two parts:

1 The *direct* costs of production are shown. For this purpose it is necessary to adjust raw material purchases for opening and closing stocks in order to identify the cost of raw materials consumed. Other direct costs, such as wages, consist of all costs which can be directly attributed to goods produced. Total direct costs are called '*prime cost*'.
2 Other costs of production embrace all the costs of running the factory which cannot be directly attributed to items produced.

The total of direct and indirect costs must then be adjusted for opening and closing work in progress which, in compliance with SSAP9, will be computed on the basis of including an appropriate portion of direct and indirect production costs.

The trading account shows sales less cost of sales, computed as production costs plus costs of goods bought in for resale, adjusted for opening and closing stocks of finished goods.

The profit and loss account shows the gross profit plus any other income, less all other expenses. Other expenses may be split, as seen above, in to administration, selling and distribution, and finance.

The procedure for preparing a manufacturing account from a trial balance is exactly the same as

Figure 55

Manufacturing Account

	Raw material stock b/f	x	Production costs carried down to Trading Account	x
+	Raw material purchases	x		
-	Raw material stock c/f	(x)		
=	Raw material cost	x		
+	Other direct costs	x		
=	Prime cost	x		
+	Indirect factory costs	x		
+	WIP b/f	x		
-	WIP c/f	(x)		
=	Production costs	x		x

Trading Account

	Finished good stock b/f	x	Sales	x
+	Production costs (see above)	x		
+	Any goods bought in for resale	x		
-	Finished good stock c/f	(x)		
=	Cost of sales	x		
	Gross profit (balancing figure)	x		
		x		x

Profit and Loss Account

Other expenses	x	Gross profit	x
Net profit (balancing figure)	x	Other income	x
	x		x

Figure 56

Talbot – Manufacturing Trading and Profit and Loss Account for the year ended 31 December 1985

	£		£
Raw material stock 1.1.85	4,000	Production cost c/d	45,400
Purchases	18,000		
	22,000		
Raw material stock 31.12.85	4,500		
	17,500		
Direct wages	17,000		
Direct overheads	4,000		
Prime cost	38,500		
Factory heat & light	1,200		
Factory rent	3,000		
Plant depreciation	2,000		
	44,700		
Work in progress 1.1.85	5,900		
	50,600		
Work in progress 31.12.85	5,200		
	45,400		45,400
Finished goods 1.1.85	9,300	Sales	66,000
Production cost	45,400		
	54,700		
Finished goods 31.12.85	10,700		
	44,000		
Gross profit c/d	22,000		
	66,000		66,000
Office salaries	12,000	Gross profit b/d	22,000
Office heat & light	750		
Office rent	1,250		
	8,000		
Net profit	22,000		22,000

described above for preparing other kinds of final accounts. Example 25 shows a simple case of the way in which a trial balance might be presented, while Figures 56 and 57 show how the accounts would be prepared. Normally an examination question would include the full range of post trial balance adjustments, excluded from this example in order to simplify the illustration. Manufacturing accounts are here presented in double entry format to illustrate the principles involved, but could equally easily be presented in vertical form.

Example 25

Talbot carries on business as a manufacturer. His trial balance at 31 December 1985 showed:

	£	£
Drawings	3,000	
Factory heat and light	1,200	
Office heat and light	750	
Factory wages	17,000	
Office salaries	12,000	

Figure 57
Talbot – Balance Sheet as at 31 December 1985

	£	£	£
Fixed assets:			
Plant: Cost			20,000
Depreciation			12,000
			8,000
Current assets:			
Stock: Raw materials	4,500		
Work in progress	5,200		
Finished goods	10,700		
		20,400	
Debtors		9,000	
Bank		2,500	
		31,900	
Less: Creditors		3,100	
Net current assets			28,800
			36,800
Capital:			
As at 1.1.85			31,800
Profit for the year			8,000
			39,800
Drawings			3,000
			36,800

Raw material purchases	18,000	
Direct overheads	4,000	
Raw material stock 1.1.85	4,000	
Work in progress 1.1.85	5,900	
Finished goods 1.1.85	9,300	
Office rent	1,250	
Factory rent	3,000	
Plant cost/depreciation	20,000	10,000
Debtors	9,000	
Bank	2,500	
Creditors		3,100
Capital		31,800
Sales		66,000
	110,900	110,900

Note:

1 Depreciation on plant at 10 per cent straight line must be provided.
2 Stock at 31.12.85 was:

Raw materials	4,500
Work in progress	5,200
Finished goods	10,700

One refinement sometimes adopted is to charge the goods produced to the trading account at wholesale prices, the difference between production cost and wholesale price being transferred to the profit and loss account as profit on manufacturing. This approach is adopted in order to identify separately the profit on manufacturing from the profit on trading, but is necessarily a somewhat artificial exercise.

Incomplete records

The term 'incomplete records' is used to describe any form of accounting records which falls short of a full double entry book-keeping system. It can cover any form of record, from the situation where no records at all have been kept to the situation where extensive records have been maintained, but not in conventional double entry format.

In the most basic position, where no information at all is available on transactions during the year, it is possible to identify profit for the year if information on the assets and liabilities of the business at the beginning and end of the year, together with drawings during the year is available. Example 26 'Bradwardine', illustrates the kind of information required. Figure 58 shows how this information would be used to compute profit for the year:

1 A *statement of affairs*, showing the assets and liabilities of the business, is produced as at the beginning of the year. The difference between assets and liabilities is the opening capital. In effect a statement of affairs can be regarded as a balance sheet which has not been derived from accounting records.
2 A statement of affairs is produced as at the end of the year.
3 Having identified the opening and closing capital figures, the profit for the year can then be computed as:
Drawings + (Closing capital – Opening capital).
Alternatively the profit can be identified by reconstructing the statement of movements in capital as it would normally be shown on the face of the balance sheet.

Example 26

Bradwardine is in business as a plumber. He has no bank account, and keeps no records of income or expenditure. He knows that during the year to 31 December 1985 he has drawn £50 a week from the business for his own use. An analysis of his position at the beginning and end of the 1985 showed:

	1.1.85	31.12.85
Equipment at valuation	800	700
Stock	220	240
Debtors	110	150
Cash in hand	50	150
Owing to suppliers	220	230

Figure 58
Bradwardine

(a) Statement of affairs 1 January 1985

Capital	960*	Equipment	800
		Stock	220
Creditors	220	Debtors	110
		Cash	50
	1,180		1,180

(b) Statement of affairs 31 December 1985

Capital	1,010*	Equipment	700
		Stock	240
Creditors	230	debtors	150
		Cash	150
	1,240		1,240

(c)
Capital

At 1.1.85	960
Profit for year	2,650*
	3,610
Drawings	2,600
At 31.12.85	1,010

* Balancing figures

The computation of profit for the year by computing an opening and closing statement of affairs is unsatisfactory in that no breakdown of income and expenditure is provided. In practice it is normally possible to identify some of the transactions during the year. In particular:

1 Bank transactions can be identified by reference to bank statements, and linked to related cheque stubs and paying-in books. It may be necessary to construct a bank reconciliation statement to identify uncleared bankings and outstanding payments.
2 Payments made out of cash may be identifiable by reference to petty cash vouchers and known regular cash outlays, e.g. drawings by the proprietor, payments to a cleaner.

In this case it may be possible to reconstruct what is effectively a summary of the double entry records for the business, identifying any missing information by deduction. Under examination conditions the procedure to be followed would be:

1 Construct a statement of affairs at the beginning of the period in order to identify opening capital.
2 Enter each item from the opening state of affairs directly onto the face of the answer if possible, or otherwise into the workings. As in the preparation of accounts from a trial balance, discussed in Chapter 4 above, 'workings' will be presented in the form either of a 'T' account or, in simple cases, on the face of the answer.
3 Enter details of bank and cash payments and receipts into the workings or, if possible, the face of the answer. Sometimes it is necessary to construct a bank reconciliation in order to ensure that payments and receipts are properly totalled.
4 Enter any normal post trial balance adjustments into the workings or answer.
5 Total all items shown in the workings and make appropriate transfers to the answer. Note that it is common to make takings from customers a balancing figure on the cash account, and sales and purchases balancing figures on their respective control accounts.
6 Total the profit and loss account, then the balance sheet.

The working of an incomplete records question is illustrated with Example 27, 'Waverley'.

Example 27

Waverley is in business as a newsagent. He does not keep proper books of account. An analysis of his bank statement for the year to 31 December 1985 showed:

	£
Payments in:	
Cash paid in	16,120
Cheque received on sale of some fittings	230
	16,350

	£
Payments out:	
Fixtures purchased	600
Payments to suppliers	14,110
Electricity	220
Rent	500
Rates	320
	15,750

There were no uncleared bankings or outstanding cheques either at the beginning or end of the year

An analysis of cash payment vouchers showed:

	£
Postage	100
Stationery	150
Sundry	70
Cleaning	500

In addition, Waverley draws £30 a week in cash for his own use.

At 1 January 1985 the accounts of Waverley showed:

	£
Fixtures	1,500
Bank	450
Debtors	320
Stock	780
Creditors	290
Prepaid rates	70
Accrued electricity	35
Cash	50

The following information on the position at 31 December 1985 is available:

1 The fixtures disposed of during the year had a written-down value of £300. Depreciation is to be provided at 10 per cent by the reducing balance method.
2 Cash in hand at 31 December 1985 was £75. Any difference on the cash account represents takings.
3 At 31 December 1985 there were:

	£
Stock	730
Debtors	350
Creditors	410
Prepaid rates	85
Accrued electricity	40

Figure 59 shows the profit and loss account for Waverley, Figure 60 shows the balance sheet, and Figure 61 shows those workings not presented on the face of the answer. The sequence of steps in producing the accounts would be:

(a) Produce a statement of affairs at 1 January 1985, as shown in the workings. This shows the opening capital. Sometimes this step is unnecessary, when the examiner presents an opening balance sheet on the face of the question.

(b) Of the items on the statement of affairs:
- (i) Capital and stock are taken straight on to the face of the answer.
- (ii) The accrual for electricity and the prepayment for rates are shown in workings on the face of the answer.
- (iii) All other items involve adjustments of sufficient complexity to justify separate 'T' accounts in the workings.

(c) The next stage is to introduce the bank payments and receipts into the answer. Of these:
- (i) Rent paid is subject to no adjustment and can be shown directly on the face of the answer.
- (ii) Electricity and rates are subject to simple adjustments for accruals and prepayments, which are most simply handled on the face of the answer.
- (iii) The remaining items, including total payments and receipts recorded in the bank account, are shown in the 'T' accounts.

(d) Similarly the various cash payments are introduced into the answer, being credited in total to the cash account. It happens in this example that all the cash payments can be shown directly on the face of the answer.

(e) The two adjustments made to fixtures, relating to an asset disposal and depreciation, are of the conventional post trial balance adjustment type.

(f) Once we have shown the balance carried down on the cash account, the balancing figure represents takings which are debited to cash and credited to debtors.

(g) The accrual and the prepayment are adjusted on the face of the profit and loss account and recorded in the balance sheet, closing stock can be recorded directly on the face of the answer as normal, and the closing balances of creditors and debtors are introduced into the respective control accounts in the workings.

(h) The various 'T' accounts in the workings are totalled, all balances carried down being transferred to the balance sheet. In addition profit and loss figures for sales and purchases are ascertained from the control accounts, and the loss on disposal is also taken to profit and loss.

(j) The workings on the face of the accounts are totalled.

(k) The profit and loss account and balance sheet are totalled.

In order to make clear the sequence of entries, the amounts derived from each of the above processes shown in Figures 59 to 61 are each designated with the appropriate paragraph letter.

In the event of a fire at the business premises it is possible that loss of the business records might be combined with a loss of cash and/or stock. In that

Figure 59

Waverley – Profit and Loss Account for the year ended 31 December 1985

		£		£
Sales				18,555
Less:				
Stock 1.1.85	(b)	780		
Purchases	(h)	14,230		
		15,010		
Stock 31.12.85	(g)	730		
Cost of sales			(k)	14,280
Gross profit			(k)	4,275
Less:				
Electricity				
(*b* –35*c* +220 *g*) +40	(j)	225		
Rent	(c)	500		
Rates				
(*b* 70 *c* + 320 *g* – 85)	(j)	305		
Postage	(d)	100		
Stationery	(d)	150		
Sundry	(d)	70		
Cleaning	(d)	500		
Depreciation	(e)	180		
Loss on disposal	(h)	70	(k)	2,100
			(k)	2,175

Figure 60

Waverley – Balance Sheet as at 31 December 1985

		£		£
Fixed assets:				
Fixtures				1,620
Current assets:				
Stock	(g)	730		
Debtors	(h)	350		
Prepayment	(g)	85		
Bank	(h)	1,050		
Cash	(h)	75		
	(k)	2,290		
Current liabilities:				
Creditors	(h)	410		
Accruals	(g)	40		
	(k)	450		
Net current assets				1,840
				3,460
Capital:				
At 1.1.85			(b)	2,845
Profit for the year			(k)	2,175
			(k)	5,020
Drawings			(d)	1,560
			(k)	3,460

case incomplete records techniques will be used to compensate for the loss of records, and also to work out the insurance claim to be made for the lost assets. In such a case it may be necessary to estimate some items of income or expenditure by reference to comparable accounting ratios for previous years; a wide range of accounting ratios are considered in Chapter 13 below.

Incomplete records are commonly found in the small business, where the proprietor does not have the skill or the time to keep full accounting records personally and the size of the business does not warrant employment of a book-keeper. Disadvantages of such a position are:

1 Although there will be a saving of the costs of running a full accounting system, there will also be additional costs in preparing the accounts at the year end.

Figure 61

Waverley – Workings, Statement of affairs 1.1.85

		£			£
Capital		2,845	*Fixtures	(a)	1,500
			Stock	(a)	780
Creditors	(a)	290	Debtors	(a)	320
Accruals	(a)	35	Prepayments	(a)	70
			Bank	(a)	450
			Cash	(a)	50
		3,170			3,170

Creditors

Bank	(a)	14,110	b/d	(b)	290
c/d	(g)	410	Purchases	(h)	14,230
		14,520			14,520

Fixtures

b/d	(b)	1,500	Disposal	(e)	300
Bank	(c)	600	P & L – depreciation	(e)	180
			c/d	(h)	1,260
		2,100			2,100

Debtors

b/d	(b)	320	Cash	(f)	18,525
Sales	(h)	18,555	c/d	(g)	350
		18,875			18,875

Bank

b/d	(b)	450	Payments	(c)	15,750
Receipts	(c)	16,350	c/d		1,050
		16,800			16,800

Cash

b/d	(b)	50	Bank	(c)	16,120
Debtors	(f)	18,525	Payments	(d)	2,380
			c/d		
		18,575			18,575

Disposal

Fixtures	(e)	300	Bank	(c)	230
			Loss on disposal	(h)	70
		300			300

* Balancing figure

2 The control mechanism of the double entry system is lost, increasing the risk of error and fraud.
3 It is very much more difficult to identify the position part way through an accounting period, and probably impossible to do so in retrospect.
4 Lack of detailed records make it more difficult to audit the accounts with confidence and may make it more difficult to defend the accounts against any dispute, e.g. from the Inland Revenue.
5 The opportunity for certain types of more detailed analysis, e.g. classifying types of sale, is lost.

Income and expenditure accounts

In Chapter 5 above we observed that organizations which do not have a profit-making objective present an *income and expenditure account* rather than a profit and loss account. The balance on the account is termed a 'surplus of income over expenditure' or 'excess of expenditure over income' and is transferred to an *accumulated fund* in the balance sheet.

The income and expenditure account will show the various items of income of the organization, setting off against each directly related costs, and then showing other items of expenditure as deducted from the total of individual sources of income.

The presentation of an income and expenditure account is illustrated in Figure 62. The range of activities of a 'not-for-profit' organization tend to be more varied that those of a business of comparable size, so that a range of sources of income have to be reported on.

Two particular problems arise in accounting for clubs and societies:

1 ***Subscriptions in arrear***
A question arises as to whether subscriptions in arrear should be treated as accrued income. In favour of this practice it is argued that following the 'matching' convention subscriptions should be regarded as income of the accounting period in which subscribers enjoy the benefit of membership. On the other hand, following the 'prudence' convention, it can be argued that the ultimate receipt of subscriptions in arrear is uncertain because subscribers may have allowed membership to lapse, and pursuit of outstanding claims may be difficult in law and because of social conventions. In practice, subscriptions may be treated either on an accruals or a cash basis providing that there is consistency of treatment.

Figure 62

Talbot Sports Club – Income and Expenditure Account for the year ended 31 December 1985

	£	£
Bar takings		25,000
Bar stock 1.1.85	2,400	
Bar purchases	20,200	
	22,600	
Bar stock 31.12.85	2,600	
		20,000
Bar surplus		5,000
Summer fete – income	7,200	
less summer fete expenses	3,700	
		3,500
Subscriptions		2,900
Investment income		700
		12,100
Less:		
Steward's wages	7,200	
Rent	2,000	
Sundry expenses	1,500	
		10,700
Surplus of income over expenditure		1,400

2 ***Life membership and entrance fees***
A club may charge an entrance fee, often of a substantial amount. This can be treated in three ways:

(a) Take the fee as income of the year in which it is received.
(b) Take the fee directly to the accumulated fund on the face of the balance sheet, on the grounds that it relates to future benefits to

be rendered to the member

(c) Credit the fee to the suspense account, and make a transfer from the suspense account to income spread evenly over each year of the member's anticipated active membership.

In the case of life membership fees option (a) is less likely to be followed, but the principles involved are the same. Option (c) is technically most correct, in accordance with the accruals convention, but in practice is rather cumbersome.

Small organizations may sometimes present a *receipts and payment account*, being a simple statement of cash inflows and outflows during an accounting period. Examiners are fond of setting questions requiring conversion of a receipts and payments account into an income and expenditure account, effectively a form of incomplete records question.

Conclusion

The presentation of the accounts is dictated by a mixture of regulation, custom, and anticipated user needs. There are special techniques for producing accounts when the conventional double entry system has not been operated.

Questions

A larger number of questions than normal are included in relation to this chapter; most of these questions draw on a range of material from across Chapters 2 to 9.

1 The financial position of the Hudson Netball Club at 31 December 1980 showed the following:

Assets	£
Premises (at cost)	4,000
Furniture, valued at	560
Investments – 5% government stock (at cost)	200
Sports equipment valued at	200
Stocks of refreshments	52
Cash and bank balance	53
Subscriptions in arrears	40
Liabilities	
Subscriptions for 1981 (received in advance)	20
One-quarter's rent of land	25
Creditor – refreshments supplied	38

The Treasurer's cash book for the year to 31 December 1981 shows:

Receipts	£	*Payments*	£
Balance in hand b/d	53	Rent of land	100
Subscriptions	725	Wages	350
Sale of refreshments	415	Purchase of sports equipment	120
Sale of dance tickets	155	Dance expenses	76
Investment interest	10	Secretary's expenses	72
		Investment – 5% government stock	100
		Balance c/d	326
	1,358		1,358

(a) You are required to prepare the club's income and expenditure account for the year ended 31 December 1981 and a balance sheet at that date, after taking into account the following points:

(i) There were no stocks of refreshments at 31 December 1981.
(ii) Wages of £20 were due but unpaid at the year end.
(iii) Depreciation is to be provided on the furniture of £50
(iv) The sports equipment was valued at £290 on 31 December 1981.
(v) The investments were purchased on 31 December 1981.
(vi) Subscriptions received during 1981 included £25 subscriptions in advance.

(b) Outline the main differences between the final accounts and balance sheets of profit and non-profit-making organizations

(c) Life membership receipts need different accounting treatment to that of yearly subscriptions. How are such receipts treated in the final accounts?

(Huddersfield Polytechnic)

2 The following balances have been extracted from the books of the Ransom Company Ltd as at 30 September 1979:

	£
Creditors	6,300
Sales	80,000
Land at cost	18,000
Buildings at cost	38,000
Furniture and fittings at cost	22,000
Bank (credit balance)	6,000
Depreciation – Buildings	6,000
– Furniture and fittings	10,000
Discounts received	1,764
Unappropriated profit at 1 October 1978	2,000
Provision for doubtful debts	816
Goodwill (Note 1)	16,400
Cash in hand	232
Stock at 1 October, 1978	14,248
Interim dividend on preference shares	600
Rates	2,124
Wages and salaries	8,000
Insurance	1,896
Return inward	372
General expenses	436
Debtors	12,640
Purchases	43,856
Debenture interest	400
Bad debts	676
5% Debentures	16,000
6% £1 Preference Shares	20,000
£1 Ordinary shares	20,000
General reserve	10,000
Share premium (Note 2)	1,000

Additional information:

(a) Stock on hand at 30 September 1979 was £15,546.
(b) Insurance paid in advance – £100.
(c) Wages owing – £280.
(d) Depreciation is to be provided at 10 per cent on cost of buildings, and at 20 per cent on the written-down value of furniture and fittings.
(e) Provision for doubtful debts is to be reduced to 5 per cent of debtors.
(f) Debenture interest outstanding of £400.
(g) The directors proposed to pay a 5 per cent dividend and the final preference dividend, and to transfer £8,000 to general reserve.

Notes:

1 The goodwill account will have arisen by the acquisition of a business at a price above the net book value of the assets acquired.
2 The share premium account arose by the issue of shares at a price above their par (or face) value, the difference between issue price and par value being the share premium.

Prepare:
(a) Profit and loss account for the year ended 30 September 1979.
(b) Balance sheet as at that date.

(Oxford Polytechnic)

3 Adam Downshire is a sole trader who does not keep proper books of account. However the undermentioned information has been extracted for the year ended 31 December 1982.

Assets and liabilities at 31 December 1981	£
Premises	50,000
Equipment and fittings	8,000
Stock	10,000
Debtors	6,000
Cash in bank	1,000
Cash in hand	50
Creditors – Trade	4,500
Expenses	600

Bank transactions

Lodgements	
Takings	2,300
Received from credit customers	11,400
Withdrawals	
Creditors	9,400
Business expenses	2,800
Proprietors drawings	1,000

At 31 December 1982 Downshire owes £4,200 to trade creditors and £440 for business expenses. Debtors owe him £5,100 and stock and equipment is valued at £9,800 and £7,400 respectively.

The proprietor tells you that £10 worth of cash takings had been retained each week and not banked to cover sundry expenses which included £200 for purchases. £80 of this sum was in hand on 31 December 1982.

You are asked to prepare a trading and profit and loss account for the year ended 31 December 1982 and balance sheet as at that date.

What are the main drawbacks of the incomplete records system of keeping accounts?

(Ulster Polytechnic)

4 Freda owns a record shop, but does not enjoy book-keeping. She does keep a note of all cash transactions and has all her cancelled cheques and bank statements.

Required:

From the following information, prepare a trading and profit and loss account for the year ended 31 October 1982 and a balance sheet as at that date.

Analysis of cash transactions

	£		£
In hand 1 November 1981	34	Paid into bank	15,574
Takings in shop	17,400	Staff wages	2,200
Receipts from credit customers	1,460	Private drawings	820
		Cleaner	140
		In hand 31 October 1982	160

Analysis of bank statements

		Balance 1 November 1981	426
Cash paid in	15,574	Paid to suppliers	10,420
Legacy from Aunt Maud	2,500	Rent and rates	1,300
		Fittings	150
		Private drawings	2,600
		Heat and light	595
		Purchase of van	1,400
		Telephone	130

Assets and liabilities

	1 November 1981	*31 October 1982*
Debtors	122	182
Creditors	1,390	1,440
Van	900	Note 1
Fittings	570	Note 2
Stocks	380	523
Prepaid rent	45	60
Accrued rates	90	76

Notes:

1 The van held at 1 November 1981 was traded-in during the year against a new van. The trade-in allowance was £750.

2 Depreciation is charged as follows:
Van 20 per cent on cost
Fittings 10 per cent reducing balance

3 During the year Freda took goods for her own use from the shop. These would have normally sold for £160.

4 At 31 October 1982 the following cheques were outstanding:
Electricity £ 26
Suppliers £210

5 Freda believes that Fred Smith's bill of £12 (included in the figure of £182) is now irrecoverable. In addition, from past experience she feels that about 10 per cent of the other debtors may be doubtful.

(University of Stirling)

5 On 1 January of the current year, James Barker began the Barker Wheel Balancing and Alignment Service with an investment of £20,000 of his personal savings. No additional investments were made during the year. Barker's business prospered during the year, with Barker and one other employee performing all the alignment and balancing work. However, Barker was too busy to keep adequate records. He engages you at the end of the year to prepare an income statement and balance sheet.

You discover that Barker has made all disbursements by cheque. Analysis of cheque book stubs indicates the following payments made during the year:

	£		£
Heat and light	450	Purchases	1,400
Garage rent	1,800	Tools	800
Wages	7,000	Partial payment on alignment equipment	4,500
Personal withdrawals	2,000		

Insurance
(current year) 150

At the end of the year, Barker's cash balance is £15,000. All bills have been paid except one for supplies of £100 and the loan due on the alignment equipment. You discover that all alignment service has been performed on a 'strictly cash' basis. You also discover that the alignment equipment being used cost £12,000, on which £7,500 is still owed. At the end of the year stock on hand amounts to £200.

Required:

(a) Prepare a balance sheet at the end of the current year. Ignore interest and depreciation.
(b) Prepare an income statement for the current year.
(c) Illustrate *two* ways of arriving at the net profit figure.

(Heriot Watt University)

6 The first draft of the final accounts of Torkard Traders disclosed a net profit of £41,004 and a capital employed of £352,600, before providing for the manager's efficiency bonus, but including £8,928 (credit balance) for errors held in suspense.

H. Huthwaithe, the manager, receives a basic salary plus an annual bonus of £300 for every complete percentage point by which the net profit to capital employed percentage exceeds 10 per cent. In this context, net profit is before charging the manager's bonus, and capital employed is defined as fixed assets plus working capital. The bonus calculation is not carried out until the figures have been audited.

During the course of the audit, it was discovered that:

(a) Discounts allowed, £536, had been credited to discounts received.
(b) The sale for cash, of some disused fixtures and fittings which had been completely written off in a previous year, had been credited to fixtures and fittings, £470.
(c) An amount of £380 owed by M & Co for goods supplied had been settled *in contra* against an amount of £850 owing to M & Co, but the ledger entries had not yet been made.
(d) A glass carboy containing chemicals, which was kept in the warehouse, had sprung a leak. The resultant seepage had caused irreparable damage to stock valued at £800 but no account has yet been taken of this fact.
(e) Due to an oversight, credit sales for the last three days of the accounting year, amounting to £1,575, have been completely omitted from the sales day book.
(f) In the purchase day book, a sub-total of £27,183.54 has been carried forward as £37,183.54. Creditors, however, have been correctly posted.
(g) A credit sale invoice of £978 has been entered in the sales day book as £789.
(h) A credit note from a supplier for £21 in respect of faulty goods, had not been posted.
(i) The proprietor of Torkard Traders sometimes, for his convenience, abstracts cash from the till for personal purposes. During the year, this has amounted to £86. The book-keeper states that he has 'reduced cash sales so that the cash book balances'.

Required:

(a) Recalculate the net profit and capital employed figures after the above errors have been corrected.
(b) Calculate the manager's bonus.
(c) Open the suspense account and post the eliminating entries.

(Association of Certified Accountants, Level 1, June 1982)

7 The balance of the accounts of Processors Ltd at 31 December 1982 are as follows:

	£	£
Administration expenses	7,400	
Bank	21,400	
Corporation tax	200	
Creditors		3,000
Debenture interest	750	
10% Debentures 1990		15,000

Debtors	26,700	
Direct labour	19,200	
Directors' remuneration	5,000	
Distributable reserves		4,200
Factory general expenses	3,050	
Factory indirect labour	4,900	
Factory rent payable	1,400	
Finished goods purchases	2,700	
Finished goods stock, at cost (as at 1.1.82)	6,100	
Ordinary share capital: Shares of 25p each		20,000
Plant, at cost	12,000	
Plant: Provision for depreciation (as at 1.1.82)		4,000
Raw materials purchases	25,700	
Raw materials stock, at cost (at 1.1.82)	4,300	
Sales		80,000
Suspense		23,500
Trade investment, at cost	5,000	
Work in progress, at cost (at 1.1.82)	3.900	
	149,700	149,700

Note: Work in progress and finished goods are all inclusive of apportioned factory overheads.

Adjustment has yet to be made in respect of the following matters:

(a) Stocks at 31 December 1982, at cost: £

Raw materials	5,800
Work in progress	3,600
Finished goods	8,000

(b) Factory electricity consumption since meter reading on last invoice entered in the books: 6,000 units at 5p per unit.

(c) Factory rent paid quarterly in advance; last payment of £300 made on due date, 1 December 1982.

(d) Depreciation of plant 25 per cent per annum of the written-down value.

(e) The Suspense account, made up of £

Proceeds of issue of 40,000 ordinary shares of 25p each at 30p per share	12,000
Proceeds of sale of the trade investment, which had been acquired in 1976, less tax paid on gain	11,500
	23,500

(f) Corporation tax on the profits of the year, payable on 1 October 1983, estimated at £3,700. (The balance found in the corporation tax account resulted from under-provision in 1981 accounts of tax payable on that year's profits.)

(g) Provision for interest due on the debentures.

(h) The directors' proposal to pay a dividend of 6p per share on ordinary shares in issue at the year end.

Required:

The manufacturing, trading and profit and loss account for the year ended 31 December 1982, and the balance sheet as at 31 December 1982.

(Preston Polytechnic)

8 Trevor and Francis, partners in a manufacturing business, have prepared from the books of account the following draft balance sheet as on 31 December 1979:

	Trevor	*Francis*	
	£	£	£
Capital 1.1.79	20,100	10,000	
Profit for year	4,770	4,770	
	24,870	14,770	
Less: Drawings	2,000	3,800	
	22,870	10,970	33,840
Creditors			7,800
Bank overdraft			2,700
			44,340

	Cost	*Dep'n*	
	£	£	£
Freeh'd buildings	12,000		12,000
Plant and Machinery	15,000	7,000	8,000
Motor vehicles	8,000	2,700	5,300
Stocks			5,000

Debtors	14,000
Cash in hand	40
	44,340

During the course of your examination of the books you ascertain that adjustments are required for the following items:

(a) Freehold buildings are shown at cost less £3,000 being the proceeds of the sale during the year of premises costing £3,500.

(b) Plant and machinery having a net book value of £215 have been scrapped during the year. The original cost was £615.

(c) Motor vehicle licences for 12-month periods costing £100 had been written off, but did not expire until 30 June 1980.

(d) Debts to the value of £521 were considered to be bad, and a further £270 doubtful requiring 100 per cent provision. Provision had previously been made for £500 doubtful debts.

(e) Stocks included at a value of £1,870 had a net realizable value of only £1,300, and scrap material having a value of £330 had been omitted from the stock valuation.

(f) The cashier had misappropriated £35.

(g) The cash book included payments amounting to £3,462, the cheques having been made but not mailed to suppliers until 1980.

(h) Interest is to be allowed on partners' opening capital account balances less drawings during the year at 9 per cent.

You are required to prepare:

(a) A summary of adjustments to the profit and loss account for the year and revised division of profit between the partners, and

(b) A revised balance sheet (in vertical form) as on 31 December 1979.

(Oxford Polytechnic)

9 Squirrel Antiques is a small one-man business run by Vic Torian the owner. He employs a book-keeper who has prepared the following trial balance and notes as at 30 April 1982.

Squirrel Antiques – Trial Balance as at 30 April 1982

	£	£
Vic Torian: Capital at 1 May 1981		16,360
Sales		22,900
Purchases	7,400	
Rent and rates	1,450	
Lighting and heating	920	
Bank interest received		190
Assistants' wages	2,700	
Furniture renovation costs	2,200	
Sundry expenses	870	
Stock at 1 May 1981	4,600	
Fixtures and fittings at cost	6,400	
Depreciation thereon to 30 April 1981		2,600
Motor vehicles at cost	11,500	
Depreciation thereon to 30 April 1981		4,100
Vic Torian: Drawings	4,200	
Bank and cash balances	3,910	
	46,150	46,150

Notes:

1 There are no credit transactions.

2 Depreciation rates are as follows:
Fixtures and fittings 10% p.a.
Motor vehicles 25% p.a.
Both are straight line, giving a full year's depreciation in the year of purchase, and none in the year of sale.

3 The original purchase price of goods still in stock at 30 April 1982 was £5,100. These goods are estimated to have a market value of £8,000 at that date.

4 Furniture renovation costs for the year of £2,200 includes expenditure of £800 on goods still in stock at 30 April 1982, and also includes £150 spent on repairing fixtures and fittings used by Squirrel Antiques.

5 Rates of £150 are prepaid at 30 April 1982, and electricity of £100 is owing at that date.

You are asked by Vic Torian to produce a

trading and profit and loss account for Squirrel Antiques for the year ended 30 April 1982, and a balance sheet at that date.

(Woverhampton Polytechnic)

10 The following balances were extracted from the ledger of Green Ltd at 31 March 1983 *after* a draft income statement for the year ended on that date had been prepared.

	£000
Freehold land and buildings	55
Bank overdraft	26
Cash in hand	3
Stock in hand at 31 March 1983	75
Creditors	18
10% Debentures	50
Share capital:	
25,000 8% Preference shares of £1 each	25
60,000 Ordinary shares of £1 each	60
Proposed dividends:	
8% on Preference shares	2
15% on Ordinary shares	9
General reserve	20
Share premium account	10
Plant and machinery at cost	80
Provision for depreciation at 1 April 1982	22
Motor vehicles	35
Provision for depreciation at 1 April 1982	8
Debtors	34
Unappropriated profit at 31 March 1983 (per draft income statement)	32

Further investigation reveals the following additional information:

(a) Depreciation should have been provided on the cost of the fixed assets of the company at the following annual rates:

Plant and machinery	10%
Motor vehicles	20%

(b) No interest has at present been paid or provided on the debenture stock for the year to 31 March 1983.

(c) The authorized share capital of the company consists of 25,000 8% preference shares of £1 each and 75,000 ordinary shares of £1 each.

(d) The balances of the company's reserves at 1 April 1982 were:

Share premium account	£10,000
General reserve	15,000
Unappropriated profit	8,000

Required:

(a) From the ledger balances and additional information given above prepare, in accordance with best accounting practice, a balance sheet for Green Ltd at 31 March 1983.

(b) Ascertain the net trading profit of the company for the year ended 31 March 1983 stating any assumptions which you may feel it necessary to make.

(Hatfield Polytechnic)

11 The trial balance extracted from the books of Hillgate Ltd at 31 December 1981 was as follows:

	£	£
Share capital		100,000
Profit and loss account 31 December 1980		34,280
Freehold premises at cost	65,000	
Machinery at cost	55,000	
Provision for depreciation on machinery account as at 31 December 1980		15,800
Purchases	201,698	
Sales		316,810
General expenses	32,168	
Wages and salaries	54,207	
Rents and rates	4,300	
Lighting and heating	1,549	
Bad debts	748	
Provision for doubtful debts at 31 December 1980		861
Debtors	21,784	
Creditors		17,493
Stock in trade 31 December 1980	25,689	
Bank balance	23,101	
	485,244	485,244

You are given the following additional information:

(a) The authorized and issued share capital is divided into 100,000 shares of £1 each.
(b) Stock in trade at 31 December 1981, £29,142.
(c) Wages and salaries due at 31 December 1981 amounted to £581.
(d) Rates paid in advance at 31 December 1981 amounted to £300.
(e) A dividend of £10,000 is proposed for 1981.
(f) The provision for doubtful debts is to be increased to £938.
(g) A depreciation charge is to be made on machinery at the rate of 10 per cent per annum at cost.

Required:
A trading and profit and loss account for 1981 and a balance sheet at 31 December 1981.

(University College of North Wales)

10

PRINCIPLES GOVERNING ACCOUNTING PRACTICE

Objectives

The basic objective of this chapter is to give a broad outline of the various types of factor which can influence accounting regulations. Specifically considered are:

1 The accounting standard setting process in the UK.
2 Factors influencing SSAPs.
3 The role of accounting theory.

Accounting standards

Accounting regulations fall into two broad categories:

1 Disclosure requirements, which prescribe what information has to be disclosed in the accounts.
2 Accounting practice requirements, which prescribe the ways in which various items should be accounted for.

Traditionally, company law has dealt mainly with disclosure requirements. Although the Companies Act 1981 introduces certain accounting practice requirements, these are adopted in the main from existing accounting standards. By and large accounting practice requirements are laid down by the accounting profession through Statements of Standard Accounting Practice, rather than by government legislation.

The Accounting Standards Committee (then known as the Accounting Standards Steering Committee) was set up in December 1969 and the first accounting standard was issued in 1971. Prior to that the various accounting bodies issued guidance to their members, probably the most widely quoted being the ICAEW's 'Recommendations on Accounting Principles', but these were widely regarded as inadequate for the following reasons:

1 On occasion the different professional bodies produced conflicting recommendations.
2 There was no procedure for consulting interested parties from outside the professional bodies concerned.
3 There was no requirement for companies to comply with these recommendations.
4 Recommendations were not always supported by thorough research and consideration before issue.

During the 1960s pressure built up for reform in the UK. Critics of the wide range and diversity of permitted accounting practices quoted the example that arose when GEC took over AEI. During the takeover bid AEI had produced a forecast, during the tenth month of their financial year, predicting a profit for the year of £10 million. GEC's bid was successful, and when the accounts for the year were produced AEI reported a loss of £4½ million. On investigation it was found that £9½ million of the difference was attributable to differences between the accounting policies of GEC and AEI. The fact that the difference between two sets of equally acceptable accounting policies could produce such a substantial difference in reported profit was held to illustrate the need for standardization of accounting practice.

Initially the ASC was set up by the ICAEW, but the other CCAB bodies became involved at an early stage. The committee is now made up of representatives from each of the six CCAB bodies. The ASC's constitution defines its objectives as being to advance accounting standards and to narrow the areas of difference in accounting practice by:

1 Keeping standards of financial reporting under review. Thus one role of the ASC is to observe developments in accounting practice which might require action; in a sense the ASC might be said to be responsible for drafting its own agenda.
2 Publishing consultative documents. These include exposure drafts, which represent a proposal for an accounting standard, and discussion papers which outline the major issues and invite comment.
3 Proposing SSAPs to the councils of the CCAB bodies. It is important to note that the ASC is responsible for the formulation of accounting standards, but the authority to issue standards remains in the hands of the individual professional bodies. It has been known for an accounting standard formulated by the ASC to be sent back for reconsideration by the council of one of the CCAB bodies.
4 Consultation with interested parties. One method of consultation is to analyse the response to exposure drafts and discussion papers. In addition the ASC has set up a consultative committee of nominees from organizations representing the major users of published accounts, including the CBI and the TUC.

It is important to note that the overall objectives of the accounting standards programme can be considered in two parts:

1 ***Improvement***
One objective of the accounting standards programme is to improve the quality of financial reporting. This raises the question of what criteria should be applied in deciding what constitutes 'improvement', an issue considered below.
2 ***Standardization***
Narrowing the areas of diversity in accounting practice can be regarded as a desirable objective in itself, irrespective of whether the new requirement constitutes an improvement. This is because it is valuable to be able to compare the accounts of different businesses. It should be noted that accounting standards can narrow the areas of difference in accounting *practice* but not in accounting *estimates*. For example it would be possible to tell all accountants to use the straight-line method of depreciation, but impossible to ensure that different accountants considering the same item of plant would produce the same estimate of asset life.

Most accounting standards in practice include a mixture of disclosure requirements and accounting practice requirements. We have seen that, by contrast, the Companies Acts contain mainly disclosure requirements. The arguments in favour of having accounting standards issued by the accounting profession rather than the government are:

1 Technical expertise. The professional accounting bodies can call on a broader range of technical expertise in accounting than would be readily available to a government formulating legislation.
2 Flexibility. The accounting profession is in a position to respond more rapidly to changes in the accounting environment than would a government operating through the legislative process.
3 Liaison with business. It can be argued that representatives of the accounting profession are likely to be involved with some aspect of the business community themselves, and will therefore have a valuable insight into the needs and problems of the business community.
4 Independence. Governments are themselves significant users of accounting information, and are also potentially under pressure from various public interest groups who may respond to accounting information. Thus governments may be biased as a source of regulations on accounting practice.

On the other hand, it can be argued that because

accounting regulations have a wide range of potential consequences, discussed in detail below, it is appropriate for governments to control the accounting standard-setting process. In practice governments in the UK have on occasion intervened in the formulation of accounting standards; examples have included the inflation accounting issue, covered in Chapter 11 below, the accounting treatment of development expenditure, and the accounting treatment of deferred taxation. The relationship between the government and the accounting profession on the issue of accounting standards can be seen as one of mutual benefit. The government allows the accounting profession to enjoy the status arising from self-regulation, and thereby avoids the technical complexities of regulating accounting practice while being able, in practice, to exercise influence in matters considered to be important.

We have already seen, in Chapter 1 above, that compliance with accounting standards in the UK is not enforced by law. The professional bodies have had a fair measure of success in using their authority over their own members to persuade companies to comply with accounting standards. However, the prospect that companies might choose to flout the authority of the ASC by refusing to comply with unpopular standards has proved a constraint on the ASC's freedom of action.

Factors influencing accounting standards

The setting of accounting standards involves an accounting setting body in making choices:

1 As to what areas of accounting practice need to be standardized.
2 As to what accounting practices are appropriate to be chosen as 'standard' in relation to each topic considered.

There have been a number of official studies which have addressed themselves to the question of what factors should influence accounting standard-setters in their decision making. These include:

1 The American Institute of Certified Public Accountants issued, in 1973, a report on 'Objectives of Financial Statements'; this report is commonly referred to as the 'Trueblood Report', after the Chairman of the committee that produced it. The Financial Accounting Standards Board in the USA have followed up the Trueblood Report with a number of studies intended to develop a conceptual framework for the development of accounting standards.
2 In the UK the ASC produced in 1976 the 'Corporate Report', a discussion paper intended to promote a major review of the objectives of financial accounting.
3 In the UK a government-appointed committee produced the 'Sandilands Report' on Inflation Accounting in 1975. This report considered in some detail what factors should influence the development of accounting standards.

Amongst the factors influencing the development of accounting standards we can identify:

1 Qualitative characteristics.
2 User needs.
3 Economic reality.
4 Economic consequences.

Each of these is considered briefly below.

Qualitative characteristics

Qualitative characteristics which various authorities have held to be desirable in accounts include:

1 ***Objectivity***
The Corporate Report argued that accounts should be unbiased in meeting all proper user needs, and neutral in that they should not be biased towards the interest of any one user group. This concept of objectivity is considered in detail in considering 'users' below. The Sandilands Report used the term 'objectivity' in a rather different way, as meaning that it is desirable that accounts should as far as possible be capable of independent verification; the Corporate Report used the term 'reliability' to cover this concept.

2 ***Comparability***
The Sandilands Report used the term 'comparability' to describe the notion that it is desirable that one company's accounts should be comparable with another and the term 'consistency' to cover the idea that successive years' accounts of a company should be comparable. The Corporate Report uses the term 'comparability' to cover both concepts.

3 ***Realism***
The Sandilands Report identified the characteristic of presenting a 'realistic' view of a company's position as similar to the concept in the Companies Acts that accounts should present a 'true and fair view'.

4 ***Ease and economy of precision***
Any accounting system should be designed bearing in mind the need to ensure that the effort and expense of presenting information should not exceed the benefits of its provision. The Sandilands Report suggests that this aspect may justify differences in the accounting requirements for large and small companies. The Corporate Report does not specifically cover this characteristic, but does point out the need to bear in mind cost and confidentiality in prescribing accounting requirements, and points out the practical desirability of 'timeliness'.

5 ***Relevance***
The Corporate Report argues that a fundamental consideration of accounting information should be its relevance to user needs.

This brief discussion of the qualitative characteristics of accounts illustrates a serious problem, that there will be unavoidable conflicts between objectives. For example 'objectivity' and 'comparability' may conflict with 'realism' and 'relevance'.

User needs

Both the Corporate Report and the Sandilands Report place a heavy emphasis on the need to respond to a range of user needs. The Corporate Report argued:

> Business enterprises can survive only with the approval of the community in which they operate and they have an interest in revealing information which displays how differing interests are being balanced for the benefit of the whole community.
>
> (para 4.29)

The Sandilands Report took a similar view, arguing for example that one desirable characteristic of the unit of measurement used in a set of accounts is that is should be:

> equally useful to all users of accounts.
>
> (para 149)

The view that accountants have a responsibility to a broad range of users has developed strongly in most European countries. For example a former president of the Dutch accounting profession and of the IASC has observed:

> we should get rid of the image of serving the needs of capital only, and associate more with other groups such as trade unions, works councils, consumer interests, environmental pressure groups, politicians, and governments.

This view of wider accountability is very much less strong in the USA.

The wide range of potential users of accounts has already been considered in detail in Chapter 1 above. An awareness of this wide range involves the accounting standard-setter in delicate judgements as to the importance and validity of different user requirements.

Economic reality

We have already seen that accounts do not, and cannot, attempt to portray the full economic reality of the position of a business. However when considering the choice between two alternative approaches to an accounting problem, it is possible to consider which best reflects the economic reality of the position. For example, one argument in favour of a 'deferral' rather than a 'write-off' approach to development expenditure (see Chapter 6 above) is that the former gives a more realistic view of a company's intention in incurring development expenditure, which is to improve the income of future periods.

Economic consequences

Accountants have become increasingly aware in recent years that accounting regulations have potential 'economic consequences'. These arise for two broad reasons:

1 ***Regulatory***
There are a number of ways in which the amounts reported in the accounts are used as a basis for regulating the economic relationships between the company and the outside world. Two examples are taxation, which is based on reported profits, and company borrowing powers, which are normally based on reported equity.

2 ***Judgemental***
We have seen that a wide range of potential users might make decisions based on the information reported in the accounts. These decisions can have serious implications both for the individual company and for the economy as a whole.

There is no doubt that economic consequence factors play a major part in determining the attitudes of interested parties on accounting issues. There is considerable controversy over how far those responsible for the formulation of accounting regulations should take economic consequence factors into account. On the one hand it can be argued that accounting regulators have a duty to society as a whole to promote the economic well-being of the community. On the other hand it can be argued that the job of the accountant is to portray economic reality as fairly as possible, and not to become involved in 'political' issues on the creation and distribution of economic wealth.

Role of accounting theory

'Theory' is defined by the *Concise Oxford Dictionary* as: 'Supposition or system of ideas explaining something'. *Accounting theory* could therefore be defined as 'supposition or system of ideas explaining accounting'.

Two broad approaches to accounting theory can be identified:

1 The *descriptive* approach. This approach seeks to provide a framework of ideas which enable us to understand how existing accounting practices have developed, and to understand how accountants are likely to respond to future developments.
2 The *normative* approach. This approach can be regarded as being concerned with understanding what accounting practices *ought* to be developed.

Above we have considered some of the factors which influence the setting of accounting standards; a descriptive theory of accounting would necessarily have to take all these factors into account; some factors are more difficult to fit into a normative approach. For example, it is easy to see how economic consequence issues affect accounting standards in practice, but more difficult to define the extent to which economic consequences ought to be considered.

Conclusion

This chapter has considered, briefly, the kinds of factors that influence accounting regulations. We have seen that there is a complex mixture of factors involved.

Questions

1 'For the annual accounts of an enterprise to be useful to various groups of users, it is vital that those users understand the bases upon which those accounts were prepared'.
Discuss, giving examples of:
(a) The information needs of the various groups of users of a set of accounts, and

(b) The 'bases of preparation' of a typical set of accounts.

(Wolverhampton Polytechnic)

2 'For financial accounting standards, disclosure standards should be a matter for legislation while measurement standards should be a matter for the accounting profession'.

Discuss.

(University of Lancaster)

3 Accounting has been defined as 'the process of identifying, measuring and communicating economic information to permit judgements and decisions by users of the information'.

Explain who are the 'users' and what information do they require, and are their needs adequately met.

(Ulster Polytechnic)

11

INFLATION AND THE ACCOUNTANT

Objectives

The basic objective of this chapter is to offer a brief review of the problems of adapting the traditional accounting framework to recognize the effects of inflation. Specifically considered are:

1 The impact of inflation on traditional historical cost accounts.
2 The current purchasing power (CPP) approach to inflation accounting.
3 The concept of 'value to the business'.
4 Current cost accounting (CCA).
5 The relative merits of CPP and CCA.

The impact of inflation

Historical cost accounts express all items in monetary amounts, as measured at the date when each item first enters the accounts. In times of inflation the 'value' of money is falling, so that the monetary unit of measurement does not have a constant value. In times of rising prices there are four major effects on the significance of the accounts:

1 Expenditure is normally incurred earlier than the related income is received, so that it will be measured at an amount which understates its 'value' at the date of consumption. Thus profit will be overstated.
2 Assets will be shown in the balance sheet measured at their monetary value at the date of acquisition, thus understating their value as at the balance sheet date.

   The combined effect of overstating profit and understating the value of assets is to overstate the return earned on capital employed.
3 The comparison of results over a period of years is misleading, because the unit of measurement used has a declining value.
4 Assets and liabilities which represent an entitlement or obligation to receive or pay amounts fixed in monetary amounts (called 'monetary items'), such as bank balances or loans, lose 'value' in times of inflation, but this change is not reflected in the accounts.

Considering each of these points in detail:

1 ***Overstatement of profit***
   There are two items in the profit and loss account where there is normally a material time gap between an item entering the accounts and being written off as an expense, the depreciation of fixed assets and the consumption of stock. Example 28 shows two simple instances of how the historical cost accounts fail to reflect the full expense to the business of items consumed in a time of rising prices.

Example 28

(a) On 1 January 1982 a business buys a machine having a five year life for £1,000. During the year to 31 December 1985 the machine's average replacement cost would be £1,800. Providing depreciation on the straight-line basis would result in an historical cost depreciation charge of:

$$\frac{1,000}{5} = £200$$

Although the cost of replacing the part of the asset consumed would be:

$$\frac{1,800}{5} = £360$$

(b) On 1 March 1986 a business bought a widget for £150, selling the widget on 30 June 1986 for £180. The cost of a replacement widget on that date would be £162. The historical cost accounts would show a profit of:

180 – 150 = £30

Although, in an ongoing business, £162 must be expended to replace stock sold so that the surplus generated is effectively:

180 – 162 = £18

2 ***Understatement of net assets***
The major non-monetary assets held by a business are fixed assets and stock. We have already seen how fixed asset revaluations are sometimes incorporated in the historical cost accounts, but this only represents a partial solution to the problem unless all assets are revalued every year.

3 Non-comparability of results over a period of years is particularly serious where inflation helps to conceal a fall in the volume of trade. For example, supposing a company has a £1,000,000 turnover in year 1; in year 2 the volume of trade falls by 10 per cent while prices rise by 15 per cent. The turnover reported in year 2 will be:

Year 1 turnover	1,000,000
Less 10% fall in volume	100,000
	900,000
Plus 15% price rise	135,000
	1,035,000

Giving an apparent 3.5 per cent increase.

4 Example 29 shows a simple , everyday example of how it is possible to make a gain as a result of borrowing money in a time of inflation. The gain is reflected when non-monetary assets financed by borrowing are revealed; the problem is deciding on which part, if any, of the gain should be regarded as 'profit'. This simple illustration shows how a variety of approaches might be justified.

Example 29

On 1 January 1975 Fred bought a house for £10,000, borrowing £9,000 to finance the purchase. At 31 December 1985 the loan outstanding is £9,000 but the house is worth £20,000. The gain of £10,000 could be regarded as follows:

1 A profit of £10,000 has been made, since this is the increase in what is 'owned'.
2 In 1975 Fred owned one-tenth of a house while in 1985 he owns eleven-twentieths of a house – a gain of nine twentieths of one house, i.e.

$$\frac{9}{20} \times 20 \text{ x } £20,000 = £9,000 \text{ profit}$$

The other £1,000 gain is a revaluation surplus, not a profit.

3 In 1975 Fred owned one house and owed £9,000. In 1985 this is still his position. Thus he has made no 'profit' and the whole £10,000 represents a revaluation surplus.

We have already seen that accountants do not claim to be able to prepare accounts which portray the full economic reality of the position of a business. However the consistent overstatement of profits over a period of some years, as a result of inflation, has been held to have contributed to the following problems in the UK:

1 Excessive dividend payments. Although the directors should take a wide range of factors into account when deciding on the level of dividends, high reported profits can raise shareholders' expectations as to dividend levels.
2 Excessive business taxation. It can be argued that when governments observe a high level of reported profits they are likely to overestimate

the amount of tax burden which the business sector can bear. In fact when, during the 1970s, there was a high level of inflation in the UK the Government did introduce a number of tax reliefs, such as 'stock relief', designed to recognize the impact of inflation on company profits.

3 Excessive wage settlements. Over-stated profits constitute an incentive to employees to press for higher wages, and may cause management to be unduly optimistic as to what can be paid.
4 Under-recovery of costs. Management may fail to appreciate the need to recover current rather than historical costs when setting selling prices.
5 Investor error. Investors may be misled by historical cost accounts. In particular, in takeover bids investors may fail to appreciate the true asset value of the company.

It should be noted that each of these perceived problems is attributable to failure by decision-makers to appreciate the significance of historical cost accounts in times of inflation. Thus the debate over an appropriate method for making accounts more meaningful in times of inflation may well have had the beneficial side-effect of making decision-makers aware of the problems and therefore less likely to make naive decisions.

Two broad types of solution have been put forward to the problem:

1 ***Current purchasing power accounting (CPP)***
This approach involves changing the unit of measurement. Instead of money a 'CPP unit' is used. All historical cost amounts are then translated into 'CPP units' which represent the value of the monetary unit at the balance sheet date.

2 ***Current cost accounting (CCA)***
This involves changing the *basis* of measurement. Instead of historical cost the 'value to the business' (defined below) is measured for all items.

Thus CPP changes the unit of measurement while CCA changes the basis of measurement.

In the UK the accounting profession produced proposals for a system of CPP accounts, to be presented as supplementary statements, in SSAP7 (May 1974). However in September 1975 a Government-appointed committee produced the Sandilands Report which recommended a CCA approach. The ASC accepted this view and, after a long and at times heated controversy, produced SSAP16 on current cost accounting in March 1980. Currently there are further proposals put forward in ED35 to make some changes to SSAP16 while retaining a CCA approach.

Current purchasing power (CPP)

The CPP approach to inflation accounting is based on using a 'current purchasing power' unit, into which all the historical cost amounts in the accounts are translated. The purchasing power of the monetary unit is computed by reference to an index of general purchasing power, such as the Retail Price Index in the UK. Historical cost amounts are translated by applying the factor:

$$\frac{\text{Index at balance sheet date}}{\text{Index at transaction date}}$$

In the balance sheet non-monetary items are shown at the translated amount, while monetary items are shown at their historical cost monetary amount because this is the actual amount receivable or payable. The difference between the CPP-adjusted amount for monetary items and the historical cost amount constitutes a gain or loss on monetary items reported in the profit and loss account; the computation of this gain or loss is considered in detail below. In the profit and loss account all items of income and expenditure are also translated into CPP units.

The principles of CPP accounting can be illustrated by the simple example 'Mount Ltd' presented in Example 30.

Example 30

On 31 December 1985 Mount Ltd was formed with an issued ordinary share capital of £40,000 and a 10 per cent loan, repayable in 1997, of £60,000. Storage facilities were purchased on the same date for £50,000, having a 10-year life with no residual value.

On 31 March 1986 Mount Ltd spent £45,000 on a purchase of 1,000 microlight aeroplane propellers. On 30 November 1986 800 propellers were sold for £70 each. £6,000 interest was paid on 31 December 1986. No other income or expenses arose in the year, so that the historical cost accounts at 31 December 1986 showed:

Profit and loss		£	£
Sales	(800 × £70)		56,000
Cost of sales	(800 × £45)		36,000
Gross profit			20,000
Depreciation		5,000	
Interest		6,000	11,000
Net profit			9,000

Balance sheet	£		£
Share capital	40,000	Fixed assets	45,000
Retained profit	9,000	Stock (200 × 45)	9,000
	49,000	Bank	55,000
Loan	60,000		
	109,000		109,000

The Retail Price Index showed:

1 January 1985	132.0
31 March 1986	143.0
30 November 1986	156.0
31 December 1986	171.6

In preparing the CPP accounts the CPP factors to be applied in respect of transactions at various dates will be:

1.1.85 $\frac{171.6}{132.0} = 1.3$

31.3.86 $\frac{161.6}{143.0} = 1.2$

30.11.85 $\frac{171.6}{156} = 1.1$

CPP accounts can then be computed as follows:

1 Translate all non-monetary items in the balance sheet by applying the CPP factor related to the date when the item first entered the accounts; the opening equity is translated at the rate applicable to the first day of the accounting period. Monetary amounts appear in the CPP balance sheet at the same amount as in the HC balance sheet, and retained profit for the year will be the balancing figure.

2 Translate all items in the profit and loss account by reference to the date when they entered the accounts. For depreciation this will be the date when fixed assets were acquired. These translations are shown in Figure 63.

3 To compute the gain or loss on monetary items would require, in principle, a detailed analysis of when each component part of monetary items first entered the accounts. In practice the gain or loss is computed as illustrated in Figure 64:

(a) Monetary items in the opening balance sheet are translated from the opening to closing purchasing power, any difference being a gain or loss on monetary items.

(b) Any difference between the CPP and the HC amount of monetary items in the profit and loss account represents a gain or loss on monetary items.

Figure 64 *Gain/loss on monetary items*

	£	£
(a) Opening loan – CPP adjusted:		
60,000 × 1.3	78,000	
less HC amount	60,000	
Gain		18,000
Opening bank – CPP adjusted		
50,000 × 1.3	65,000	
less HC amount	50,000	
Loss		(15,000)
(b) Profit and loss items:		
Sales – CPP	61,600	
less HC	56,000	
Loss		(5,600)
Purchases – CPP	54,000	
less HC	45,000	
Gain		9,000
		6,400

Figure 63 *Translation of the accounts of Mount Ltd*

Balance Sheet

		HC	CPP translation factor		CPP
	£	£		£	£
Share capital		40,000	1.3 (a)		52,000
Retained profit		9,000	*		12,300
		49,000			64,300
Loan		60,000	— (a)		60,000
		109,000			124,300
Fixed assets		45,000	1.3 (a)		58,500
Stock		9,000	1.2 (a)		18,800
Bank		55,000	—		55,000
		109,000			124,300

* Balancing figure

Profit and Loss Account

Sales		56,000	1.1 (b)		61,600
Cost of sales		36,000	1.2 (b)		43,200
Gross profit		20,000			18,400
Depreciation	5,000		1.3 (b)	6,500	
Interest	6,000		1 (b)	6,000	
		11,000			12,500
		9,000			5,900
Gain on monetary items		—	(c)		6,400
Net profit		9,000			12,300

Value-based accounting

The alternative to measurement based on historical cost is measurement based on *value*. Value can be measured in a variety of ways, but the three main measures of value are:

1 *Replacement cost*, being the cost of buying a replacement asset at the point in time under consideration.
2 *Net realizable value*, being the amount for which the asset could be sold less all cost of disposal.
3 *Present value*, also called *economic* value, being the present value of the net inflows of cash which are going to arise in the future as a result of using the asset. In principle the *present value* of a future cash flow is found by *discounting* the expected cash flow by a factor which allows for the fact that, because of the time value of money (commonly represented by a rate of interest), an amount of money to be received in the future has less value than if it were received immediately.

Both replacement cost and net realizable value have been put forward as the basis of measurement to be used in an accounting system. However the basis of measurement most commonly used is *value to the business* also known as *deprival value*. Value to the business can be defined as the *lower* of replacement cost and recoverable amount, while *recoverable amount* is the *higher* of net realizable value and present value. The logic behind this definition is that if a business possesses an asset it has a choice of either selling or using the asset, and can be expected to make the choice which will yield the highest return (the recoverable amount); if a business were deprived of an asset it would incur the cost of replacing the asset if, and only if, the recoverable amount were greater.

In practice, if we consider the two major categories of non-monetary asset:

1 Stock is bought with a view to resale at a profit, so we would normally expect net realizable value to exceed replacement cost. Since stock is held for resale rather than use, no 'present value' will arise.
2 Fixed assets are bought with a view to use in the business, so we would expect present value to exceed replacement cost in an viable business.

Thus for both stock and fixed assets value to the business will normally be replacement cost. Accountants are already used to computing the net realizable value of stock for the purpose of following the 'lower of cost and net realizable value' rule in the historical cost accounts. However the computation of 'present value' is more difficult, because of:

1 The extent of estimation involved in predicting future cash flows.
2 The problem of separately identifying expected future cash flows attributable to each asset.
3 The problem of choosing an appropriate 'discount rate' to reflect the time-value of money.

In practice accountants preparing current cost accounts do not normally attempt a precise computation of present value, assuming that in a viable continuing business present value must exceed replacement cost. However it can happen in practice that a fixed asset is in use which would not be replaced if the business were deprived of it, in which case some method of estimating present value is necessary.

Current cost accounting

Current cost accounting is similar to historical cost accounting in using money as the unit of measurement. Where current cost accounting differs from historical cost is in using *value to the business* as the basis of measurement. In the current cost accounts the balance sheet will therefore, in principle, aim to show all assets and liabilities at their value to the business at the balance sheet date; the profit and loss account should show as expenses the value to the business of all items consumed as at the time of consumption. Current cost accounting is based on the capital maintenance concept of *operating capability*. By operating capability is meant the ability of the business to continue to be able to maintain the output of goods and services which it is able to supply with its existing resources.

Current UK requirements on current cost accounting are included in the SSAP16, 'Current Cost Accounting'. SSAP16 requires most listed, and some other large, companies to include a current cost balance sheet and profit and loss account in their annual report; in practice this is normally effected by means of a supplementary statement.

When an asset is acquired it will be recorded at historic cost, which at the date of acquisition will be equal to replacement cost. However when the same asset is recorded in the balance sheet it may be that the 'value to the business' has changed, in which case the change in value is shown as an unrealized revaluation surplus (or deficit); these differences are taken to a *current cost reserve*, sometimes known as a *capital maintenance reserve*. Similarly when an asset is consumed its 'value to the business' must be recorded as an expense in the current cost profit and loss account and the difference between value to the business and historical cost is shown as a realized revaluation surplus (or deficit) taken to the current cost reserve.

A practical problem in the preparation of current cost accounts is the computation of 'value to the business'. As we have already seen, this will most commonly be 'replacement cost' both for fixed assets and stock, and it is normal to assume that value to the business will be equal to replacement cost unless there is evidence to the contrary. There are a variety of ways in which replacement cost can be estimated, including professional valuation and obtaining estimates from suppliers. The most common method of computing replacement cost is to use a 'specific price index' related to the specific category of asset under consideration. The UK government publish *Price Index Numbers for Current Cost Accounting* (PINCCA) which cover a wide range of types of asset. When an index is used to estimate the replacement cost the amount is computed as follows:

$$\text{Historical cost} \times \frac{\text{Index at reporting date}}{\text{Index at acquisition date}}$$

Example 31 is used to illustrate the preparation of current cost accounts in accordance with SSAP16. It relates to a company Bond PLC, whose historical

Figure 65

Bond PLC
Balance Sheet as at 31 December 1985

	1985		1984	
	£000	£000	£000	£000
Share capital – ordinary shares of £1		500		500
Retained profits		370		270
		870		770
Plant – Cost		1,200		1,200
Depreciation		480		360
		720		840
Current assets:				
Stock	280		240	
Debtors	300		180	
Bank	100		20	
	680		440	
Current liabilities:				
Creditors	160		150	
Taxation	70		60	
	230		210	
Net current assets		450		230
		1,170		1,070
10% Debentures		300		300
		870		770

Profit and Loss Account for the year ended 31 December 1985

	£000	£000
Sales		1,800
less:		
Goods consumed	960	
Wages	320	
Expenses	200	
Depreciation	120	1,600
Net profit before interest		200
Interest		30
Profit before taxation		170
Taxation		70
Retained profit		100

Figure 66

Bond PLC
Current Cost Balance Sheet as at 31 December 1985

	£000	£000
Share capital		500
Current cost reserve		447
Retained profits (270 + 25)		295
		1,242
Plant – Cost		1,800
Depreciation		720
		1,080
Current assets:		
Stock	292	
Debtors	300	
Bank	100	
	692	
Current liabilities:		
Creditors	160	
Taxation	70	
	230	
Net current assets		462
		1,542
10% Debentures		300
		1,242

Figure 67

Bond PLC
Current Cost Profit and Loss Account for the year ended 31 December 1985

	£000	£000
Turnover		1,800
Profit before interest and taxation on a historical cost basis		200
Less: Current cost operating adjustments:		
Depreciation	54	
Cost of sales	32	
Monetary working capital	9	
		95
Current cost operating profit		105
Gearing adjustment	(20)	
Interest payable	30	
		10
Current cost profit before taxation		95
Taxation		70
Retained current cost profit for the year		25

cost accounts are shown in Figure 65. Figure 66 shows the current cost balance sheet, Figure 67 shows the current cost profit and loss account, and Figure 68 the related workings.

Example 31

1 There have been no additions or disposals of fixed assets during the year. An official index related to the type of plant owned by the company showed:

At date of acquisition	100
At 31 December 1984	140
Average in 1985	145
At 31 December 1985	150

2 Monetary working capital is to be regarded as including only debtors and creditors. Stock, debtors, and creditors, are all to be regarded as arising on average six weeks prior to the year end. An official index related to stock showed:

Mid-November 1984	120
At 31 December 1984	125
Average in 1985	130
Mid-November 1985	136
At 31 December 1985	142

The monetary items in the current cost balance sheet are shown at the same amount as in the historical cost balance sheet, since the actual monetary amount receivable or payable represents 'value to the business'. This leaves two non-monetary items to consider:

1 Both the original cost and the accumulated depreciation of plant are adjusted to reflect changes in an appropriate index since the date of

acquisition, as illustrated in working 1 (Figure 68). If different items of plant had been acquired at different times it would be necessary to 'age list' plant and adjust each year's acquisitions by reference to the index at date of acquisition. Note that the opening fixed asset revaluation surplus is also computed, so that the total increase in the revaluation surplus can be identified.

2 The revaluation of stock is shown in working 3. Note that in computing the current cost of stock it is normal to estimate the average date of acquisition of all stock, rather than trying to analyse each individual item.

The current cost profit and loss account is shown in Figure 66. The profit is computed in two stages:

1 Current cost operating profit is arrived at by adjusting historical cost profit before interest and tax by the three current cost operating adjustments considered below.
2 Current cost operating profit is then adjusted for interest charges and the gearing adjustment (see below) to give current cost profit before taxation.

The three current cost operating adjustments are:

1 ***The depreciation adjustment***
This adjustment reflects the difference between the value to the business of fixed assets consumed in the year and the historical cost depreciation. Working 2 (Figure 68) shows how this is computed by multiplying the historical cost depreciation on each asset by the factor:

$$\frac{\text{Average plant index for the accounting period}}{\text{Index acquisition date}}$$

This gives the CCA depreciation charge. The difference between CCA and HC depreciation will then be the depreciation adjustment.

2 ***The cost of sales adjustment (COSA)***
This represents the difference between the value to the business and the historical cost of stock consumed during the year. Thus a precise computation of the COSA would involve identifying the realized revaluation surplus on each item of stock sold in the year, clearly not normally a practical accounting task. An approximation, using relevant specific price indices, can be computed by the *averaging method*. This is calculated by adjusting both opening and closing stock to the average price for the accounting period, using the factor:

$$\frac{\text{Average of index}}{\text{Index at acquisition date}}$$

Sometimes the index at the related balance sheet date is used in place of the acquisition date, for the sake of simplicity.

Cost of sales is then recomputed using the average price rather than the historical cost of stock; since the purchases are the same on either basis, to calculate the COSA it is only necessary to consider the change in stock, as illustrated in working 4.

3 ***The monetary working capital adjustment (MWCA)***
Monetary working capital consists of trade debtors, trade creditors, and any cash balances which are required to finance trading transactions. In a time of rising prices a higher level of debtors has to be financed to cover a constant volume of trade, and a higher level of creditors will finance part of the increased cost of stock. The MWCA reflects the impact of price changes on the funds necessary to maintain net operating assets. Working 5 illustrates how the MWCA is computed in the same way as the COSA using the averaging method, employing the same index as is applicable to stock.

Having computed the three current cost operating adjustments, and so arriving at the current cost operating profit, the next stage is to show the effect of the net borrowing on profit. SSAP16 defines the net borrowing as the excess of all monetary liabilities and provisions, excluding all monetary working capital items and proposed dividends, over current assets other than stock and monetary working capital items. Net borrowing has two effects on profit:

1 Interest charges arise on the net borrowing.
2 A gearing adjustment reflects the fact that part of the cost of the current cost operating adjustments will be financed by borrowing rather than by the proprietors.

The gearing adjustment is computed as:

$$\frac{\text{Average net borrowing}}{\text{Average net operating assets}} \times \text{CCA operating adjustments}$$

This is illustrated in working 6. Note that unrealized revaluation surpluses have to be taken into account in computing net operating assets. Working 7 confirms the net operating assets position.

Finally, working 8 shows how the movement on the current cost reserve is broken down. Note that 'realized' surpluses are only included in the current cost reserve as from the date that current cost accounts are first prepared. Thus the retained profits shown in the CCA balance sheet are a mixture of historical cost retained profit up to the date when current cost accounts were first prepared, and current cost profits thereafter.

Figure 68 *Bond PLC: Workings*

1 Plant – per balance sheet

1985	*HC*	*CCA factor*	*CCA*
Cost	1,200	150/100	1,800
Depreciation	480	150/100	720
	720		1,080
			720
Revaluation surplus			360

1984	*HC*	*CCA factor*	*CCA*
Cost	1,200	140/100	1,680
Depreciation	360	140/100	504
	840		1,176
			840
Revaluation surplus			336

2 Depreciation adjustment

	HC	*CCA factor*	*CCA*
Charge for year	120	145/100	174
			120
Depreciation adjustment			54

3 Stock – per balance sheet

1985	*HC*	*CCA factor*	*CCA*
Stock	280	$\frac{142}{136}$	292
			280
Revaluation surplus			12

1984	*HC*	*CCA factor*	*CCA*
Stock	240	$\frac{125}{120}$	250
			240
Revaluation surplus			10

4 Cost of sales adjustments

	HC	*CCA factor*	*CCA*
Closing stock	280	$\frac{130}{136}$	268
Opening stock	240	$\frac{130}{120}$	260
Increase in stock	40		8
			40
COSA			32

5 Monetary working capital adjustment

	HC	*CCA factor*	*CCA*
Closing MWC (300 – 160)	140	$\frac{130}{136}$	134
Opening MWC (180 – 150)	30	$\frac{130}{120}$	33
Increase	110		101
			110
MWCA			9

Figure 68 (cont.)

6 Gearing adjustment

		1985		*1984*
Bank		(100)		(20)
Taxation		70		60
Debentures		300		300
Net borrowing		270		340
Share capital	500		500	
Retained profits	370		270	
Revaluation surpluses	372		346	
		1,242		1,116
Net operating assets		1,512		1,456

$$\text{Average net borrowing} = \frac{270 + 340}{2} = 305$$

$$\text{Average net operating assets} = \frac{1{,}512 + 1{,}456}{2} = 1{,}484$$

$$\therefore \text{Gearing adjustment} = \frac{305}{1{,}484} \times (54+32+9) = 20$$

7 Net operating assets

	1985	*1984*
Plant	1,080	1,176
Stock	292	250
Debtors	300	180
Creditors	(160)	(150)
	1,512	1,456

8 Movements on current cost reserve

B/fwd:		
Plant		336
Stock		10
		346
Increase in – Plant (360 – 336)		24
– Stock (12 – 10)		2
Total 'unrealized surpluses'		372
Depreciation adjustment	54	
COSA	32	
MWCA	9	
	95	
Gearing adjustment	(20)	
'Realized surpluses'		75
C/fwd		447

Relative merits of CPP and CCA

The basic difference between the two systems is in the capital maintenance concept. CPP aims to preserve the purchasing power of the shareholders' equity while CCA aims to maintain the operating capability of the business.

In favour of CPP it can be argued:

1 Inflation is generally defined as referring to the decline in the general purchasing power of money, so that strictly defined CPP is the only form of 'inflation accounting' system.
2 CPP accounts are more easily verifiable than CCA accounts, because a single index is used.
3 CPP is evolutionary in its approach, preserving all the principles of historical cost accounting except for the unit of measurement.
4 CPP provides a way of adjusting the comparative figures for previous years for the effects of inflation.
5 CPP is easier and so less costly to implement.

In favour of CCA it is argued:

1 The CCA concept of operating capability capital maintenance is applicable to a wider range of users than the CPP concept, based on the purchasing power of the shareholders' equity.
2 CCA measures the individual company's experience of inflation, as it affects the company's own pattern of consumption.
3 Management planning has to be based on the replacement cost of assets consumed. Thus CCA seems more compatible with useful management accounting systems.
4 Investment analysts have developed techniques for making CCA adjustments to historical cost accounts, finding these useful for decision-making purposes.

Conclusion

In response to the problems of inflation accountants have considered two possible approaches:

1 A change in the unit of measurement (CPP).
2 A change in the basis of measurement (CCA).

The latter approach is currently favoured by the accounting profession in the UK, but the debate is by no means concluded.

Questions

1 (a) Discuss the limitations of financial accounts based upon generally accepted accounting principles.
(b) In what way do inflation-adjusted accounts endeavour to overcome one of the limitations outlined in (a)?

(Huddersfield Polytechnic)

2 The 'inflation accounting' debate in the UK has centred on the relative merits of CPP accounting, based on a unit of current purchasing power, and current cost accounting, based on the concept of 'value to the business'. You are required:
(a) To explain the nature of a unit of current purchasing power.
(b) To define 'value to the business' and discuss the logic underlying the concept.

3 'Current value financial statements present more useful information to external users than do historic cost statements.' Discuss.

(Manchester University)

4 Outline the main features of SSAP16, 'Current Cost Accounting'.

12

CASH BUDGETS AND FUNDS FLOW

Objective

The objective of this chapter is to consider two tools used by accountants to monitor the flow of resources through a business, the *cash budget* and the *funds flow statement*. In detail the chapter covers:

1. The relationship between cash and working capital.
2. The preparation of a cash budget.
3. The principles of the funds flow statement.
4. The preparation of a funds statement.
5. The interpretation of the funds statement.

The control of working capital

We have already seen, when considering the nature of current assets and current liabilities, that every business will have part of its resources tied up in the 'working capital' involved in the firm's operating cycle. Figure 69 shows a simplified diagram of the flow of resources through a business. Within the operating cycle there is a constant flow of resources between the different working capital items, while there are also flows both into and out of the working capital via the bank.

In practice the term 'working capital' is often used in two different ways. The strict definition of

Figure 69 *An example of resource flows in a business*

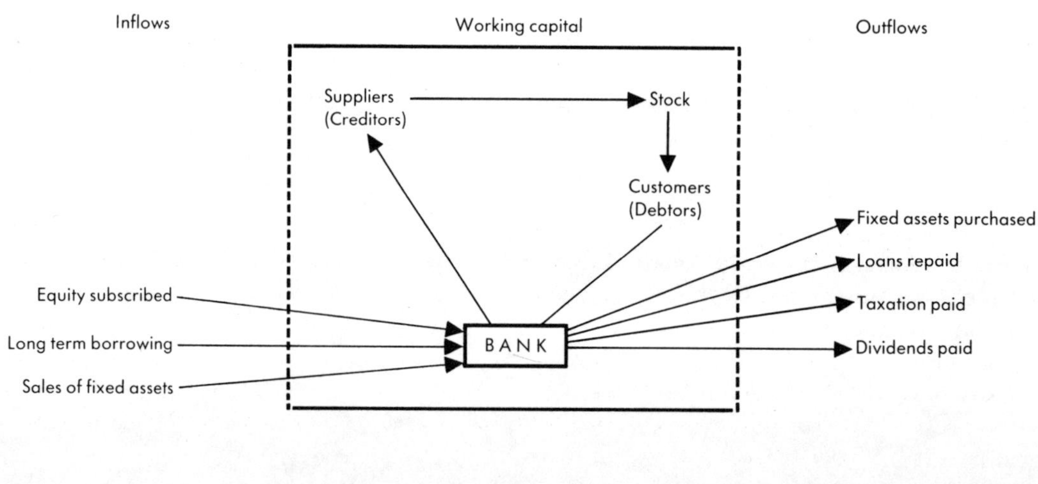

'working capital' is as given above, but often in practice the term is used to refer to the cash resources of the business. The confusion is understandable, because any failure in working capital management is likely to manifest itself in a cash shortage.

Below we consider two tools used by accountants to analyse and control the flow of resources through a business. One, the cash budget, is used to analyse the effects of all planned future activities on fluctuations in the cash position. Although the cash budget focuses on the cash position, it takes into account the effects of plans for the future on all aspects of working capital. The other, the funds statement, is a statement used to analyse the movements of resources through the business during an accounting period. The funds statement can focus on either cash or working capital. It is normally prepared in relation to an accounting period which has passed, although it may be prepared on the basis of forecast information.

The cash budget

The *cash budget* is a statement which shows an estimate of the cash receipts and cash payments which will arise from the planned activities of the business, and the effect of these on the cash balances that will be held during the period of the forecast. The analysis is generally made on a month-by-month basis, but sometimes a week-by-week forecast is made when the cash position is particularly sensitive.

The cash budget is a vital management tool, enabling management to identify times when the cash resources of the business will be insufficient to meet the requirements of the business and to adjust their plans accordingly. When the cash budget indicates that the business plans will require greater financial resources on a long-term basis than the business currently has available, then management will either have to revise their plans or seek new long-term financial resources. It frequently happens, however, that the cash budget indicates a short-term problem in that the outflow of cash exceeds available resources only for a short period of time. This is a particularly common situation where the business plans an expansion of activity, because the additional outlay on stock and promotional expenditure precedes the inflows generated by the increased level of sales. Where the cash budget suggests a short-term financing problem it may be possible to use the cash budget to identify a solution. For example:

1 Cash shortages may be attributable to amounts taken out of the business as dividends or drawings, and might be avoided by reducing the amount or postponing the date of payment.
2 Cash shortages may be caused by a particularly substantial fixed asset purchase; it may be possible to delay acquisition of the fixed asset, or to defer payment in some way.
3 A particularly large order may involve heavy outlays on raw materials and other expenses, with a delay while payment is awaited. It may be possible to negotiate performance of the order in stages with payments received on account.

These three instances do not constitute a comprehensive list of problems or of solutions; they do illustrate the type of problem which might be revealed by producing a cash budget.

One possible solution to a short-term cash shortage revealed by a cash budget is to negotiate a bank overdraft facility; in such a case a cash budget is an essential document to present to the bank as part of the loan application. Any knowledgeable lender is likely to insist on production of a cash budget, sometimes called a 'cash flow forecast', when considering a loan application.

When preparing the cash budget the accountant will need to be aware of the plans for each department of the business, and will compute the amount and timing of the cash flows relating to each transaction. The forecast sales are likely to be of particular significance, since these affect not only the amounts to be raised from debtors but will also be related to production, selling, and distribution costs.

Under examination conditions the amount of data relating to forecasts provided will necessarily be restricted. Examination questions on cash budgets are often used by examiners as an opportunity to test the student's grasp of accounting principles, in recognizing the relationship between cash flow and the amounts reported in the accounts.

Example 32 offers an illustration of the way in which a question on cash budgets might be presented; the period of two months is shorter than normally required, and has been chosen to simplify the illustration.

Figure 70 shows how the cash budget would be presented. A column is shown for each month covered. Forecast inflows are totalled, forecast outflows are totalled, so that the net inflow or outflow can be computed. The cash balance brought forward is then adjusted to reflect the net inflow or outflow, and the new cash balance is carried forward to the following month.

The workings prepared in drawing up the cash budget are shown in Figure 71. The steps taken are:

1 The estimate of future sales is the basis of computing the expected cash inflows from debtors; in so far as a proportion of bad debts is expected, it follows that no cash inflow will arise from that part of sales. The workings in Figure 71 show the way in which the cash inflow from debtors for each month would be computed.

2 There are a number of ways in which the cost of sales information can be presented. In some cases it will be necessary to reconstruct the cost of sales account in order to identify purchases, and then to reconstruct the creditors control account in order to identify cash payments. In our example we can see that the gross profit is 25 per cent so that the cost of sales must represent 75 per cent of sales; it follows that raw material costs must represent 50 per cent of sales ($\frac{2}{3}$ × 75%) and other production costs 25 per cent ($\frac{1}{3}$ × 75%). The workings show how the cost of sales relating to sales must break down.

We are told that raw materials are bought one month before production and goods are produced one month before sale, so that there is a two-

Figure 70

Varney Ltd – Cash budget

	March	April
	£000	£000
Inflows		
From sales	87	87
Outflows		
Wages	27.5	32.5
Creditors	55	65
Administrative expenses	10	10
Plant	100	
Dividend		30
	192.5	137.5
Net inflow/(outflow)	(105.5)	(50.5)
Cash b/f	200	94.5
Cash c/f	94.5	(44)

Figure 71 *Workings*

1 Cash from sales

		Month cash received			
		Jan	Feb	March	April
Month of sale	Jan	30	18	20	
	Feb		20	27	30
	March			40	27
	April				30
				87	87

2 Cost of sales – make up

	April	May
Sales in	110	130
Raw material (50%)	55	65
Wages etc. (25%)	27.5	32.5
	82.5	97.5

month gap between purchase of raw materials and related sales. We are also told that creditors are paid one month after purchase. Thus the cash outflow in respect of goods purchased is one month before related sales.

Wages will be paid in the month of production, which is the month before related sales.

3 Other cash outflows take place in this example in the months specified by the examiner. Note that information on how fixed assets are going to depreciate has no impact on the cash budget, since the only cash flows relating to a fixed asset occur when the asset is purchased.

Example 32

Varney Ltd has been in business for many years as a manufacturer of gloves. In response to an increased demand for the company's products it is planned to increase output during 1985.

The following information is available in relation to estimated sales for the first half of 1985:

	Jan.	*Feb.*	*March*	*April*	*May*	*June*
	£000	*£000*	*£000*	*£000*	*£000*	*£000*
Cash sales	30	20	40	30	30	30
Credit sales	40	60	60	80	100	120
	70	80	100	110	130	150

45 per cent of debtors normally pay after one month, 50 per cent after two months, and on average 5 per cent prove to be bad debts.

The company earns a consistent gross profit percentage of 25 per cent; production costs consist of raw materials two-thirds and wages and other expenses one-third. The company's policy is to pay for raw materials one month after they have been received, while wages and other expenses are paid in the month incurred. It is the company's policy to hold in stock sufficient raw material to cover the next one month's production and sufficient manufactured goods to cover the following month's sales. Administrative expenses, paid in the month incurred, are £10,000 a month.

The company plans to buy an item of plant costing £100,000 with a five year life and no residual value in March 1986, and to pay a £30,000 dividend in April 1986. At 1 March 1986 the cash balance is £200,000.

Prepare a cash budget for March and April.

The funds flow statement

Of the two traditional financial statements, the profit and loss account shows the difference between resources generated and consumed in the course of the operations of the business during a period of time while the balance sheet shows the form in which the resources are held at a certain point in time. The funds flow statement is a third accounting statement designed to report the flow of resources through a business during an accounting period. SSAP10, 'Statements of Source and Application of Funds', defines the objective of the funds flow statement as being:

> To show the manner in which the operations of a company have been financed and in which its financial resources have been used.

SSAP 10 also adds:

> the format selected should be designed to achieve this objective.

Figure 69 shows, in simple form, the flow of resources through a business. In the box marked 'Working Capital' is shown the trading cycle:

1 Payments made to suppliers of goods and services to the business; some of these suppliers will have offered credit terms and therefore become creditors.
2 The goods supplied to the business will pass into stock.
3 Stock will be sold to the customer, some of whom may buy on credit terms and therefore become debtors.
4 Payments are made by customers, thus constituting an inflow of cash.

Since the business should normally be expected to trade profitably, we would expect the trading cycle to produce a flow of resources into the business. This inflow of resources will not necessarily be reflected in an increase in cash, because extra resources may be tied up in increased stock or in increased debtors; conversely, resources may be derived from an increase in creditors.

The profit for the year will not, therefore, necessarily represent an inflow of *cash* into the business as a result of trading because the inflow of resources may be tied up in other aspects of working capital. Moreover, the profit for the year will not even necessarily represent the inflow of *working capital* from trading, because there may be items of income and expenditure in the profit and loss account which do not represent movements within the working capital cycle. An example is the depreciation charge.

Figure 69 shows that normally, apart from the working capital cycle, movements of resources involve inflows or outflows of cash.

It is generally agreed that the figures in a funds statement should be linked to the figures shown in the profit and loss account and balance sheet. It is also generally agreed that it is useful to identify the resources generated from operations separately from other inflows and outflows of resources. The major area of disagreement is in deciding whether the funds statement should focus on cash or on working capital. The difference between the two approaches is illustrated in Figure 72 below, considering the difference between the two approaches:

1 When the funds statement focuses on cash the profit as reported in the accounts has to be adjusted both for non-working-capital items in the profit and loss account and for non-cash working capital movements.
2 When the funds statement focuses on working capital the profit as reported only has to be adjusted for non-working-capital items in the profit and loss account.

The term 'funds' is used to describe the focal point of the 'funds statement'; thus funds can be defined either as cash or as working capital.

SSAP 10 requires:

1 That all companies with a turnover in excess of £25,000 should present a funds statement.
2 That the statement should show the profit or loss for the year and any adjustments for non-funds items in the profit and loss account.
3 The statement should identify dividends paid, acquisition costs or disposal proceeds of fixed assets, and funds raised by increasing or expended in redeeming long-term loans and shares.
4 The statement should identify movements in net liquid funds (being cash and bank balances and short-term investments), and the increase or decrease in working capital subdivided into its components.

Figure 72

1 Funds statement focusing on cash

	£000
Profit for year	598
Non working capital P & L items	80
Working capital from operations	678
Increase in working capital apart from cash	(60)
Cash from operations	618
Other inflows	490
	1,108
Other outflows	(1,183)
Net cash flow in year	(75)

2 Funds statement focusing on working capital

Profit for year	598
Non working capital P & L items	80
Working capital from operations	678
Other inflows	490
	1,168
Other outflows	(1,183)
Net working capital outflow	(15)

3 Analysis of net working capital outflow

	£000	*£000*
Non cash inflow	60	
Cash outflow	(75)	
		(15)

SSAP 10 also includes a general requirement that there should be a minimum of 'setting off' in the funds statement; for example, it is desirable to show additions to fixed assets as an outflow of funds and disposal proceeds as an inflow, rather than to set one figure off against the other.

It is interesting to observe that SSAP 10 does not state whether funds should be defined as 'cash' or as 'working capital', but ensures that the disclosures in respect of cash and working capital are sufficiently detailed to give as much information as is to be found in either form of the funds statement.

In addition to the requirements laid down by SSAP 10 the statement also offers an example of how a funds statement might be perpared. The format from SSAP 10 has been used in presenting the example 'Tressilian Ltd' in Figure 73 below. SSAP 10 does not require use of this format, and alternative forms of presentation can be equally acceptable. What is particularly ingenious about the SSAP 10 format is that although the focal point in the statement is 'working capital' the separate identification of cash movements accommodates those analysts who prefer to focus on cash.

The funds statement: preparation

The normal starting point in preparing a statement of source and application of funds is to compare the balance sheets for the beginning and end of the year to be covered. The balance sheet movements will be of two kinds:

1 Some movements will reflect sources or applications of funds during the year. These can be entered directly onto the funds statement.
2 Some movements will be the result of several different inflows of funds during the year. It is necessary to enter these into working schedules and to break them down into the separate elements so that the individual movements of funds can then be shown on the funds statement.

Items which commonly involve several different movements of funds are:

Retained profits

The balance sheet movement on the retained profits reserve will represent the net profit for the year less all appropriations. It is normal to show the net profit *before* appropriations as a source of funds from operations, so it is necessary to add back to the retained profit taxation, dividends, and any transfers to general reserve, for the year.

Share capital

Where there has been a bonus issue of shares no movement of funds will have been involved, the balance sheet movements being an increase in share capital and a reduction in whichever of the reserve accounts has been utilized; these movements cancel one another out and should be ignored in the funds statement. Share capital may also have moved because of a share issue, which would involve an increase both in the share capital account and, if the shares were issued at a price in excess of nominal value, in the share premium account. It is important that in the funds statement the total funds raised from a share issue should be shown as a single source of funds, *not* split into the two elements of nominal value and share premium.

Fixed assets

Movements in the balance sheet amount at which each category of fixed asset is shown can be split into four parts:

1 Revaluation surpluses. These do not represent any movement of funds, and will be balanced by an equal balance sheet movement on the revaluation reserve; both movements should be ignored in preparing the funds statement.
2 Additions. These should be shown as an application of funds.
3 Depreciation. We have already seen that this is an example of an expense in the profit and loss account which does not involve the movement of funds. It should therefore be added back to profit on the face of the funds statement.
4 Disposals. the removal of the written-down value of disposals will be a part of the balance sheet movement on fixed assets. On the face of the funds statement the disposal proceeds will be shown as a source of funds. The gain or loss on disposal is treated as an 'item not involving

movement of funds', a loss being added to profit and a gain being deducted; the reason for this is that the gain or loss on disposal represents an adjustment to depreciation already charged and must therefore be treated in the same way as depreciation on the face of the funds statement.

Taxation

The provision for taxation shown in the balance sheet can change for two reasons:

1 Tax on the profit for the year. As we have already seen, this is added back to retained profit in arriving at the profit figure shown in the funds statement.
2 Tax paid during the year. This will normally be tax on the profit of the previous years. It is shown as an application of funds.

Dividends

Dividends for the year are added back to profit while the dividend actually paid in the year is shown as an application of funds.

The preparation of a funds statement is illustrated by Example 33, Tressilian Ltd.

Example 33

Tressilian Ltd – Balance sheet as at 31 December 1985

		1985		*1984*
	£000	*£000*	*£000*	*£000*
Fixed assets				
Land and buildings		1,000		800
Plant		1,205		920
		2,205		1,720
Current assets				
Stock	380		350	
Debtors	400		360	
Bank	—		40	
Cash	5		10	
	785		760	
Current liabilities				
Creditors	120		110	
Taxation	200		180	
Overdraft	30		—	
Proposed dividend	160		120	
	510		410	
Net current assets		275		350
		2,480		2,070
Long-term loan		100		250
		2,380		1,820
Ordinary shares of 25p		1,200		800
Share premium		250		330
General reserves		800		600
Retained profits		130		90
		2,380		1,820

Notes to Tressilian Ltd

1 During 1985 plant with a written-down value of £120,000 was sold for £170,000, the profit on disposal being included in the profit for the year. During 1985 depreciation on plant was £130,000; no depreciation was provided on land and buildings.
2 On 1 March 1985 800,000 ordinary shares were issued at a price of 40p per share. On 30 June 1985 a bonus issue of one share for every five held was made.
3 The tax paid during 1985 was £178,000. No interim dividend was paid during the year.

The statement of source and application of funds for Tressilian Ltd is shown in Figure 73, and the related workings are shown in Figure 74. The funds statement would be prepared by taking each balance sheet movement in turn as follows:

(a) *Fixed assets* The workings show how we can combine the information in the balance sheet on fixed assets with the information in (1) to the example. Since we know the written-down value of disposals and the depreciation charge for the year additions must be the balancing figure. The additions and depreciations are then shown in the appropriate parts of the statement. In respect of the disposal it is necessary to identify the sale proceeds and the profit on disposal, which are then transferred to the statement.

(b) *Stock* The balance sheet movement can be shown directly on the face of the funds statement.

(c) *Debtors* The balance sheet movement is shown on the face of the funds statement.

(d) *Bank* When a bank balance is shown as an asset in one year and as a liability in the other then clearly there has been a move between having cash at the bank and having an overdraft. To show the true change in position the two movements must be added together.

(e) *Cash* The cash movement is shown on the face of the statement.

(f) *Creditors* The balance sheet movement is shown directly on the face of the statement.

(g) Movements in taxation are most easily identified by reconstructing the taxation account. Note that it often happens that the provision for taxation estimated at the end of a year is slightly different from the amount which actually has to be paid.

(h) *Overdraft* Already dealt with by (d) above.

(j) *Proposed dividend* The proposed dividend at the end of the year is added back to profit, while the proposed dividend at 31 December 1984 is assumed to have been paid during the year and is shown as an application.

(k) *Loan* In the absence of other information, the reduction in the loan is assumed to represent a repayment and is shown as an application of funds.

(l) *Ordinary shares and share premium* The information on note (2) to the example enables us to verify (in working 2) that the bonus issue has been covered from the share premium account. The issue of shares is shown as a single source of funds and the bonus issue has no effect on the funds statement.

(m) *General reserve and retained profit* The movement on general reserve is assumed to represent an appropriation of profit. On this basis the profit for the year can be computed (see working 4).

In practice the preparation of the funds statement is often undertaken by using a columnar working schedule, in which three pairs of columns are used:

1 The first pair of columns show the balance sheet movements in the year.

2 The second pair of columns show the adjustments made in preparing the funds statement.

Figure 73

Tressilian Ltd – Statement of Source and Application of Funds for the year ended 31 December 1985

			£000	£000
Source of funds				
(m)	Profit before tax			598
	Adjustments for items not involving the movement of funds:			
(a)	Depreciation		130	
(a)	Profit on sale of plant		(50)	
				80
	Total generated from operations			678
Funds from other sources				
(l)	Issue of shares for cash		320	
(a)	Disposal of plant		170	
				490
				1,168
Application of funds				
(k)	Loan repaid		150	
(j)	Dividend paid		120	
(g)	Tax paid		178	
(a)	Purchase of land & buildings		200	
(a)	Purchase of plant		535	
				1,183
				(15)
Increase/(Decrease) in working capital				
(b)	Increase in stock		30	
(c)	Increase in debtors		40	
(f)	Increase in creditors		(10)	
			60	
(d)	Bank – decrease	(70)		
(e)	Cash – decrease	(5)		
			(75)	
				(15)

Figure 74 *Workings*

1 Fixed assets

	Land & buildings	*Plant*
	£000	*£000*
B/fwd	800	920
Additions*	200	535
Disposals (net)		(120)
Depreciation	—	(130)
	1,000	1,205
Profit on disposal		
Sale proceeds		170
Written down value		120
		50

* Balancing figure

2 Movement on share capital and share premium

	Share capital	*Share premium*
B/fwd	800	330
Share issue	200	120
	1,000	450
Bonus issue	200	(200)
	800	250

3 Movement on taxation

Cash	178	Bal b/f	180
Bal c/f	200	P & L	198
	378		378

4 Profit and Loss – reconstruction

Net profit	598
Taxation (per working 3)	198
	400
Dividend	160
	240
Transfer to general reserve	200
Increase in retained profit	40

3 The third pair of columns show the applications and sources.

Figure 75 shows how such a schedule might be prepared for Example 33, 'Tressilian Ltd', while Figure 76 explains the adjustments made.

Some students find this form of working schedule helpful in examinations, while others find it too time-consuming.

Funds statement: interpretation

There are two reasons for preparing a funds statement. One is in order to comply with the requirements of SSAP 10. The other is as an aid to the interpretation of the accounts.

In order to interpret a funds statement it is necessary to be familiar with the variations in practice which arise in presentation, and the significance of the items shown on the statement.

We have seen that the normal starting point in a funds statement is the profit figure, and that normally this is taken as profit before tax. An alternative approach is that the statement can start with profit *after* tax. In this case tax is being treated as a type of business expense, and accordingly tax owing will be treated as a part of working capital so that any increase or decrease in the tax liability will be shown as part of the working capital section of the funds statement.

It would also be possible to start the statement showing retained profit, treating dividends in the same way as tax above; however such an approach would be in breach of the SSAP 10 requirement to show dividends paid separately as an application of funds.

The heading 'items not involving the movement of funds' was discussed in introducing the funds statement. In principle this can cover any item in the profit and loss account which involves a transfer between profit and loss and any 'non-working capital' balance sheet item; depreciation is the most common example. It is important to note, in view of the widespread misunderstanding as to the nature of depreciation, that depreciation is *not* shown under this heading as being a source of funds; on the contrary, depreciation is added back to profit because it does not involve any movement of funds.

In practice, sometimes companies show individual working capital items as applications or sources of funds rather than as a separate total at the end of the statement.

Figure 75 *Form of working schedule for preparation of funds statement*

	Balance sheet movements		*Adjustments*		*Funds statement*	
	Dr *£000*	*Cr* *£000*	*Dr* *£000*	*Cr* *£000*	*Application* *£000*	*Source* *£000*
Land & buildings	200				200	
Plant	285		(a) 120		535	
			(b) 130			
Stock	30				30	
Debtors	40				40	
Bank		40		(c) 30		70
Cash		5				5
Creditors		10				10
Taxation		20	(d) 198		178	
Overdraft		30	(c) 30			
Dividend		40	(e) 160		120	
Loan	150				150	
Ordinary shares		400	(f) 200	(g) 120		320
Share premium	80		(g) 120	(f) 200		
General reserve		200	(h) 200			
Retained profit		40	(a) 50	(b) 130		678
				(d) 198		
				(e) 160		
				(h) 200		
Disposal				(a) 170		170
	785	785	1,208	1,208	1,253	1,253

Figure 76 *Adjustments to balance sheet movements*

(a) *Dr* Plant 120
P & L 50
Cr Disposal 170
Reversing entries relating to disposal of plant

(b) *Dr* Plant 130
Cr P & L 130
Reversing entries relating to depreciation

(c) *Dr* Overdraft 30
Cr Bank 30
To combine in liability overdraft with decrease in asset bank

(d) *Dr* Taxation 198
Cr P & L 198
To write back tax charge for year

(e) *Dr* Dividend 160
Cr P & L 160
To write back dividend for year

(f) *Dr* Share capital 200
Cr Share premium 200
To reverse entries for bonus issue

(g) *Dr* Share premium 120
Cr Share capital 120
To show share premium as part of proceeds of shares issued

(h) *Dr* General reserve 200
Cr Retained profit 200
To reverse transfer from P & L to general reserve

When funds statements published by two companies are compared it may be necessary to adjust the way in which they are presented in order to make them comparable, because of the potential variations in practice noted above.

When preparing a funds statement as an aid to interpretation it may sometimes happen that not all the detail needed to prepare a complete statement will be available; in that case some degree of improvisation may be necessary. For example, if a breakdown of fixed asset movements is not available it may be necessary to show additions net of the written-down value of disposals as a single application.

As a tool in the interpretation of accounts the funds statement is likely to be used in conjunction with ratio analysis techniques, considered in detail in Chapter 13 below. The statement is likely to be particularly useful in explaining changes in a company's liquidity position, and will also help to identify changes in a company's earning position.

Conclusion

The cash budget and the funds statement are both working documents, designed to aid in analysing and planning the affairs of the business. Thus it is important both to be able to prepare these statements and to be able to understand them.

Questions

1 The management of Duswell Ltd plan to increase production and sales during the next year as follows:

	Units	
	Production	*Sales*
January	1,000	800
February	1,200	1,000
March	1,200	1,200
April	1,400	1,300
May	1,500	1,400
June	1,500	1,600
July	1,500	1,600
August	1,600	1,600
September	1,600	1,700
October	1,800	1,900
November	2,000	2,000
December	2,000	2,000

The selling price should remain constant at £10 per unit, the expansion resulting most likely from increased advertising. Payments to the advertising agents are likely to be £1,000 in January, £1,500 in April, £1,800 in July and £2,400 in October.

Raw materials cost £4 per unit. Payment is made to suppliers one month after delivery, and the materials are held in stock for an average of one month before issue to production. Wages and other variable expenses cost £3 per unit. Salaries and other administrative and production expenses are expected to be £1,600 per month for the first five months and then £2,000 per month.

New production equipment has been ordered at a cost of £6,000. This should be delivered in March and the agreement is to pay for it by three equal instalments in April, May and June. Dividend payments of £600 are due in April.

All goods are sold on credit terms and the average interval before payment is two months. Sales during the previous November and December were 700 and 800 units respectively.

The bank balance at 1 January was £7,500.

Required:

(a) Prepare a cash budget for the year. What overdraft facilities would the company be seeking?
(b) Assuming depreciation for the year was £5,000, calculate the estimated profit for the year.
(c) Reconcile the reduction in the bank balance during the year with the profit.
(d) 'Cash Budgeting is an essential aid to the management control process'. Discuss.

(Huddersfield Polytechnic)

2 Leutasch Ltd plans to commence business on 1 June 1983. The company is to produce one product only. Production will start on 1 July 1983 and it is anticipated that 3,700 units will be produced each month.

The company plans to issue 74,000 £1 ordinary

shares. The shares are to be issued for cash on 1 June 1983 at £1.20 each.

Plant and machinery costing £88,800 will be purchased for cash in June 1983. Depreciation will be charged at £740 each month from 1 July 1983.

The sales department estimates that 2,775 units will be sold in August and that 3,700 units will be sold in each subsequent month. Each unit is to be sold for £14.

It is estimated that raw materials will amount to £5 per unit produced. Sufficient material is to be purchased each month to meet the planned production for the following month.

Direct wages are expected to amount to £4 per unit produced and will be paid on the last day of each month.

Factory overheads (excluding depreciation) are expected to amount to £7,400 per month, administration overheads to £3,700 per month. These overhead costs will begin in July 1983 and will be paid one month in arrears.

Nick's Newsmart

Balance sheets as at 31 March

1981 £	1981 £		1982 £	1982 £
		Fixed assets		
16,000		Premises at cost	16,000	
3,600		Less: Depreciation	3,900	
	12,400			12,100
3,000		Fixtures & fittings at cost	8,200	
1,000		Less: Depreciation	1,300	
	2,000			6,900
	14,400			19,000
		Current assets		
5,400		Stocks – magazines, periodicals	8,060	
1,480		sweets, tobacco etc.	3,240	
2,200		Debtors – trade	4,900	
140		other	420	
6,400		Bank	—	
280		Cash	500	
15,900			17,120	
		Less:		
		Current liabilities		
4,200		Creditors – trade	3,600	
100		other	120	
—		Bank overdraft	4,000	
4,300			7,720	
	11,600	*Working capital*		9,400
	26,000	*Net assets employed*		28,400
24,600		Opening capital	26,000	
6,800		Add: net profit	8,600	
31,400			34,600	
5,400		Less: Drawings	6,200	
	£26,000	Closing capital		£28,400

Suppliers will allow two months' credit and one months' credit is to be allowed to customers.

Required:

(a) A cash budget for Leutasch Ltd for the six months to 30 November 1983 showing the surplus or deficit at the end of each month.
(b) The manufacturing, trading and profit and loss account for the six months ending 30 November 1983 (appropriate subtotals should be shown), and a balance sheet as at that date.

(University College Cardiff)

3 A friend of yours who owns a newsagent's and confectionery business has asked for your help. he is very worried because he suspects that a shop assistant is stealing money from his till. He comments as follows: 'For the year to 31 March 1982 my shop made a profit of £8,600 and yet I have had to ask the bank for an overdraft', then adds, 'Will you check the figures for me please?' You agree to help and he supplies the information shown on page 159 (balance sheets as at 31 March).
You confirm that he has not disposed of any fixed assets during the year.

Required:

Prepare a statement of source and application of funds (funds flow statement) to show Nick where his profit has gone.

(Association of Certified Accountants)

4 Consecutive balance sheets for Corrigan Ltd for two years were as follows:

		31 December		
	1980		*1981*	
	£000	*£000*	*£000*	*£000*
Fixed assets				
Land and buildings		1,297		1,277
Plant and equipment		1,054		1,000
		2,351		2,277
Goodwill		200		150
Current assets				
Stocks	2,549		2,785	
Debtors	1,732		1,629	
Cash	1	4,282	3	4,417
		6,833		6,844
Current liabilities				
Creditors	1,246		1,249	
Taxation	400		345	
Bank overdraft	300		—	
Proposed dividends	200	2,146	250	1,844
		4,687		5,000
Capital				
Ordinary shares	1,400		1,500	
Preference shares	1,500		1,500	
Revenue reserves	1,787	4,687	2,000	5,000

Notes:

1 The profit and loss account for 1981 shows the following amounts for depreciation:

	£
Land and buildings	40,000
Plant and equipment	105,000
Goodwill	50,000

2 The balance on the profit and loss account at the end on 1981 was transferred to revenue reserves.
3 Plant and equipment costing £20,000 with an accumulated depreciation of £15,000 was sold in 1981 for £3,000. The difference between the sale price and the net book value was written off the the profit and loss account.
4 The exact amounts provided for taxation and dividends in the 1980 accounts were paid in 1981.

Prepare a statement of the source and application of funds for 1981, in line with SSAP 10.

(Oxford Polytechnic)

---

5 ***Happy Holidays Ltd***

Balance sheet at 31 December

	1981		*1982*	
	£000	*£000*	*£000*	*£000*
Fixed assets				
Land and buildings		30		46
Other fixed assets	70		80	
Less: accumulated depreciation	30		40	
		40		40
		70		86
Research and development Expenditure		10		30
Current assets				
Debtors	15		20	
Inventory	20		16	
Cash	5		4	
		40		40
		£120		£156
Share capital and reserves				
Ordinary shares		50		60
Share premium		5		5
Undistributed profits		6		16
		61		81
Debenture loans		30		44
Current liabilities				
Creditors	19		29	
Dividend payable	10		2	
		29		31
		£120		£156

Notes:

1 The company does not depreciate its land and buildings. There were no sales of land and buildings during the year.
2 Certain other fixed assets, which had cost £30,000 some years previously and had a current net book value of £12,000, were sold in 1982 for £6,000.
3 The company shows research and development expenditure at cost less amounts written off. The amount written off in 1982 was £4,000.
4 An issue of debentures was made in 1981. No debentures were redeemed in the year.

You are asked to prepare

(a) A statement of sources and application of funds.

(b) A schedule of changes in working capital.

(Stirling University)

6 Harry has an opportunity to buy a hotel in the seaside town of Whitelake at a price of £40,000; he will have to pay the purchase price on 1 January 1983 and has been offered a 60 per cent mortgage at 15 per cent interest; the mortgage is repayable by monthly instalments of £350 and you may assume that in the first year this will be made up of:

	£
Interest	300
Repayment of capital	50
	350

Harry expects to open the hotel from April to October, takings coming in:

	£
April	2,000
May	3,000
June	4,000
July	6,000
August	6,000
September	6,000
October	3,000
	30,000

All takings are in cash, except that a school party which has booked the entire hotel in June have agreed to pay in October.

For these seven months Harry will have to employ staff at £800 per month. Food is expected to cost 20 per cent of takings and will be paid for in cash, while laundry is expected to cost 5 per cent of takings and will be paid one month in arrears. Rates of £1,500 must be paid in April and electricity bills of £200 are expected to be paid in each of February, May, August, and November. Harry explains this position to you and then says:

I have £18,000 to pay the deposit and cover my initial working capital needs. I expect to draw out £400 per month for personal expenses and in August I will draw an additional £4,000 for a new motor car – that's in the middle of the season so I should have plenty of cash by then.

Required

Prepare a cash flow forecast for 1983 on a monthly basis and suggest how any cash shortage might be met.

7 You have recently been made redundant by the company which has employed you as a sales manager for a number of years. You propose to set up your own business using your redundancy payment of £15,000. Any additional finance you require will have to be borrowed.

You have negotiated to buy fixed assets costing £8,000, for which you will pay at the end of June. They are expected to be of use in the business for five years by which time they will have no residual value. You plan to charge depreciation on a monthly basis.

You calculate that you will need stock costing £5,000 for delivery at the end of June to start the business. Subsequent purchases of stock will be sufficient to replace forecast sales for the month. One month's credit will be given by suppliers of stock.

You forecast that sales will be £3,000 in July, £6,000 in August and September and £10,500 per month from October 1984 onwards. Selling price is fixed at the cost of stock plus 50 per cent. Two months' credit will be allowed to customers.

You estimate that running expenses, including rent but excluding depreciation of fixed assets, will be £1,600 per month payable in the month in which they arise.

You intend to withdraw £1,000 cash per month from the business to meet your personal expenses.

Required:

(a) A cash budget for the six months to 31

December 1984 showing the accumulated cash surplus or deficit at the end of each month.

(b) A forecast trading and profit and loss account (income statement) for the six months ending 31 December 1984.

(c) A forecast balance sheet at 31 December 1984.

(d) The arguments you will use to convince the bank manager that he/she should lend you the money for your business.

(Kingston Polytechnic)

13

THE INTERPRETATION OF ACCOUNTS

Objective

The objective of this chapter is to introduce some techniques used in the interpretation of accounts. Specifically covered are:

1 The nature and limitations of ratio analysis.
2 Techniques for looking at the working capital position.
3 Techniques for analysing the financial structure.
4 Uses of the primary ratio for assessing performance.
5 Uses of the secondary ratios, for investigating performance in depth.
6 Earnings per share.

Ratio analysis: nature and limitation

A *ratio* is a way of expressing the relationship between two amounts as a proportion or percentage. *Ratio analysis* is used as a technique in the interpretation of accounts, for the purpose of expressing the relationship between two figures in the accounts in a way that can be used for the purposes of comparison.

The need for ratio analysis can be illustrated by a simple example. Suppose that you are told that a business made a profit of £250,000 last year, and are asked whether you feel this was a creditable performance. Before you answer this question you would wish to know what kind of business was involved, and the size of the business; you would also need to have some sort of standard against which to measure the performance of this particular business, in order to decide what can be regarded as 'creditable'.

The various kinds of ratio used to express different aspects of a company's position are considered in detail below. The various aspects of a company's position we consider can be classified into three broad headings:

1 Liquidity, considering the ability of the business to meet liabilities as they fall due and the management of working capital.
2 Gearing, considering the financial structure of the business.
3 Performance, considering how the company has performed during the year.

Having computed accounting ratios it is necessary to find other ratios against which they can be compared. Possible sources of comparison are:

1 Previous years' accounts. Comparison with a company's own past performance helps to identify whether a company's position is improving, and also helps to identify the situation where the company's trading pattern is changing.
2 Other companies. It is important to make comparisons with other companies in a similar line of business, because the operating structure of companies in different industries can vary substantially.
3 Industrial averages. Sometimes average ratios for an industry are available. These may be published, or may be available privately from

some form of inter-firm comparison exercise.

4 Target ratios, laid down inside the business as objectives to be achieved.

The main benefits of ratio analysis are:

1 It enables the user to identify the relationship between figures in the accounts.
2 It facilitates comparison between companies of different size.
3 It enables use of industrial average ratios for comparison.
4 It is a tool which enables the large amount of data in a set of accounts to be sumarized quickly.

The main limitations are:

1 The information in accounts is not necessarily a fair representation of economic reality, particularly in times of inflation. Thus any form of economic judgement based on the accounts is of limited value, whatever tools of interpretation are used.
2 In published accounts key information is sometimes omitted, particularly for smaller companies. This may limit the amount of analysis that can be undertaken.
3 Accounts are normally presented some months after the year end date, by which stage the affairs of the business may have changed.
4 There are a number of terms in ratio analysis which can be used in a variety of ways. These must therefore, be used with considerable care.
5 Concentration exclusively on accounting ratios can distract attention from the significance of key amounts in isolation.

None of these limitations constitute a reason for not employing ratio analysis techniques, but they do make it important to use accounting ratios with caution.

In considering specific ratio analysis techniques we will refer to the accounts of Verinder Ltd set out in Example 34.

Example 34

Verinder Ltd

Profit and loss account for the year ended 31 December 1985

	£	£
Turnover		2,525
Less: Stock 1.1.85	420	
Purchases	2,065	
	2,485	
Stock 31.12.85	465	
Cost of Sales		2,020
Gross Profit		505
Distribution costs	132	
Administrative expenses	70	
		202
		303
Interest payable:		
On current borrowings	23	
On long-term borrowings	25	
		48
Net profit before taxation		225
Taxation		111
Profit attributable to shareholders		144
Dividends – Preference paid	14	
– Ordinary proposed	50	
		64
Retained Profit		80

Verinder Ltd

Balance sheet as at 31 December 1985

	£000	£000
Fixed assets		1,255
Current assets		
Stock	465	
Debtors	500	
Cash at bank	25	
	990	
Less: Proposed dividend	50	
Creditors	285	
Bank overdraft	160	
	495	
Net current assets		495

Total assets less current liabilities	1,750
Less: Debentures 10% 1997	250
	1,500
Ordinary shares of £1	600
7% Preference shares of £1	200
Share premium	240
Retained profit	460
	1,500

In the management of cash a firm's objective will be to achieve a balance, having sufficient cash available to meet all liabilities as they fall due but at the same time not tying up too high a proportion of the firm's resources in unproductive cash balances. In the management of other working capital items the objective will be to allow resources to be tied up only to the extent that they yield a profit to the firm.

In considering the overall working capital position two ratios are commonly used:

1 ***The current ratio***

This ratio measures the relationship between current assets and current liabilities, being measured as:

$$\frac{\text{Current assets}}{\text{Current liabilities}}$$

Thus the current ratio for our example Verinder Ltd (Example 34) will be:

$$\frac{990}{495} = 2$$

2 ***The liquidity ratio***

This ratio is known by a number of names, including *quick asset ratio* and *acid test*. In principle it is regarded as expressing the relationship between *quick assets*, being those assets which are expected to be converted into cash in the short term, and current liabilities. In practice quick assets are normally computed as current assets excluding stock, so that the ratio is computed as:

$$\frac{\text{Current assets} - \text{Stock}}{\text{Current liabilities}}$$

In our example Verinder Ltd this will be:

$$\frac{990 - 465}{495} = 1.1$$

There is no standard acceptable level for these two ratios; in most industries a current ratio less than 1.5 or a liquidity ratio of less than 0.7 would be regarded as indicative of danger. The significance of these ratios is particularly dependent on the industry in which a business operates. For example a retail store, which may well be able to sell goods for cash before payment is due to creditors, can survive on a very much lower current ratio than a manufacturer who has to buy goods for stock, hold those goods while processing them, hold them while awaiting sale, and finally must wait for debts to be paid by customers.

The liquidity ratio is generally regarded as giving earlier warning of liquidity problems than the current ratio.

As we have already seen working capital is employed in the activities of the business. Thus if we wish to see how efficiently working capital is being used then we will wish to find a way of expressing the relationship between the level of activity in the year and the working capital position. One way to do this is by computing the *working capital turnover* measured as:

$$\frac{\text{Turnover}}{\text{Working capital}}$$

In our example this ratio would be:

$$\frac{2{,}525}{495} = 5.1$$

The higher this ratio, the higher the level of activity being obtained from working capital and so working capital can be said to be used more efficiently.

This approach can be applied to each individual component part of working capital.

Stock is best measured by expressing the relationship between cost of sales and stock, because stock is shown at cost in the accounts.

The most common way of measuring how efficiently stock is being used is by computing the *stock turnover ratio*, being:

$$\frac{\text{Cost of sales}}{\text{Stock}}$$

In our example this ratio will be:

$$\frac{2,020}{465} = 4.3$$

The ratio could also be expressed in a rather different way as a number of days stock, being:

$$\frac{\text{Stock}}{\text{Cost of sales}} \times 365$$

In our example this would be:

$$\frac{465}{2,020} \times 365 = 84$$

For weeks the multiple would be 52, for months 12, etc.

Sometimes the cost of sales figure is not published in the accounts. In that case sales would be taken as the level of activity, and the stock turnover would be:

$$\frac{\text{Turnover}}{\text{Stock}}$$

In our example being:

$$\frac{2,525}{465} = 5.4$$

It is unfortunate that the term 'stock turnover' can have these two different meanings, the first expressing the number of times stock turns over in the year and the second expressing the relationship between stock and turnover.

The objective of good stock control will be to ensure that stock is available when required while keeping the amount of resources tied up in stock-holding to a minimum.

Debtors are related to turnover, since debtors are shown at selling price. The most common way of expressing the relationship is:

$$\frac{\text{Debtors}}{\text{Credit sales}} \times 365$$

It is normal to assume that all sales are on credit unless we are told otherwise, so that in our example this ratio will be:

$$\frac{500}{2,525} \times 365 = 72 \text{ days}$$

It is also possible to express a debtors' turnover ratio, computed as:

$$\frac{\text{Turnover}}{\text{Debtors}}$$

This might be a particularly appropriate where it is known that turnover includes a mix of cash sales and credit sales but the split is not known, since otherwise a misleading impression of the terms of credit being taken might be formed.

The management of debtors is known as credit control. The objective of credit control is to ensure that debtors pay within the terms of credit. The company's terms of credit will be designed to balance two objectives on the one hand offering sufficiently long credit to attract sales and on the other hand collecting debts sufficiently rapidly to avoid tying up excessive resources in debtors.

Creditors are best considered in relation to the purchases figure, so that where this is available the *number of days' creditors* will be computed as:

$$\frac{\text{Creditors}}{\text{Purchases}} \times 365$$

In our example the ratio will be:

$$\frac{285}{2,065} \times 365 = 50$$

Where the purchases figure is not available then the creditors turnover ratio will be computed as:

$$\frac{\text{Turnover}}{\text{Creditors}}$$

In our example this will be:

$$\frac{2,525}{285} = 8.9$$

Trade credit is an attractive source of finance since apart from any cash discount forgone, it involves no obvious costs. Nevertheless an excessive delay in paying creditors will cause ill will with suppliers, and may force a business to buy goods from more expensive sources than otherwise would be available.

Working capital ratios have to be used with care, for two reasons in particular:

1 In a business subject to seasonal fluctuations the balance sheet figures may not be representative. For example a toy manufacturer may have very different figures for stock and debtors at the end of May as compared to the end of November because of retailers ordering goods for Christmas.
2 Special circumstances may distort the working

capital figures at a particular balance sheet date. For example a heavy advertising campaign in the month before the balance sheet date may increase sales levels for that month, so that the number of days' debtors might be distorted.

Thus the expression of stock, debtors, and creditors in 'numbers of days', is a useful tool in giving us a vision of the firm's trading pattern but must be used with caution.

In our examples we have used year-end balance sheet figures. Some accountants prefer to use the average of the opening and closing figures for stock, debtors, and creditors, when working out the working capital activity ratios. An examiner who has this preference is likely to express it by asking for 'average' ratios (e.g. 'average stock turnover'), or by making a point of saying that opening balance sheet figures should be used.

Gearing

The nature and significance of gearing has been discussed in detail in Chapter 7 above. Users of accounts will be interested in making an assessment of a company's gearing position for two broad reasons:

1 The higher the level of gearing, the higher the risk of the company having difficulty in meeting its obligations.
2 The higher the level of gearing, the greater the potential degree of fluctuation in the profit attributable to shareholders.

The various users of accounts will be interested in looking at the gearing position not only as it affects them directly but also as it affects the decisions of others. For example, a shareholder who observes that a company is highly geared will note that potential lenders are likely to find this undesirable so that the company will have difficulty in raising further borrowings.

In computing a ratio to express a company's gearing position the following points must be considered:

1 There are two broad approaches to the measurement of gearing, *income-based* measures and *capital-based* measures. An income-based measure compares the cost of borrowing shown in the profit and loss account with the profit available to cover the cost of borrowing. The most common method of expressing this relationship is with the *interest cover ratio*, being:

$$\frac{\text{Profit before tax + Interest}}{\text{Interest}}$$

A capital-based measure compares the borrowings shown in the balance sheet with the shareholders' funds. The most common way of expressing this relationship is as a percentage:

$$\frac{\text{Borrowings}}{\text{Borrowings + Shareholders' funds}}$$

Some authors prefer to express the relationship directly as borrowing in proportion to shareholders' funds, Borrowings: Shareholders' funds following American terminology, some call this the 'Debt : Equity' ratio.

2 Gearing can be measured in relation to long-term borrowings or in relation to total borrowings. The argument for looking just at the long-term position is that this avoids short-term fluctuations and is more likely to represent the company's policy on gearing. On the other hand the distinction between long-term and short-term borrowings can be artificial, and exclusion of short-term borrowings gives an incomplete picture.

3 We have already seen, in Chapter 7 above, that preference shares are akin to equity in that they only receive any payment in a liquidation after all liabilities have been paid and in that they can only receive dividends out of realized profits. On the other hand they receive a fixed rate of return, like lenders. In practice it is more common to treat preference shares as a form of borrowing when computing the gearing ratios, but a case can be made for either approach depending on the aspects of a company's position being considered.

Thus we can see that, combining the various possible different approaches above, there are a number of ways in which ratios relating to gearing can be computed. Figure 77 shows these various approaches applied to our example Verinder Ltd, and these are discussed as follows:

1 An income-based measure relating to long-term funds, treating preference shares as part of equity.
2 When preference dividends are treated as part of loan interest the ratio is renamed 'fixed charge cover'. Note that preference dividend is not added to profit because it is already included.
3 When total borrowings are referred to short-term as well as long-term interest is added back.
4 As in '2' above, preference dividend is added, this time to total interest.
5 This is a capital-based ratio. Although both income- and capital-based ratios are measure of 'gearing', when the term 'gearing ratio' is used this normally means a capital-based measure.
6 In this case the preference shares are treated as a form of loan.
7 Note that current liabilities are added to both sides of the equation.
8 As 6 above.

Figure 77 *Various measures of gearing for Verinder Ltd*

(1) Interest cover, based on long term borrowings and treating preference shares as part of equity.

$$\frac{255 + 25}{25} = 11.2$$

(2) Fixed charge cover, based on long term funds and treating preference shares as a form of loan.

$$\frac{255 + 25}{14 + 25} = 7.2$$

(3) Interest cover, based on total borrowings and treating preference shares as part of equity.

$$\frac{255 + 48}{48} = 6.3$$

(4) Fixed charge cover, based on total funds and treating preference shares as a form of loan.

$$\frac{255 + 48}{48 + 14} = 4.9$$

(5) Gearing ratio based on long term borrowings and treating preference shares as part of equity.

$$\frac{250}{1500 + 250} = 14.3\%$$

(6) Gearing ratio based on long term funds treating preference shares as a form of loan.

$$\frac{200 + 250}{1500 + 250} = 25.7\%$$

(7) Gearing ratio based on total funds treating preference shares as part of equity.

$$\frac{250 + 495}{1500 + 250 + 495} = 33.2\%$$

(8) Gearing ratio based on total funds treating preference shares as a form of loan.

$$\frac{250 + 495 + 200}{1500 + 250 + 495} = 42.1\%$$

In principle when computing the fixed charge cover ratio the preference dividend should be multiplied by the factor:

$$\frac{1}{1 - \text{Corporation tax rate}}$$

The reason for this adjustment is that in order to cover a preference dividend it is necessary to earn enough profit before tax to be able to pay tax on the profit and have enough left over to cover the dividend. In practice this adjustment is rarely made.

Measuring performance: the primary ratio

The basic question to be asked about the performance of any business might be phrased as: 'How successfully has the business employed the resources at its disposal?'

The profit and loss account offers us a measure of the success of the business, while the balance sheet shows the resources of the business. The ratio which relates these two is the *primary* ratio, being the *return on capital employed (ROCE)*. In principle this can be regarded simply as:

$$\frac{\text{Return}}{\text{Capital}}$$

In practice there are a number of ways in which this ratio can be computed, including:

1 The *after-tax return on equity*, computed as:

$$\frac{\text{Profit after tax - preference dividend}}{\text{Ordinary share capital + resources}}$$

This ratio tells us what the company has managed to achieve on behalf of the ordinary shareholders with the funds they have entrusted to the business. For our example Verinder Ltd the ratio would be:

$$\frac{144 - 14}{600 + 240 + 460} = 10\%$$

2 The *pre-tax return on equity*, computed as:

$$\frac{\text{Profit before tax - preference dividend}}{\text{Ordinary share capital + reserves}}$$

This ratio tells us what the company has managed to achieve on behalf of the ordinary shareholders with the funds they have entrusted to the business, before taking taxation into account. For our example the ratio would be:

$$\frac{255 - 14}{600 + 240 + 460} = 18.5\%$$

Note that in principle the preference dividend should be adjusted for tax, as discussed under 'gearing' above, but in practice this is rarely done.

3 The *pre-tax return on long-term funds*, computed as:

$$\frac{\text{Profit before tax + Long-term interest}}{\text{All share capital + Reserves + Long-term loans}}$$

This ratio tells us what the directors have managed to achieve with the funds entrusted to them on a long-term basis. For our example:

$$\frac{225 + 25}{1500 + 250} = 16\%$$

4 The *pre-tax return on total funds,* computed as:

$$\frac{\text{Profit before tax + All interest}}{\text{All share capital + Reserves + All liabilities}}$$

This ratio tells us what the directors have managed to achieve with the total funds they control. For our example:

$$\frac{255 + 48}{1500 + 250 + 495} = 13.5\%$$

We have seen that the return on equity can be compared either after tax or before tax. The arguments in favour of taking the 'after-tax' return are:

1 Tax is a burden which has to be borne in the same way as any other form of expense, and therefore should be taken into account when computing the return earned for ordinary shareholders.
2 Efficient tax planning is one of the functions for which management are responsible, and should be taken into account in a full analysis of the company's position.

On the other hand it can be argued:

1 In a comparison between different years after-tax ratios may be distorted by changes in tax rates.
2 Different accounting policies on deferred taxation can distort comparisons between companies.
3 Tax planning is a highly specialized function which should be judged separately from other aspects of management.

The difference between the return on equity and the other two forms of ROCE ratio, based on long-term funds and total funds, is attributable to gearing (discussed above). It should be remembered that gearing has two significant effects on our analysis of ROCE ratios:

1 It explains why a different rate of return is earned on different definitions of 'capital'.
2 It explains why any fluctuation in the return on long-term or total funds leads to a greater fluctuation in the return in equity.

After taking into account the impact of taxation and gearing, we can try to assess how succesfully the operations of the company have been managed. Whether this is best done by reference to the return on long-term funds will depend on circumstances. Points to take into account in choosing between the two include:

1 Total funds embrace current liabilities; which are more prone to fluctuation through circumstances or even manipulation by management.
2 Long-term funds exclude current liabilities; this may not present a realistic picture where a business relies on short-term borrowing as a source of finance

In brief, 'total funds' give a fuller picture but where current liabilities are subject to violent fluctuation 'long-term funds' may be preferred.

A full analysis of return on capital might involve computing each of the above ratios, and explaining any differences between the ratios and between any trends they show.

Having considered the primary ratio, a further analysis can be made computing the secondary ratios, these being:

1 The *net profit percentage*, computed as

$$\frac{\text{Return}}{\text{Turnover}}$$

2 The *asset turnover* ratio, being

$$\frac{\text{Turnover}}{\text{Capital}}$$

These two ratios can be used to examine any type of primary ratio, since

$$\frac{\text{Return}}{\text{Turnover}} \times \frac{\text{Turnover}}{\text{Capital}} = \frac{\text{Return}}{\text{Capital}}$$

In practice the secondary ratios would normally be computed by reference to either long-term funds or total funds, depending on which of these definitions of the ROCE is considered the more useful in assessing management performance. Detailed analysis of the secondary ratios is considered below.

There are a number of adjustments in computing the ROCE which are sometimes made:

1 In comparing two companies with different accounting policies adjustments might be made to the accounts to reflect common policies.
2 Sometimes when computing return on long-term funds a bank overdraft (and the related interest) will be treated as a long-term item, where there is evidence that the overdraft is in fact a long-term financing agreement.
3 When comparing two companies one of which owns freehold property and the other rents similar accommodation, sometimes the property is deducted from 'capital' and a notional sum of 'rent' is deducted from return.
4 In looking at the accounts of a small unincorporated business it is necessary to bear in mind that the proprietor's own services are not rewarded by wages, and it may be conversely, in a small private company directors' remuneration often includes an element of 'profit', which should be added back.

Measuring performance: the secondary ratios

We have seen that the way in which the two secondary ratios are defined relates to the definition of the primary ratio. Thus supposing we define the ROCE as return on long-term funds then the ratios computed for our example will be:

Net profit % $\frac{255 + 25}{2,525} = 11.1\%$

Asset turnover $\frac{2,525}{1,500 + 250} = 1.44$

Multiplied together: 11.1% × 1.44 = 16%
16 per cent is the return on long-term funds computed above.

Depending on the amount of detail given in the accounts, either of these ratios can be investigated further.

The net profit percentage is normally investigated in two stages:

1 An examination of the gross profit percentage.
2 A comparison of items of expenditure with turnover or with the previous year.

The gross profit percentage is computed as:

$$\frac{\text{Gross profit}}{\text{Sales}}$$

In our example the ratio would be:

$$\frac{505}{2,525} = 20\%$$

We would normally expect the gross profit percentage of a business to remain fairly similar from year to year, so that even a fairly small change would be investigated. Reasons for a change might include:

1 Change in management policy. The management of a business might choose to reduce the gross profit percentage to increase business, or increase prices in a bid to move up-market.
2 Change in sales mix. A business which sells different types of goods, each at a different gross profit percentage, might have a change in the mix of goods sold.
3 Loss of goods through damage, theft, etc.
4 Accounting error. In particular, an error in the valuation of stock in one year distorts the following year's accounts in the opposite direction, leading to an exaggerated trend in gross profit percentage.

Investigation of the expenses depends on the amount of detail available in the accounts. In our example we can compute the following in relation to sales:

Distribution costs $\frac{132}{2,525} = 5.2\%$

Administrative expenses $\frac{70}{2,525} = 2.8\%$

These percentages can be compared with previous years or with other businesses. In addition, when comparing successive years of the same company it is possible to compute the increase or decrease in different types of expense.

The asset turnover ratio can be analysed in more detail by computing the relationship between each type of asset and the turnover. Thus in our example fixed asset turnover would be:

$$\frac{\text{Turnover}}{\text{Fixed assets}} = \frac{2,525}{1,255} = 2$$

We have already seen how a range of working capital activity ratios can be computed in relation to turnover or, in some cases, other measures of the activity level.

To summarize, the asset turnover ratio tells us what level of activity the business is managing to achieve from its resources, while the net profit percentage tells us how much profit the business is generating from its activities.

Earnings per share

The earnings per share ratio is computed as:

$$\frac{\text{Profit after tax} - \text{Preference dividend}}{\text{Number of ordinary shares}}$$

Thus for Verinder the earnings per share would be:

$$\frac{144 - 14}{600} = 21.7\text{p}$$

SSAP3, 'Earnings per share', requires listed companies to show the earnings per share figure on the face of the profit and loss account. There can be three types of problem in computing the earnings per share:

1 When part of the tax charge is attributable to ACT which cannot be recovered.
2 When ordinary shares have been issued during the year.
3 When there is a commitment to issue shares in the future, resulting in a potential 'dilution' of earnings.

The solutions to those problems can be complex, and fall outside the scope of this text. They are covered in SSAP3.

Two ratios follow on from the earnings per share:

1 *Dividend cover*, computed as:

$$\frac{\text{Earnings per share}}{\text{Dividend per share}}$$

This tells us how far dividends are covered by profits.

2 *Price earnings (P/E)* ratio, computed as:

$$\frac{\text{Share price}}{\text{Earnings per share}}$$

The P/E ratio is often quoted in the financial press.

Because the earnings per share figure is shown on the face of the accounts it can often be the starting point in a user's inquiry into a company's financial position.

Conclusion

Using the ratios

When undertaking a ratio analysis exercise the following approach can be helpful:

1 Compute a small number of key ratios, designed to identify key areas of concern. The ratios chosen will depend on the reason for the inquiry being undertaken, but might include:

(a) Pre-tax return on equity
(b) Return on total funds*
(c) Net profit percentage
(d) Asset turnover
(e) Gearing ratio
(f) Current ratio
(g) Acid test

*In some cases long-term funds may appear more suitable.

2 Consider the above ratios in order to identify the areas for further inquiry.
3 Compute additional ratios in order to pursue further enquiry. For example if the net profit percentage is the major area of interest, look at the gross profit percentage and at the expenses in relation to turnover. It may sometimes also be useful to prepare a funds statement.
4 Consider the ratios computed to help further enquiry. Summarize your conclusions, ensuring they are consistent with each other.
5 Present your conclusions in a clearly written report, showing the computation of ratios in a separate appendix. Be careful not to make your report too long.

Under examination conditions the examiner may guide you as to the ratios to be prepared, either by giving a selection of industrial average ratios or by specifying ratios to be computed; normally there is nothing in such cases to prevent a student computing a small number of additional ratios to help clarify a point.

Most students find time constraints a problem in examinations. In planning your time it is important to allow time for thought and consideration.

To conclude, ratio analysis is a valuable tool in the use of the accounts. Remember that ratios are a *tool*, and that it is necessary to develop skills in their use as well as their computation.

Questions

1 The following information relates to Macdonald Ltd:

On 31 March 1982

Issued ordinary share capital	£150,000
Fixed assets, in relation to share capital	1.3 to 1
Net current assets	£90,000
Ratio of current assets to current liabilities	1.9 to 1

Current liabilities as a ratio of liquid assets (balance at bank and debtors)	1 to 1.4
Ratio of fixed assets to shareholders' equity	39 to 50
Ratio of sales to net profit	10 to 1
General reserve as a percentage of the net profit for the year	120%
Sales for the year ended 31 March, 1982	£730,000
Collection period for debtors	40 days
Stock turnover for the year	12 times

Current assets were stock, debtors and bank balance. The only other assets were fixed assets. The liability side of the balance sheet comprised issued share capital, profit and loss account, general reserve, debentures and current liabilities.

On 1 April, 1981 the balance on the profit and loss account was £6,700, and the stock figure was £30,000.

Required:

Construct, as far as you are able from the figures given:

(a) Profit and loss account for the year ended 31 March 1982.

(b) A balance sheet as at that date.

(Oxford Polytechnic)

2 The following shows the trading and profit and loss accounts and balance sheets of two companies S. Acorn and T. Oak Ltd.

Trading and profit and loss account for the year ended 31 December 1982

	Acorn	*Oak*		*Acorn*	*Oak*
Stock (1.1.82)	57,500	37,000	Sales	300,000	150,000
Add: Purchases	185,000	92,000			
	242,500	129,000			
Less: Stock (31.12.82)	42,500	29,000			
Cost of goods sold	200,000	100,000			
Gross profit c/d	100,000	50,000			
	£300,000	£150,000		£300,000	£150,000
General expenses	70,000	38,000	Gross profit b/d	100,000	50,000
Net profit	30,000	12,000			
	£100,000	£ 50,000		£100,000	£ 50,000

Balance sheets as at 31 December 1982

	Acorn	*Oak*		*Acorn*	*Oak*
Share capital	180,000	96,000	Fixed assets	166,500	77,000
Profit and Loss a/c	30,000	12,000	*Current Assets*		
Current Liabilities			Stock	42,500	29,000
Creditors	29,000	15,500	Debtors	26,000	14,000
			Cash	4,000	3,500
	£239,000	£123,500		£239,000	£123,500

You are required to:

(a) Calculate in respect of each company:

(i) Gross and net profit for the year as a percentage of sales;
(ii) The acid test ratio;
(iii) Net profit for the year as a percentage of net assets employed;
(iv) Debtors and creditors ratio.

(b) Comment on the results obtained. What are the main limitations to the use of ratio analysis in the interpretation of financial statements?

(Ulster Polytechnic)

3 The following are summarized accounts of two companies, Rex Ltd and Regis Ltd at 31 October 1982:

Trading and profit and loss accounts

		Rex Ltd		Regis Ltd
	£	£	£	£
Sales		1,080,000		1,080,000
Opening stock	144,000		24,000	
Purchases	957,000		932,000	
	1,101,000		956,000	
Closing stock	156,000		36,000	
Cost of goods sold		945,000		920,000
Gross profit		135,000		160,000
Overheads		48,600		52,800
Net profit		86,400		107,200

Summarized balance sheets

	Rex Ltd	Regis Ltd		Rex Ltd	Regis Ltd
	£	£		£	£
Issued Shares	300,000	200,000	Fixed Assets	383,400	204,000
Reserves	240,000	48,000	Stock	156,000	36,000
Profit and Loss Account	180,000	43,000	Debtors	120,000	72,000
Creditors	191,400	137,000	Bank	252,000	116,000
	911,400	428,000		911,400	428,000

Required:

(a) Compute the following for each company:
Stockturn (times)
Debtors ratio (months)
Creditors ratio (months)
Current ratio
Liquid ratio
Working capital

(b) Assuming that both companies sell the same type of products in similar markets, comment on the relative performance of each.

(University of Stirling)

---

4 ***Lisburn Electrics PLC***

Summarized profit and loss accounts for the year ended 31 December

	1981	1982
	£000	£000
Turnover	400	420
Profit before interest and taxation	40	45
Interest payable	5	5
Taxation	12	15
Profit after taxation	23	25
Ordinary dividends	10	15
Retained profits	13	10

Summarized balance sheets as at 31 December

		£000		£000
Fixed assets		200		180
Current assets				
Stocks	120		200	
Debtors	130		70	
Cash	20	270	180	450
Less: Current liabilities		70		150
		400		480

Financed by:		
Ordinary share capital	200	250
Share premium	50	67
Retained profits	100	113
10% Debentures	50	50
	400	480

The chairman of Lisburn Electrics reports that 1982 was a very good year. Sales, profits and dividends had increased and careful control of working capital had produced a very healthy cash balance.

Required:

Making use of appropriate ratios comment on the financial position and performance of Lisburn Electrics.

(Queen's University Belfast)

5 The following information has been extracted from the books of Leek Ltd.

Balance sheets at 31 December

	1980	*1981*	*1982*
	£	£	£
Freehold property	30,000	30,000	30,000
Plant & machinery	40,000	70,000	120,000
Stocks	60,000	85,000	100,000
Sundry debtors	25,000	35,000	70,000
Cash at bank	40,000	30,000	—
	195,000	250,000	320,000
Issued share capital	105,000	120,000	120,000
Profit and loss account	25,000	27,000	30,000
10% Debentures	—	—	40,000
Sundry creditors	65,000	103,000	100,000
Bank overdraft	—	—	30,000
	195,000	250,000	320,000

	£	£	£
Sales	300,000	350,000	600,000
Gross profit	75,000	70,000	100,000
Net profit	20,000	14,000	42,000

The stock as at 1 January 1980, was valued at £50,000.

Required:

Your comments on the financial policy followed by Leek Ltd during the period covered by the balance sheets, together with your recommendations for the future.

(University College Cardiff)

6 A colleague submits the accounts of Rysouth Ltd for your advice. He cannot understand why the company has earned £52,000 in profit over two years yet, having started with a bank balance of £7,000 in its favour, the company has ended with an overdraft of £19,000.

You are given the following figures for Rysouth Ltd:

Balance sheet as at 31 December

	1976	*1977*	*1978*
	£000	*£000*	*£000*
Issued £1 shares	110	110	155
Reserves	28	39	34
Proposed dividends	9	11	10
Trade creditors	31	39	52
Bank overdraft	—	7	19
	178	206	270
Fixed assets, at cost at start of year	130	142	153
Net additions during year	12	11	14
	142	153	167
Less: Cumulative Depreciation	40	48	64
	102	105	103
Stocks	27	35	49
Trade debtors	42	66	118
Bank	7	—	—
	178	206	270

Profit statements for year ending 31 December

		1977		*1978*
		£000		*£000*
Sales – Credit		300		430
Cash		220		130
		520		560
Less cost of goods sold	352		379	
Sundry expenses	129		135	
Depreciation	12		16	
Loss on sale of fixed assets	5	498	—	530

Net profit	22	30
Less proposed dividend	11	10
Retained profit	11	20

You are also told:

(a) There was a bonus issue during 1978 of £25,000 shares.

(b) Fixed assets which had cost £12,000 were sold for £3,000.

Required:

(a) Prepare a source and application of funds (or funds flow) statement.

(b) Comment on the financial position and performance of the company, illustrating your answer with calculations of appropriate ratios.

(University College of North Wales)

7 Binns runs a mobile grocery business from a small rented stall and garage.

His balance sheets as at 31 March in successive years were as follows:

	1982		*1983*	
	£	£	£	£
Van at cost	3,200		6,400	
Less: Depreciation to date	2,400	800	800	5,600
Fixtures at cost	1,100		1,100	
Less: Depreciation to date	470	630	520	580
Stock	1,370		2,750	
Debtors	1,040		1,500	
Rent paid in advance	—		30	
Cash at bank	590	3,000	—	4,280
		4,430		10,460
Capital: as at previous 1 April	4,270		3,490	
Add: Profit in year	2,920		6,680	
	7,190		10,170	
Less: Drawings in year	3,700		4,130	
		3,490		6,040
Loan: 5 years from 1.10.82		—		3,000
				9,040
Creditors	890		1,050	
Rent accrued unpaid	50		—	
Bank overdraft	—	940	370	1,420
		4,430		10,460

During the year ended 31 March 1983 Binns had sold his old van for £500 in part-exchange for a new van. There had been no other requisitions or disposals of fixed assets.

Required:

(a) A statement in conventional form showing the sources and applications of funds in the year ended 31 March 1983.

(b) Explain to Binns the changes in his performance and position, giving comparable ratios for the two years in respect of profitability and liquidity.

(Preston Polytechnic)

APPENDIX
THE COMPANIES ACT 1981 – DISCLOSURE REQUIREMENTS

Schedule 1 of the Companies Act 1981 contains detailed requirements as to the disclosures provided in company accounts. The schedule is split into six parts:

> Part 1 deals with the form and content of the accounts.
> Part 2 covers certain accounting principles to be followed.
> Part 3 lays down disclosure requirements to be complied with in the notes to the accounts.
> Part 4 covers special requirements relating to holding and subsidiary companies.
> Part 5 covers investment companies.
> Part 6 covers definitions.

Below we consider Parts 1 and 3 in detail and Part 2 in outline.

Form and content

Schedule 1 provides two permitted balance sheet formats and four permitted profit and loss formats.

The two balance sheet formats are shown at the end of this appendix. Format 1 arrives at a total of all assets less all liabilities, and a total of all shareholders' funds, while format 2 arrives at a total of all assets and a total of shareholders' funds and all liabilities.

Of the four permitted profit and loss account formats two are shown at the end of this appendix. Format 1, presented in the vertical format shows costs analysed by type of operation while format 2, also presented in the vertical format shows costs analysed by type of expenditure. The two formats not reproduced show the same information in horizontal form, format 3 on a type of operation basis and format 4 on a type of expenditure basis.

The directors are required to choose a balance sheet format and a profit and loss account format, and to show the items listed in the same order, and under the same headings and subheadings, as in the format. It is not necessary to reproduce the letter or number attached to each heading or subheading in the format. Once a format is chosen it should only be changed where there are 'special reasons', and in the year of change these reasons should be disclosed in the notes to the accounts.

For each item in the balance sheet and profit and loss account the corresponding amount reported the previous year must be shown; where the corresponding amount reported the previous year is not comparable then the amount should be adjusted, details being given in the notes to the accounts.

Companies are permitted to show items in greater detail, or to include in their accounts items not included in the formats, with the provision that the following items are not to be shown as assets in the balance sheet:

1 Preliminary expenses.
2 Expenses and commission relating to the issue of shares or debentures.
3 Costs of research.

The directors may adapt the arrangement and headings of items in the formats to which an arabic number is assigned where the special nature of the company's business requires such adaptation. Items to which an arabic number is assigned may be combined if either the individual amounts are not material or the combination facilitates use of the accounts; in the latter case the individual amounts must be laid out in a note to the accounts.

No set-off between assets and liabilities or income and expenditure is permitted.

Whatever format is chosen, the profit and loss account must identify:

1 Profit and loss on ordinary activities before taxation.
2 Any transfer to or from reserves.
3 The aggregate amount of dividends paid and proposed.

Schedule 1 includes detailed notes relating to the formats. In the balance sheet these cover:

1 Items where alternative positions within the format are permitted. These are:
   (a) Called-up share capital net paid, at either A or C II 5 in both formats.
   (b) Prepayments and accrued income, at either C II 6 or D in both formats.
   (c) Accruals and deferred income, which in format 1 are shown either at J or appropriately split between E 9 and H 9, and in format 2 are shown under liabilities either at C 9 or D.
2 Concessions, patents, etc. (item B I 2 in both formats) are only to be shown as assets if acquired for valuable consideration or created by the company itself.
3 Goodwill (item B I 3 in both formats) is only to be included if acquired for valuable consideration.
4 Where the company holds its own shares the nominal value is to be shown separately.
5 Debtors (listed at C II in each format) falling due after more than one year are to be identified separately. Similarly creditors shown under format 2 should distinguish between amounts falling due within one year and other items, with the aggregate of each being shown separately.
6 Convertible loans should be shown separately from the other debentures.
7 Other creditors (item E 8 and H 8 in format 1, C 8 in format 2) must identify creditors for taxation and social security separately from other items.
8 Under the heading 'called-up share capital' there should be identified separately allotted share capital and called-up share capital.

The detailed notes on the profit and loss account include the following requirements:

1 Where a type of operation format is used the various types of operating expense may include an element of depreciation, which must be identified in a note to the accounts.
2 Income from fixed asset investments, interest receivable and interest payable should identify separately amounts relating to group companies.

Accounting principles

Part 2 of Schedule 1 lays down the five accounting principles considered in Chapter 4 above, i.e. going concern, consistency, prudence, accruals, and that the component parts of asset and liability items are to be valued individually. Companies are allowed to follow either *historical cost accounting rules* or *alternative accounting rules*; the latter, in effect, allow current cost accounting as outlined in SSAP16, discussed in Chapter 11 above. Rules in relation to specific kinds of asset and liability have been considered in the main text above.

Disclosure requirements

The principal items to be disclosed in the notes to the accounts can be summarized as follows:

Accounting policies

Accounting policies adopted by the company must be disclosed.

Share capital and debentures

1 Both the total *authorized* share capital and the number and nominal value of each class of share *issued*.
2 Full details on the rights and terms for the redemption of any redeemable shares.

3 Details of, and the reasons for, any issue of shares of debentures during the year.
4 Details of any options to buy shares which are outstanding.

Fixed assets

1 In respect of each class of fixed asset there must be shown the cost or valuation brought forward, any revaluation during the year, and any additions or disposals in the year. Similarly there should be shown for each class of asset accumulated depreciation brought forward, and the charge for the year, depreciation on disposals, and any other adjustment.
2 Where fixed assets have been revalued the year of the valuation should be shown. In addition in the year of valuation there should be shown the basis of valuation and either the name or the qualifications of the valuer.
3 The classes into which fixed assets are broken down must identify separately freehold land and buildings, long leaseholds (over 50 years) and short leaseholds (under 50 years).

Investments

1 The amount of investments which represents listed investments.
2 The market value of listed investments, and their Stock Exchange value if that is lower.

Reserves and provisions

Details of all movements to or from any reserve or provision shown in the accounts must be given.

Indebtedness

1 The total of long-term creditors repayable other than within five years must be disclosed.
2 The total of long-term creditors repayable by instalments part of which are due for repayment after more than five years must be shown, together with the total of instalments falling due after five years.
3 In respect of (1) and (2) above the repayment terms and interest rate must be shown.
4 An indication of the nature of the security given to support any loan must be shown.
5 Arrears of cumulative preference dividends must be shown.

Financial commitments

1 Any guarantee given by the company on behalf of another person.
2 Details of any contingent liability.
3 Capital commitments split between those contracted for and those authorized but not contracted for.
4 Details of pension commitments.

Profit and loss details

There must be disclosure of:

1 Interest payable on loans repayable wholly within five years.
2 Other interest payable.
3 Amounts set aside for redemption of shares or loans.
4 Income from listed investments.
5 Rents received from land, if they are a substantial part of revenue.
6 Amounts payable for hire of plant and machinery.
7 Auditors' remuneration.

Taxation

1 The basis on which the tax charge is computed.
2 Particulars of any special circumstances affecting the tax position.
3 Details of UK tax, any double tax relief, and UK income tax, and overseas tax charged.

Turnover

1 Where more than one class of business is carried on, turnover and pre-tax profit attributable to each class of business.
2 Where the company supplies markets (as defined by geographical bounds) that differ substantially from each other the amount of turnover attributable to each market must be shown.

Staff details

1 The average number of persons employed by the company, analysed into appropriate categories.
2 Totals of wages and salaries, social security costs, and other pension costs.

Miscellaneous

1 Extraordinary items.
2 Exceptional items.
3 Prior-year adjustments.

Directors' emoluments

Provisions from the Companies Acts 1948 and 1967 which are unchanged by the Companies Act 1981 require disclosure of:

1 Total amount of directors' emoluments, by whomsoever paid, split between:
   (a) Fees
   (b) Other emoluments
   (c) Pensions
   (d) Compensation for loss of office

2 If total directors' emoluments (*including* pension contributions) exceed £40,000 there must be disclosed the emoluments (*excluding* pension contributions) of the chairman and the highest paid director. In respect of other directors the number of directors whose emoluments fall within each band of £5,000 must be shown.

Profit and loss account format 1

			£
1	Turnover		x
2	Cost of sales		(x)
3	Gross profit or loss		x
4	Distribution costs		(x)
5	Administrative expenses		x
6	Other operating income		(x)
7	Income from shares in group companies		x
8	Income from shares in related companies		x
9	Income from other fixed asset investments		x
10	Other interest receivable and similar income		x
11	Amounts written off investments		(x)
12	Interest payable and similar charges		(x)
13	Tax on profit and loss on ordinary activities		(x)
14	Profit or loss on ordinary activities after taxation		x
15	Extraordinary income	x	
16	Extraordinary charges	(x)	
7	Extraordinary profit or loss		x
18	Tax on extraordinary profit or loss		(x)
19	Other taxes not shown under the above items		(x)
20	Profit or loss for the financial year		£x

Profit and loss account format 2

			£
1	Turnover		x
2	Change in stocks of finished goods and work in progress		(x)
3	Own work capitalized		x
4	Other operating income		x
5	(a) Raw materials and consumables	(x)	
	(b) Other external charges	(x)	(x)
6	Staff costs		
	(a) Wages and salaries	(x)	
	(b) Social security costs	(x)	
	(c) Other pension costs	(x)	(x)
7	(a) Depreciation and other amounts written off tangible and intangible fixed assets	(x)	
	(b) Exceptional amounts written off current assets	(x)	(x)
8	Other operating charges		(x)
9	Income from shares in group companies		x
10	Income from shares in related companies		x
11	Income from other fixed asset investments		x
12	Other interest receivable and similar income		x
13	Amounts written off investments		(x)
14	Interest payable and similar charges		(x)
15	Tax on profit or loss on ordinary activities		(x)
16	Profit or loss on ordinary activities after taxation		x

17 Extraordinary income	x	
18 Extraordinary charges	(x)	
19 Extraordinary profit or loss		x
20 Tax on extraordinary profit or loss		(x)
21 Other taxes not shown under the above items		(x)
22 Profit or loss for the financial year		x

Balance sheet format 1

	£	£	£
A CALLED UP SHARE CAPITAL NOT PAID			x
B FIXED ASSETS			
I *Intangible Assets*			
1 Development costs	x		
2 Concessions, patents, licences, trade marks and similar rights and assets	x		
3 Goodwill	x		
4 Payments on account	x		
		x	
II *Tangible Assets*			
1 Land and buildings	x		
2 Plant and machinery	x		
3 Fixtures, fittings, tools and equipment	x		
4 Payments on account and assets in course of construction	x		
		x	
III *Investments*			
1 Shares in group companies	x		
2 Loans to group companies	x		
3 Shares in related companies	x		
4 Loans to related companies	x		
5 Other investments other than loans	x		
6 Other loans	x		
7 Own shares	x		
		x	
TOTAL OF B			x
C CURRENT ASSETS			
I *Stocks*			
1 Raw materials and consumables	x		
2 Work in progress	x		
3 Finished goods and goods for resale	x		
4 Payments on account	x		
	x		
II *Debtors*			
1 Trade debtors	x		
2 Amounts owed by group companies	x		
3 Amounts owed by related companies	x		
4 Other debtors	x		
5 Called up share capital not paid	x		
6 Prepayments and accrued income	x		
	x		
III *Investments*			
1 Shares on group companies	x		
2 Own shares	x		
3 Other investments	x		
IV *Cash at bank and in hand*	x		
TOTAL OF C		x	
D PREPAYMENTS AND ACCRUED INCOME		x	
TOTAL OF D AND C		x	
E CREDITORS: AMOUNTS FALLING DUE WITHIN ONE YEAR			
1 Debenture loans	(x)		
2 Bank loans and overdrafts	(x)		
3 Payments received on account	(x)		
4 Trade creditors	(x)		
5 Bills of exchange payable	(x)		
6 Amount owed to group companies	(x)		
7 Amounts owed to related companies	(x)		
8 Other creditors including taxation and social security	(x)		
9 Accruals and deferred income	(x)	(x)	
F NET CURRENT ASSETS (LIABILITIES) (C+D–E)			x
G TOTAL ASSETS LESS CURRENT LIABILITIES (A+B+F)			x
H CREDITORS: AMOUNTS FALLING DUE AFTER MORE THAN ONE YEAR			
1 Debenture loans	(x)		
2 Bank loans and overdrafts	(x)		
3 Payments received on account	(x)		
4 Trade creditors	(x)		
5 Bills of exchange payable	(x)		
6 Amounts owed to group companies	(x)		
7 Amounts owed to related companies	(x)		
8 Other creditors including taxation and social security	(x)		
9 Accruals and deferred income	(x)		
I PROVISIONS FOR LIABILITIES AND CHARGES			
1 Pensions and similar obligations	(x)		
2 Taxation, including deferred taxation	(x)		
3 Other provisions	(x)		
			(x)
J ACCRUALS AND DEFERRED INCOME			(x)
			£x

K	CAPITAL AND RESERVES		
	I *Called up share capital*		x
	II *Share premuim account*		x
	III *Revaluation reserve*		x
	IV *Other reserves*		
	1 Capital redemption reserve fund	x	
	2 Reserve for own share	x	
	3 Reserve provided for by the articles of association	x	
	4 Other reserves	x	x
	V PROFIT AND LOSS ACCOUNT		x
			£x

Balance sheet format 2

		£	£	£
A	CALLED UP SHARE CAPITAL NOT PAID			x
B	FIXED ASSETS			
	I *Intangible Assets*			
	1 Development costs	x		
	2 Concessions, patents, licences, trade marks and similar rights and assets	x		
	3 Goodwill	x		
	4 Payments on account	x		
			x	
	II *Tangible Assets*			
	1 Land and buildings	x		
	2 Plant and machinery	x		
	3 Fixtures, fittings, tools and equipment	x		
	4 Payments on account and assets in course of construction	x		
			x	
	III *Investments*			
	1 Shares in group companies	x		
	2 Loans to group companies	x		
	3 Shares in related companies	x		
	4 Loans to related companies	x		
	5 Other investments other than loans	x		
	6 Other loans	x		
	7 Own shares	x		
			x	
	TOTAL OF B			x
C	CURRENT ASSETS			
	I *Stocks*			
	1 Raw materials and consumables	x		
	2 Work in progress	x		
	3 Finished goods and goods for resale	x		
	4 Payment on account	x		
		x		
	II *Debtors*			
	1 Trade debtors	x		
	2 Amounts owed by group companies	x		
	3 Amounts owed by related companies	x		
	4 Other debtors	x		
	5 Called up share capital not paid	x		
	6 Prepayments and accrued income	x		
		x		
	III *Investments*			
	1 Shares in group companies	x		
	2 Own shares	x		
	3 Other investment	x		
	IV *Cash at bank and in hand*	x		
	TOTAL OF C		x	
D	PREPAYMENTS AND ACCRUED INCOME		x	
	TOTAL OF C+D		x	x
	LIABILITIES			x
A	CAPITAL AND RESERVES			
	I *Called up share capital*			x
	II *Share premium account*			x
	III *Revaluation reserve*			x
	IV *Other reserves*			
	1 Capital redemption reserve fund	x		
	2 Reserve for own shares	x		
	3 Reserves provided for by the articles of association	x		
	4 Other reserves	x		x
	V PROFIT AND LOSS ACCOUNT			x
				x
B	PROVISIONS FOR LIABILITIES AND CHARGES			
	1 Pensions and similar obligations	x		
	2 Taxation, including deferred taxation	x		
	3 Other provisions	x		
				x
C	CREDITORS			
	1 Debenture loans	x		
	2 Bank loans and overdrafts	x		
	3 Payments received on account	x		
	4 Trade creditors	x		
	5 Bills of exchange payable	x		
	6 Amounts owed to group companies	x		
	7 Amounts owed to related companies	x		
	8 Other creditors including taxation and social security	x		
	9 Accruals and deferred income	x		
				x
D	ACCRUALS AND DEFERRED INCOME			x
				x

SPECIMEN SOLUTIONS

Specimen answers are included for all questions requiring computational solutions. Answers to questions on Chapters 1, 10 and 11 are not included, because these simply involve repeating material already in the text.

Chapter 2

1 (a) A
(b) L
(c) E
(d) E
(e) A
(f) L
(g) A
(h) I

2 ***S. Perceval balance sheet as at 30 September 1985***

	£		£
Capital	86,000	Building	20,000
Loan	22,000	Plant	51,000
Trade creditors	10,000	Stock	24,000
		Debtors	15,000
		Deposit account	7,000
		Cash	1,000
	118,000		118,000

3 (a) Dr Bank Cr Capital
(b) Dr Purchases Cr F. Green
(c) Dr Van 14,000 Cr Cash 7,000 Cr J. White 7,000
(d) Dr A. Pink Cr Sales
(e) Dr Bank Cr M. Black
(f) Dr Cash Cr Bank
(g) Dr F. Green Cr Bank
(h) Dr Wages Cr Bank
(j) Dr Cleaning Cr Petty Cash
(k) No entry because no transaction completed

4 ***Joseph Anton***

(a) – (d) *Ledger*

Bank

(a)	1.7.85 Capital	5,000	(b)	2.7.85 Rent	250
(b)	29.7.85 F. Williams	450	(c)	3.7.85 Equipment	4,000
			(e)	19.7.85 Wages	300
				31.7.85 Bal c/f	900
		5,450			5,450
	1.8.85 bal b/f				

Equipment

(c)	3.7.85 Bank	4,000		31.7.85 Bal c/f	4,000

Fees Receivable

	P & L	1,740	(d)	12.7.85 F. Williams	800
			(h)	30.7.85 C. Sinclair	940
		1,740			1,740

Goods Consumed

(f)	28.7.85 J. Austen	400		31.7.85 P & L	400

C Sinclair

(h)	30.7.85 Fees	940		31.7.85 Bal c/f	940
	1.8.85 Bal b/f	940			

Capital

	31.7.85 Bal c/f	5,790	(a)	1.7.85 Bank	5,000
				31.7.85 P & L	790
		5,790			5,790
				1.8.85 Bal b/f	5,790

Rent

(b)	2.7.85 Bank	250		31.7.85 P & L	250

F Williams

(d)	12.7.85 Fees	800	(g)	29.7.85 Bank		450
				31.7.85 Bal c/f		350
		800				800
	1.8.85 Bal b/f	350				

Wages

(e)	19.7.85 Bank	300	31.7.85 P & L	300

J Austen

31.7.85 Bal c/f	400	(f)	28.7.85 Goods consumed	400
			1.8.85 Bal b/f	400

Profit and Loss

31.7.85 Rent	250	31.7.85 Fees	1,740
31.7.85 Wages	300		
31.7.85 Goods	400		
31.7.85 Capital (net profit)	790		
	1,740		1,740

(b) *Trial balance*

	Dr £	Cr £
Bank	900	
Capital		5,000
Equipment	4,000	
Rent	250	
Fees Receivable		1,740
F. Williams (Debtor)	350	
Wages	300	
Goods consumed	400	
J. Austen (Creditor)		400
C. Sinclair (Debtor)	940	
	7,140	7,140

(c) *Profit and loss account for the month ended 31 July 1985*

	£	£
Fees Receivable		1,740
Less:		
Rent	250	
Wages	300	
Materials	400	
		950
Net Profit		790

(c) *Balance sheet as at 31 July 1985*

	£		£
Capital:		Equipment	4,000
Introduced	5,000	Debtors	1,290
Profit	790	Bank	900
	5,790		
Creditor	400		
	6,190		6,190

Chapter 3

1 *Dover Company*

Adjustments to cash account

	£
Per question	3,105.15
Service charge	(5.00)
Error in cheque record	20.00
	3,120.15

Bank reconciliation statement

	£
Balance per statement	3,150.25
Bank error	150.00
	3,300.25
Add:	
Uncleared bankings	454.00
	3,754.25
Less:	
Outstanding cheques	634.10
	3,120.15

2 (a) *Smithers Ltd*

30.11.82 Correction of opening balance	180	30.11.82 Balance b/d	1,110
		30.11.82 Interest	29
		30.11.82 Correction of cheque error (2 × 60)	120
		30.11.82 Dishonoured cheque	45
30.11.82 Balance c/d	1,154	30.11.82 Discount	30
	1,334		1,334
		30.11.82 Balance b/d	1,154

Bank reconciliation statement

	£
Balance as per bank statement	5,154 (o/d)
Outstanding cheques	3,300
	8,454 (o/d)
Uncleared bankings	7,300
Per cashbook	1,154 (o/d)

(b) (i) Reconciliation of trade creditor accounts with suppliers' statements. This serves as a check on the accuracy of the purchase ledger, and also gives a useful check on the 'cut-off' procedures which ensure that all goods included in stock have been recorded as purchases.

(ii) Debtor and creditor ledger control accounts, whereby the total of a list of the individual ledger balances is checked against the balance on a control account which includes the totals of individual amounts posted to the ledgers.

3 *Control accounts*

(a) purposes

(i) There are certain types of error which can be revealed by a comparison of the control account balance and the total of individual ledger balances.

(ii) They can be useful in making it possible to identify in which part of the trial balance an error is to be found, so that the search for the cause can be confirmed to one type of account.

(iii) Where responsibility for the control account is separated from the responsibility for the individual accounts in the ledger some measure of protection against fraud is established.

(iv) They are a valuable management tool in giving immediate access to total debtor and creditor figures.

(b) *Sales ledger control account*

7 May 1982 Balance b/d	9,123	1 May 1982 Balance b/d	211
May 1982 Sales	36,755	May 1982 Bank	27,370
May 1982 Bank	489	May 1982 Contra	3,046
May 1982 Bank	53	May 1982 Allowance	1,720
31 May 1982 Balance c/d	136	May 1982 Bills	6,506
		May 1982 Cash	4,201
		May 1982 Discounts	732
		31 May Bal. c/d	2,770
	46,556		46,556
1 June 1982 Balance b/d	2,770	1 June 1982 Balance b/d	136

Purchase ledger control account

1 May 1982 Balance b/d	88	1 May 1982 Balance b/d	4,490
May 1982 Allowances	629	May 1982 Purchases	18,135
May 1982 Discounts	1,105	31 May 1982 Balance c/d	67
May 1982 Bank	15,413		
May 1982 Contra	3,046		
31 May 1982 Balance c/d	2,411		
	22,692		22,692
1 June 1982 Balance b/d	67	1 June 1982 Balance b/d	2,411

4 *Hannay Limited*

Journal

31.1.86 a.	E. Leithen	18	
	Suspense account		18
	Correction of error in posting of sales invoice		
31.1.86 b.	Suspense account	120	
	Sundry income		120
	Item omitted from trial balance		
31.1.86 c.	Sales	9	
	Blenkiron PLC		9
	Correction of error in entering invoice in sales day book		
31.1.86 d.	D. Black	52	
	P. Black		52
	Correction of error in entering invoice in purchase ledger		
31.1.86 e.	Suspense account	900	
	Motor expenses		900
	Correction of error in cast of purchase day book		
31.1.86 f.	Suspense account	80	
	Motor expenses		80
	Correction of error in posting refund of road tax to motor expenses		

Suspense account

31.1.86 Sundry income	120	31.1.86 Balance b/d	1,082
31.1.86 Motor expenses	900	31.1.86 E. Leithen	18
31.1.86 Motor expenses	80		
	1,100		1,100

Chapter 4

1 *Aramis – Insurance Account*

1.4.85 Bal b/d	175	31.3.86 Bal c/d	205
30.5.85 Cash	572	31.3.86 P & L	1,362
30.6.85 Cash	820		
	1,567		1,567
1.4.86 Bal b/d	205		

2 ***Planchet – Profit and loss account for the year ended 31 December 1985***

	£	£
Sales		60,000
Less:		
Stock 1.1.85	2,800	
Purchases	46,000	
	48,800	
Stock 1.1.86	3,700	
Cost of Sales		45,100
Gross Profit		14,900
Less:		
Telephone (310–20)	290	
Motor expenses (450+40)	490	
Wages (4,200+70)	4,270	
Rates (1,260–270)	990	
Depreciation	500	
		6,540
Net Profit		8,360

Plancet – Balance sheet as at 31 December 1985

	£	£
Fixed Assets:		
Premises		21,000
Van (2,000–500)		1,500
		22,500
Current Assets:		
Stock	3,700	
Debtors	2,120	
Prepayments (20+270)	290	
Current Liabilities:		
Creditors	3,040	
Accruals (40+70)	110	
Bank	1,120	
	4,270	
Net current assets		1,840
		24,340
Capital:		
At 1.1.85		23,080
Profit for the year		8,360
		31,440
Drawings		7,100
At 31.12.85		24,340

(Questions 3 to 6: answers follow the main text)

Chapter 5

1 A good answer would pick up the points made in Chapter 5 in the section contrasting partnerships and limited companies.

2 ***Martin, Robertson and Stoneham – Trading and profit and loss account for the year ending 30 June 1982***

		£	£
Sales			24,160
Less:			
Opening Stock		10,000	
Purchases		18,730	
		28,730	
Closing profit		12,400	16,330
Gross Profit			7,830
Wages		1,200	
Expenses		1,750	
Interest on Advance		100	3,050
Net Profit			4,780
Interest on capital:	M	600	
	R	500	
	S	300	
			1,400
			3,380
Salaries	M	500	
	R	500	
			1,000
			2,380
Profit share	M	952	
	R	833	
	S	595	
			2,380

Balance sheet as at 30 June 1982

		£	£
Capital accounts:	M	12,000	
	R	10,000	
	S	6,000	
			28,000
Advance			2,000
Current Accounts:			
M (2,052+100–800)		1,352	
R (1,833–700)		1,133	
S (895)		895	
			3,380
			33,380
Fixed Assets			
Freehold Property			10,200
Plant			3,560
			13,760
Current Assets			
Stock		12,400	
Debtors		6,720	
Bank		4,200	
		23,320	
Less: Creditors		3,700	
Net current assets			19,620
			33,380

(b)

Realization Account

30.6.82 Property	10,200	30.6.82 Cash			9,000
30.6.82 Plant	3,560	30.6.82 Cash			3,000
30.6.82 Stock	12,400	30.6.82 Martin			18,000
30.6.82 Debtors	6,720	30.6.82 Capital a/c			
			M	1,152	
			R	1,008	
			S	720	
					2,880
	32,880				32,880

Bank

30.6.82 Bal b/d	4,200	30.6.82 Creditors	3,700
30.6.82 Realization	9,000	30.6.82 Robertson	10,125
30.6.82 Realization	3,000	30.6.82 Stoneham	6,175
30.6.82 Martin	3,800		
	20,000		20,000

Martin – Advance

30.6.82 Capital	2,000	30.6.82 Bal b/d	2,000

Capital Accounts

	M	*R*	*S*		*M*	*R*	*S*
30.6.82 Realization	18,000			30.6.82 Bal b/d	12,000	10,000	6,000
30.6.82 Realization	1,152	1,008	720	30.6.82 Current a/c	1,352	1,133	895
30.6.82 Bank		10,125	6,175	30.6.82 Loan a/c	2,000		
				30.6.82 Bank	3,800		
	19,152	11,133	6,895		19,152	11,133	6,895

Current Accounts

	M	*R*	*S*		*M*	*R*	*S*
30.6.82 Capital a/cs	1,352	1,133	895	30.6.82 Bal b/d	1,352	1,133	895

3

(a) Debenture interest is an *expense*, paid to those who have lent money to the company. Dividends are an *appropriation* of profit, paid to the shareholders who own the company.

(b) A transfer of profits to the general reserve signals the company's intention of regarding the resources which represent the general reserve as to be retained in the business, rather than being distributed as dividends, but does not involve a binding commitment on the company to continue with such a policy.

(c) 'Share premium account' is a capital reserve, while both 'general reserve' and 'unappropriated profits' are revenue reserves.

(d) 'Share premium' represents the excess of the price at which shares are issued over their nominal value.

(e) Revenue reserves may be distributed to shareholders as dividends; capital reserves may not.

(f) 'Working capital' is a term used to describe the current assets and current liabilities which circulate in the course of the operations of the business.

(g) The net worth of Kenmar is £161,650*. This is unlikely to be the 'real' worth for two reasons:

(i) Assets are shown at historical cost less depreciation where appropriate. This does not necessarily reflect their true value.

(ii) The accounts do not report the 'inherent goodwill' of the business, i.e. the extent to which the value of the business as a whole exceeds the value of the individual assets.

*Taking net worth as *total* shareholders' funds, but excluding proposed dividends.

(h) £2.0825. We would expect this to be greater than par because some shares have been issued at a premium and because profits have been retained in the company.

(i) This is a private company, being 'Limited'. A public company would be 'PLC'.

4

(a) *Revaluation*

31.3.82 Plant		1,500	31.3.82 Freehold	6,000
31.3.82 Capital:				
B	2,250			
R	1,500			
L	750			
		4,500		
		6,000		6,000

(b)

Capital Accounts

	B	*R*	*L*	*E*		*B*	*R*	*L*	*E*
31.3.82 Goodwill		3,691	1,846	1,846	31.3.82 Bal b/d	12,000	6,000	3,000	
31.3.82 Bank	5,000				31.3.82 Revaluation	2,250	1,500	750	
31.3.82 Loan					31.3.82 Goodwill	3,691	2,461	1,231	
31.3.82 Bal b/d	13,901	6,270	3,135	3,154	31.3.82 Current a/c	960			
					31.3.82 Bank				4,000
					31.3.82 Plant				1,000
	18,901	9,961	4,981	5,000		18,901	9,961	4,981	5,000

(c) ***Balance sheet as at 1.4.82***

Fixed assets:		
Freehold premises		12,000
Plant		8,900
		20,900
Current assets:		
Stock	4,600	
Debtors	5,600	
Cash	7,060	
	17,260	
Current liabilities:		
Creditors	10,300	6,960
		27,860
Capital accounts:		
Rose	6,270	
Larch	3,135	
Elm	3,154	12,559
Current accounts:		
Rose	840	
Larch	560	1,400
Loan account		13,901
		27,860

Workings

Goodwill – £7,383*

Split in old ratio:

B	3,691
R	2,461
L	1,231

Split in new ratio:

R	3,691
L	1,846
E	1,846

*In the absence of information on the 'weighting' to be used, a simple average has been computed.

5 A good answer is likely to include notes on the following:

Loan interest
Interest on loans is usually paid. The Partnership Act 1890 provides for 5 per cent interest on loans in absence of agreement between partners. Current market rates of interest are such that the partners are likely to agree a higher rate.

Other interest
The Partnership Act 1890 makes no provision for any other form of interest payment between partners. However where, as in this case, the capital subscribed by each partner differs substantially, it is common in appropriating profits for the year to agree on a rate of interest to be allowed on capital in order to compensate partners making the largest capital contribution

The partners will also wish to consider on what basis each partner should be permitted to make drawings from the business on account of profits, and whether interest should be charged on such drawings

Partners' salaries
In sharing out profits it is common to allocate an agreed sum by way of 'salary' to each partner; this is particularly appropriate where, as in this case, there are substantial variations in the amount of time devoted to the business by different partners.

Allowance for expenses
Where a partner incurs expenses personally on behalf of the firm, as in the case of Dee and his van, it is normal to agree on a system for such expenses to be paid by the firm, this cost being shown as an expense rather than as an appropriation of profit.

Residual profit or loss
The Partnership Act 1890 provides that in the absence of agreement to the contrary profits and losses should be shared equally. The partners might wish to vary this, depending on their view of the total contribution made by each partner.

Minimum profit share
Sometimes it is agreed that a partner should enjoy a minimum profit share, to be borne by one or more of the other partners if necessary. In this example Cee, who apparently has little in the way of personal resources and will be working full-time in the business, may wish to seek such an arrangement.

Limited Partnership Act 1907
It appears that Bee may be in a position to be treated as a limited partner, since he plays no part in the management of the business. The partners may wish to register Bee as a limited partner.

Chapter 6

1 A number of points could be made in answering this question. They might include:

(a) A definition of depreciation, emphasizing that it involves allocating the cost of a fixed asset to the accounting periods when it is consumed.
(b) A discussion of the concept of value, with an explanation that although a fixed asset will be shown at cost at the point of purchase and at estimated disposal value when fully depreciated there is no reason why the depreciated cost of the asset should relate to any concept of value in between.
(c) Consideration of the relationship between depreciation and replacement, noting that depreciation does not directly involve retention of any cash resources in the business.
(d) Explanation of the link between profit and capital maintenance, so that indirectly the charging of depreciation as an expense may result in retaining resources in the business. Note, however, that those resources will not necessarily be in liquid form.

2 *Depreciation*

(a) (i) *Machinery*

	£		£
1.1.81. Balance b/d	90,000	30.6.81. Disposal	30,000
1.1.81. Acquisition	35,000	31.10.81. Disposal	30,000
		31.12.81. Balance c/d	65,000
	95,000		95,000

Provision for Depreciation

	£		£
30.6.81. Disposal	14,640	1.1.81. Balance b/d	43,920
31.10.81. Disposal	14,640	31.12.81. Profit and Loss	10,072
Balance c/d	24,712		
	53,992		53,992

Asset Disposal

	£		£
30.6.81. Machinery	30,000	30.6.81. Cash	10,000
30.10.81. Machinery	30,000	30.6.81 Depreciation	14,640
		31.10.81. Cash	12,000
		31.10.81. Depreciation	14,640
		31.12.81. Profit and Loss	8,720
	60,000		60,000

(ii) Machinery:

Cost	65,000
Less: Accumulated depreciation	24,712
	40,288

(b) An answer to this question could be quite extensive. Major points to include would be:

(i) There is not a direct link between depreciation, which represents an allocation of the cost or value of an asset to the accounting periods in which it is used, and the planning of cash management for asset replacement.

(ii) There is an indirect link between depreciation and replacement, because of the capital maintenance concept implicit in computing profit.

(iii) Increasing the depreciation rate will write off the asset more rapidly, but if the asset is held until the end of its useful life, total depreciation accumulated will not change.

(iv) The solution to the manufacturer's problem may be some form of value accounting – replacement cost would seem most appropriate.

(v) As a separate issue, the losses on disposal would suggest that depreciation rates are low.

Workings

Accumulated depreciation on each machine:

	£	£ *Cumulative depreciation*
Cost 1978	30,000	
Less: 20%	6,000	6,000
WDV 1.1.79.	24,000	
Less: 20%	4,800	4,800
WDV 1.1.80.	19,200	
Less: 20%	3,840	3,840
WDV 1.1.81.	15,360	14,640

Therefore accumulated depreciation 1.1.81. = 3 × £14,640 = £43,920.

Charge for year:	£
Cost	65,000
Less: Accumulated depreciation	14,640
	50,360
× 20% =	10,072

3

(a)

Freehold Land and Buildings

1.1.81	Balance b/d	25,000	31.12.81	Balance c/d	25,000
1.1.82	Balance b/d	25,000			

Plant and Machinery

1.1.81	Balance b/d	12,800	1981	Disposal	3,000
1981	Bank	4,000	31.12.81	Balance c/d	13,800
		16,800			16,800
1.1.82	Balance b/d	13,800			

Depreciation on Plant and Machinery

1981	Disposal	2,100	1.1.81	Balance b/d	6,200
31.12.81	Balance c/d	5,480	31.12.81	Profit and Loss	1,380
		7,580			7,580
			1.1.82	Balance b/d	5,480

Motor Vehicles

1.1.81.	Balance b/d	10,450	1981	Disposal	4,000
1981	Acquisition	6,000	31.12.81	Balance c/d	12,450
		16,450			16,450
1.1.82	Balance b/d	12,450			

Depreciation on Motor Vehicles

1981	Disposal	2,628	1.1.81	Balance b/d	6,100
31.12.81	Balance c/d	6,165	31.12.81	Profit and Loss	2,693
		8,793			8,793
			1.1.81	Balance b/d	6,165

Fixtures and Fittings

1.1.81	Balance b/d	1,800	31.12.81	Profit and Loss	350
1981	Bank	600	31.12.81	Balance c/d	2,050
		2,400			2,400

Fixed Asset Disposal

1981	Plant	3,000	1981	Depreciation on plant	2,100
1981	Vehicles	4,000	1981	Disposal proceeds	200
				Depreciation on m/vs	2,628
			1981	Disposal proceeds	1,500
			31.12.81	Profit and Loss	572
		7,000			7,000

Workings

Depreciation on assets sold:

Plant – 7 years @ 10% p.a. × 3,000 = 2,100

Vehicle

	Written-down value	*Depreciation*
1978 – Cost	4,000	
Less: Depreciation	1,200	1,200
1979 – Balance b/d	2,800	
Less: Depreciation	840	840
1980 – Balance b/d	1,960	
Less: Depreciation	588	588
	1,372	
		2,628

(b) ***Profit and loss account extract***

	£	£
Depreciation		
Plant	1,380	
Motor vehicles	2,693	
Fixtures	350	
		4,423
Loss on disposal of fixed assets		572

Balance sheet

Fixed Assets

	Cost/ Valuation £	*Accumulated depreciation* £	*Net book value* £
Freehold land and buildings	25,000	—	25,000
Plant and machinery	13,800	5,480	8,320
Fixtures and fittings	2,050	—	2,050
Motor vehicles	12,450	6,165	6,285
	53,300	11,645	41,655

4

(a) *Motor Vehicles*

1.7.81	Balance b/d	61,850	30.6.82	Disposals	7,100
30.9.81	Cash	8,600	30.6.82	Balance c/d	78,150
31.10.81	Cash	10,800			
28.2.82	Cash	4,000			
		85,250			85,250
1.7.82	Balance b/d	78,150			

(b) *Provision for Depreciation of Motor Vehicles*

30.6.82	Disposals	4,335	1.7.81	Balance b/d	32,426
30.6.82	Balance c/d	42,038	30.6.82	Profit and Loss	13,947
		46,373			46,373
			1.7.82	Balance b/d	42,038

(c) *Disposal of Motor Vehicles*

30.6.82	Motor Vehicles	7,100	31.10.81	Cash	300
			31.12.81	Cash	540
			31.3.82	Cash	420
			30.6.82	Depreciation	4,335
			30.6.82	Profit and Loss	1,505
		7,100			7,100

(d) ***Balance sheet extracts as at 30 June, 1982***
Note to the accounts

Motor vehicles

	£
Cost:	
At 1.7.81	61,850
Additions	23,400
Disposals	(7,100)
At 30.6.82	78,150
Depreciation:	
At 1.7.81	32,426
Charge for year	13,947
Disposals	(4,335)
At 30.6.82	42,038
WDV 30.6.82	36,112
WDV 1.7.81	29,424

Workings
Depreciation on vehicles:

Car	$2{,}800 \times \frac{4}{5}$	=	2,240
Tractor	$2{,}400 \times \left(2 + \frac{7}{12} \div 5\right)$	=	1,240
Van	$1{,}900 \times \left(2 + \frac{1}{4} \div 5\right)$	=	855
			4,335

Depreciation for year:			
	$\frac{1}{5} \times (61{,}850 - 7{,}100)$	=	10,950
Van	$\frac{9}{12} \times \frac{1}{5} \times 8{,}600$	=	1,290
Car	$\frac{8}{12} \times \frac{1}{5} \times 10{,}000$	=	1,400
Lorry	$\frac{4}{12} \times \frac{1}{5} \times 4{,}000$	=	267
			13,947

5

(a) Depreciation must have been computed on a time basis, because we have no data on usage. The same plant was in use in 1979 and in 1980, but the depreciation charge in 1979 was £16,000 and in 1980 £12,800 – thus the straight-line method cannot be used. Testing to see if the reducing balance method was used we find the depreciation rate in 1979 was:

$$\frac{16{,}000}{80{,}000} = 20\%$$

and in 1980:

$$\frac{12{,}800}{64{,}000} = 20\%$$

Thus it appears likely that the method used is in fact reducing balance.

(b) *Depreciation*

	1979	*1980*	*1981*	*1982*
B/fwd	—	10,000	28,800	36,720
Less: Disposals	—	—	5,400	14,640
	—	16,000	23,400	22,080
Charge for year	16,000	12,800	13,320	17,584
C/fwd	16,000	28,800	36,720	39,664

Workings

Charge for year

1979 20% × 80,000 = 16,000
1980 20% × 64,000 = 12,800
1981 20% × (90,000 – 23,400) = 13,320
1982 20% × (110,000 – 22,080) = 17,584

Accumulated depreciation on disposals

			Accumulated depreciation
First disposal:			
1979 – Cost		15,000	
	Less: 20%	3,000	3,000
1980 – b/d		12,000	
	Less: 20%	2,400	2,400
		9,600	5,400
Second disposal:			
1979 – Cost		30,000	
	Less: 20%	6,000	6,000
1980 – b/d		24,000	
	Less: 20%	4,800	4,800
1981 – b/d		19,200	
	Less: 20%	3,840	3,840
		15,360	14,640

(c)

	£
Plant at Cost	110,000
Accumulated depreciation	39,664
Net (written-down value)	70,336

(d)

	Disposal 1		*Disposal 2*	
	£	£	£	£
Sale proceeds		8,000		21,000
Cost	15,000		30,000	
Less: Depreciation	5,400		14,640	
		9,600		15,360
Profit/(Loss)		(1,600)		5,640

Chapter 7

1

(a) Stock can be ascertained at any time providing that the company has a continuous stock-recording system. Such a system identifies and records all items of stock received and issued, so that the balance of stock held at any point in time can be identified.

(b) Even where a company has a system of continuous stock recording it will be necessary to have a system for counting all items of stock at least once a year as a check on the accuracy of the records. Where a continuous stock-taking system is in use a small number of items will be test counted each day, so that every item is counted at least once a year. The advantages of this approach over annual stock-taking are:

(i) It avoids the disruption of a total close-down of business activity while a complete count is made.

(ii) Any irregularities or changes in procedure by those responsible for the custody of stock are revealed more rapidly.

(iii) In some cases the volume of stock may be such as to make a complete count in one day impossible.

(iv) In a large business it is possible to employ staff specifically as stock-takers, so that a greater degree of skill in performing the job is built up.

2

	£	£
Stock as reported		187,033
Less:		
Adjustment 2	140	
Adjustment 4	6,480	
Adjustment 7	152	
		6,772
		180,261
Add		
Adjustment 3	8,010	
Adjustment 5	1,200	
		9,210
		189,471

(a) SSAP 9 requires companies to value stock at the lower of cost and net realizable value, which in this case would be cost £11 each. This is in accordance with the prudence concept, whereby losses are provided for as soon as they are foreseen but income is only recognized when established by a legal transaction. It would not be appropriate within the historical cost convention to write down stock to replacement cost because no loss has been made.

(b) Net realizable value consists of the expected sale proceeds less any costs to be incurred before selling the goods. In this case net realizable value is:

	£
Sale proceeds	6,321
Less	804
	5,517

so that a write down of (5657–5517) = £140 should be made.

(c) This error, of (9105 – 1095) = £8,010, represents an amount which has been excluded from the stock figure in error and must be added back.

(d)

	£
Units as shown in stock sheet 480 x 15	7,200
Units at actual cost 480 x 1.5	720
Excess amount deducted from stock	6,480

(e) Since these goods are the property of the company, they should be included in stock at cost £1,200.

(f) Since these goods are the property of Cranfleet Commodities, they are quite properly included in stock.

(g) Free samples distributed are no longer the company's property, and therefore should not be included in stock.

(a) ***CCL – Profit and loss account for the year ended 31 December 1981***

	£000	*£000*
Sales		2,100
Cost of sales:		
Steel purchases	1,200	
Wages	450	
Rent (225–45)	180	
Electric (70+20)	90	
Depreciation	90	
	2,010	
Less: Closing stock	360	
		1,650
Gross Profit		450
Administrative expenses	230	
Bad debts	25	
		255
Net Profit		195
Proposed Dividend		75
Retained Profit		120

CCL – Balance sheet as at 31 December 1981

	£000	*£000*
Share Capital – £1 ordinary shares		500
Retained Profit		120
		620
Plant – Cost		600
Less: Depreciation		90
		510
Current Assets:		
Stock	360	
Debtors (500–25)	475	
Prepayment	45	
	880	
Current Liabilities:		
Creditors	450	
Accrual	20	
Proposed Dividend	75	
Bank	225	
	770	
Net current assets		110
		620

(b) We are told that stock is valued at £360,000 but are not told the basis of valuation. In order to try and work out the basis of valuation we first compute the amount of the raw material value of stock at the year end as follows:

(i) Number of containers sold

$$= \frac{\text{Total sales}}{\text{Selling price per container}} = \frac{2{,}100{,}000}{3{,}000} = 700$$

(ii) Steel purchases are sufficient to make

$$\frac{\text{Total purchases}}{\text{Cost of steel content per container}} = \frac{1{,}200{,}000}{1{,}200} = 1{,}000$$

(iii) Therefore steel stock is sufficient to make:

1,000 – 700 = 300 containers

(iv) Raw material value = 300 × £1,200 =£360,000

Therefore stock is valued by reference to raw material content only.

SSAP9 states that the cost of stock should include related production costs. Total production costs are:

	£000
Wages	450
Rent	180
Electric	90
Depreciation	90
	810

We are told that at the end of the year two-thirds of stock, i.e. 200 units, has been converted to containers. Thus total production must have consisted of 700 units sold plus 200 in stock = 900 units.

Therefore production cost per unit =

$$\frac{£810{,}000}{900} = £900$$

And total cost per unit is material cost + production cost =
£1,200 + £900 = £2,100

On a SSAP9 basis we would therefore value stock:

200 complete units @ £2,100	=	£420,000
100 raw material units @ £1,200	=	120,000
		540,000

The increase of £180,000 in stock valuation would increase CCL's profit by the same amount.

4 *Sam Martin*

(a) (i)

		1979		1980		1981		1982
	£	£	£	£	£	£	£	£
Sales		16,000		22,000		27,600		24,000
Cost of Sales		8,000		13,200		18,400		16,800
Gross Profit		8,000		8,800		9,200		7,200
Expenses	3,000		3,000		3,000		3,000	
Depreciation	3,300		2,211		1,481		1,008	
		6,300		5,211		4,481		4,008
Profit for the Year		1,700		3,589		4,719		3,192

(ii)

		1979		1980		1981		1982
Sales		16,000		22,000		27,600		24,000
Cost of Sales		8,000		14,000		19,200		15,200
Gross Profit		8,000		8,000		8,400		8,800
Expenses	3,000		3,000		3,000		3,000	
Depreciation	2,000		2,000		2,000		2,000	
		5,000		5,000		5,000		5,000
Profit for the year		3,000		3,000		3,400		3,800

(b) ***Comments***

(i) Illustrates the way in which different accounting policies can give completely different impressions of trends.

(ii) LIFO – in times of rising prices normally uses most recent stock prices and therefore gives lower gross profit. But note how in the final year a reduction in stock brings in 'old' price levels and therefore artificially high gross profit.

(iii) Reducing balance depreciation depresses early years profit and boosts later years.

Workings

Cost of sales

FIFO

	1979	1980	1981	1982
Stock b/fwd	—	2,000	5,600	9,600
Purchases	10,000	16,800	22,400	7,200
	10,000	18,800	28,000	16,800
Stock c/fwd	2,000	5,600	9,600	—
	8,000	13,200	18,400	16,800

LIFO

	1979	1980	1981	1982
Stock b/fwd	—	2,000	4,800	8,000
Purchases	10,000	16,800	22,400	7,200
	10,000	18,800	27,200	15,200
Stock c/fwd	2,000	4,800	8,000	—
	8,000	14,000	19,200	15,200

5 *Eidelweiss*

	£	£
(a) Dr Profit and loss	1,600	
Cr Provision for bad debts		1,600

Adjustment to bad debt provision at year end

(b)

Current Assets		
Debtors	91,500	
Less: Provision	2,100	
		89,400

Workings

Provision:

80,000 × 1%	800
6,000 × 5%	300
4,000 × 10%	400
1,500 × 40%	600
	2,100

Chapter 8

1 Gearing has two effects:

(a) The higher the level of gearing, the more responsive is the return on shareholders' funds to fluctuations in operating profit. (Income effect).

(b) The higher the level of gearing, the greater the risk of a default on repayment of borrowings. (Capital effect).

In measuring gearing, preference shares have an ambiguous position being akin to borrowings from the point of view of the income effect but being more akin to ordinary capital from the point of view of the capital effect. Preference dividends are paid out of profit after tax, whereas interest is a tax-allowable expense.

The income effect of gearing can be illustrated if we compare Sam PLC with an imaginary company Jim PLC which is totally financed by equity. The comparison is shown in Appendix A. If we consider the effect on shareholders of an operating profit of £100,000 (a), then compare that with a 20 per cent increase in operating profit to £120,000 (b) we can see that in Sam PLC, which has some fixed interest finance, profit available to shareholders goes up by 33 per cent while in Jim PLC, with no fixed interest finance, profit available to shareholders only goes up by 20 per cent. This is because the share of profit taken by preference shareholders and debenture holders is a fixed amount irrespective of the level of operating profit; the greater this fixed claim, the more significant will be the effect on the residue of any fluctuation in operating profit.

The capital effect of gearing can be illustrated if we consider what proportion of the total assets of Sam PLC would have to be lost before the company was unable to repay loans. The answer is:

$$\frac{100 + 200 + 100}{560} = 71\%$$

This is because preference shareholders receive no payment in a liquidation until all claims by lenders have been met in full.

Appendix A

Assume another company Jim PLC totally financed from equity:

	Sam PLC £	*Jim PLC* £
Equity	300,000	560,000
Preference shares	100,000	
Debentures	160,000	
	560,000	560,000

Assume:

(a) Each company earns profit before interest and tax £100,000

	Sam PLC £	*Jim PLC* £
Profit before interest and tax	100,000	100,000
Interest	19,200	—
	80,800	100,000
Taxation	40,400	50,000
	40,400	50,000
Preference dividends	10,000	—
Profit available to ordinary shareholders	30,400	50,000

Profit as % equity $\frac{30,400}{300,000} = 10.1\%$ $\frac{50,000}{560,000} = 8.9\%$

(b) Each company improves profit before interest and tax by 20 per cent.

	Sam PLC £	*Jim PLC* £
Profit before interest and tax	120,000	120,000
Interest	19,200	—
	100,800	120,000
Taxation	50,400	60,000
	50,400	60,000
Preference dividend	10,000	—
	40,400	60,000

Profit as % equity $\frac{40{,}400}{300{,}000} = 13.5\%$ $\frac{60{,}000}{560{,}000} = 10.7\%$

Increase in profit for shareholders

$\frac{40{,}400-30{,}400}{30{,}400} = 33\%$ $\frac{60{,}000-50{,}000}{50{,}000} = 20\%$

Note: Assumes corporation tax rate 50 per cent

2

(a) This is a very broad question, which can be answered in a wide number of ways. A good answer might:

(i) List the various possible sources of finance, discussing the risks and costs associated with each.

(ii) Define gearing and explain both the income effect and gearing effect. The figures in part (b) might be referred to in illustrating the income effect.

(iii) Discuss the factors which will influence the company in its attitude to gearing.

(b) (i) Profits £40,000:

	(1)	(2)
Profit	40,000	40,000
Interest	—	4,000
	40,000	36,000
Tax	20,000	18,000
	20,000	18,000
Preference dividend	—	1,000
Earnings	20,000	17,000

E P S $\frac{20{,}000}{100{,}000} = 20p$ $\frac{17{,}000}{40{,}000} = 42.5p$

(ii) Profits £40,000:

	(1)	(2)
Profit	10,000	10,000
Interest	—	4,000
	10,000	6,000
Tax	5,000	3,000
	5,000	3,000
Preference dividend	—	1,000
Earnings	20,000	17,000

E P S $\frac{5{,}000}{100{,}000} = 5p$ $\frac{2{,}000}{40{,}000} = 5p$

Recommendation:

Assuming the two profit figures represent the range of expected profit, the high-geared structure (2) seems preferable since in the worst envisaged position it offers as good an earnings per share as option (1), while above that level it will offer higher earnings. However this is subject to the shareholders' attitude to risk.

3 The points made in answer to this question would largely be those listed under the heading 'Controlling the financial structure' in Chapter 8. Special points to make relating to the data in the question are:

(a) Both the capital equipment and the working capital need to be financed on a long-term basis.

(b) Capital equipment can be made the subject of a fixed charge, working capital a floating charge.

(c) If not already listed, the firm is obviously large enough to consider seeking listing on the Stock Exchange.

(d) If the sum of £6m is large in relation to the current size of the firm then a mixture of equity and borrowing may be appropriate in order to maintain the current gearing ratio.

Chapter 9

1 (a) *Hudson Netball Club – Income and expenditure for the year ended 31 December 1980*

	£	£
Sale of refreshments		415
less:		
Stock 1.1.80	52	
Purchases (214 – 38)	176	
	228	
Stock 31.12.80	—	
		228
Surplus on supply of refreshments		187
Income from dance	155	
less: Dance expenses	76	
Surplus on dance		79
Subscriptions (20 – 40 + 725 – 25)		680
Investment interest		10
		956
less:		
Rent (100 – 25 + 25)	100	
Wages (350 + 20)	370	
Secretary's expenses	72	
Depreciation – Furniture	50	
– Sports equipment	30	
		622
Surplus of income over expenditure		334

Hudson Netball Club – Balance Sheet as at 31 December 1980

	£	£
Fixed assets		
Premises		4,000
Furniture (560 – 50)		510
Sports equipment (200 + 120 – 30)		290
		4,800
Investments (200 + 100)		300
		5,100
Current assets:		
Bank	326	
less:		
Accruals (20 + 25 + 25)	70	
Net current assets		256
		5,356
Accumulated fund		
At 1.1.80		5,022
Surplus of income over expenditure		334
At 31.12.80		5,356

Note: It is assumed that £25 rent is again outstanding at the year end.

(b) Non-profit-making organizations
   (i) Show an 'income and expenditure account' rather than a 'profit and loss account', reporting a surplus of income over expenditure or an excess of expenditure over income, rather than a 'profit' or 'loss'.
   (ii) The income and expenditure account on a non-profit-making organization often has to identify the surplus or deficit on a variety of activities, compared with the simpler pattern of activity of most small businesses.
   (iii) The 'proprietor's' interest section of the Balance Sheet in a non-profit-making organization is represented by an 'accumulated fund'

(c) Two approaches are possible:
   (i) Take life membership fees direct to the accumulated fund on the face of the balance sheet.
   (ii) Credit each life membership to a suspense account and transfer to income in even instalments over the period of expected active membership.

Ransom Company Ltd – Profit and loss account for the year ended 30 September 1979

	£	£
Sales (80,000 – 372)		79,628
less:		
Stock 1.10.78	14,248	
Purchases	43,856	
	58,104	
Stock 30.9.79	15,546	
Cost of sales		42,558
Gross profit		37,070
Add: Discounts received		1,764
		38,834

less:		
Rates	2,124	
Wages (8,000 + 280)	8,280	
Insurance (1,896 – 100)	1,796	
General expenses	436	
Interest (400 + 400)	800	
Depreciation – Buildings	3,800	
– F & F	2,400	
Bad debts (676 – 184)	492	
		20,128
		18,706
Dividends		
Preference – Paid	600	
– Proposed	600	
Ordinary proposed	1,000	2,200
		16,506
Unappropriated profit 1.10.78		2,000
		18,506
Transfer to general reserve		8,000
Unappropriated profit		10,506

Ransom Company Ltd – Balance Sheet as at 30 September 1979

	£	£
Tangible Fixed Assets (Note 1)		55,800
Goodwill		16,400
Current Assets:		
Stock	15,546	
Debtors (12,640 – 632)	12,008	
Prepayment	100	
Cash	232	
	27,886	
Current Liabilities:		
Creditors	6,300	
Accruals (280 + 400)	680	
Bank	6,000	
Proposed dividend – Preference	600	
Ordinary	1,000	
	14,580	
Net current assets		13,306
		85,506
5% Debentures		16,000
		69,506
Share Capital – Preference shares at £1		20,000
– Ordinary shares at £1		20,000
		40,000
Share Premium		1,000
General Reserve (10,000 + 8,000)		18,000
Unappropriated profit		10,506
		69,506

Note 1 Tangible Fixed Assets

	Land	*Buildings*	*F & F*	*Total*
Cost	18,000	38,000	22,000	78,000
Depreciation	—	9,800	12,400	22,200
	18,000	28,200	9,600	55,800

Workings

Provision for doubtful debts

c/d	632	b/d	816
P & L	184		
	816		816

3 (b) *Adam Downshire – Trading Profit and Loss Account for the year ended 31 December 1982*

	£	£
Sales (10,500 + 2,850)		13,350
Less:		
Stock 1.1.82	10,000	
Purchases	9,300	
	19,300	
Stock 31.12.82	9,800	
Cost of sales		9,500
Gross profit		3,850
less:		
Expenses	2,960	
Depreciation	600	
		3,560
Net profit		290

Adam Downshire – Balance Sheet as at 31 December 1982

	£	£
Fixed Assets		
Premises		50,000
Equipment (8,000 – 600)		7,400
		57,400
Current Assets		
Stock	9,800	
Debtors	5,100	
Bank	1,500	
Cash	80	
	16,480	

Current Liabilities		
Creditors – Trade	4,200	
– Expenses	440	
	4,640	
Net Current assets		11,840
		69,240
Capital:		
At 1.1.82		69,950
		290
		70,240
Drawings		1,000
At 31.12.82		69,240

Workings

Adam Downshire – Statements of Affairs as at 31 December 1981

		£			£
Capital		59,950	*Fixed Assets*		
			Premises		50,000
			Equipment		8,000
Creditors –			*Current Assets*		
Trade	4,500		Stock	10,000	
Expenses	600		Debtors	6,000	
		5,100	Bank	1,000	
			Cash	50	
					17,050
		75,050			75,050

Debtors

B/d	6,000	Bank	11,400
Sales	10,500	c/d	5,100
	16,500		16,500

Bank

B/d	1,000	Payments	13,200
Receipts	13,700	c/d	1,500
	14,700		14,700

Cash

B/d	50	Bank	2,300
Sales	2,850	Purchases	200
		Expenses	320
		c/d	80
	2,900		2,900

Creditors – Trade

Bank	9,400	B/d	4,500
c/d	4,200	Purchases	9,300
Cash	200		
	13,800		13,800

Creditors – Expenses

Bank	2,800	B/d	600
c/d	440	Expenses	2,960
Cash	320		
	3,560		3,560

(b) Disadvantages include:

(i) Loss of control – risk of error/fraud.

(ii) Extra costs of preparing accounts at year end.

(iii) No easy access to figures in mid-year.

(iv) Difficulty of detailed analysis.

(v) Problem of audit, and proof of figures if required.

4 *Freda – Trading and Profit and Loss Account for the year ended 31 September 1982*

	£	£
Sales (17,400 + 160 + 1,520)		19,080
less:		
Stock 1.11.81	380	
Purchases	10,680	
	11,060	
Stock 31.12.82	523	
Cost of Sales		10,537
Gross Profit		8,543
less:		
Rent & Rates (45 – 90 + 1,300 – 60 + 76)	1,271	
Heat & Light (595 + 26)	621	
Telephone	130	
Wages	2,200	
Cleaner	140	
Bad debts (12 + 17)	29	
Depreciation – Van	430	
– Fittings	72	
Loss on disposal	150	
		5,043
Net Profit		3,500

Freda – Balance Sheet as at 31 October 1982

	£	£
Fixed Assets		
Van (1,400 + 750 – 430)		1,720
Fittings (570 + 150 – 72)		648
		2,368
Current Assets		
Stock	523	
Debtors (170 – 17)	153	
Prepaid	60	
Bank (1,053 – 236)	817	
Cash	160	
	1,713	
Current Liabilities		
Creditors	1,440	
Accruals	76	
	1,516	
Net current assets		197
		2,565
Capital at 1.11.81		145
Add: Introduced in year		2,500
		2,645
Profit for the year		3,500
		6,145
Drawings (820 + 2,600 + 160)		3,580
		2,565

Workings

Statement of Affairs 1 November 1981

	£	£		£	£
Capital*		145	Fixed assets:		
			Van		900
Current liabilities			Fittings		570
Creditors	1,390		Current assets		
Accruals	90		Stock	380	
Bank overdraft	426		Debtors	122	
		1,906	Prepaid	45	
			Cash	34	
					581
		2,051			2,051

* Balancing figure

Disposal Account

Van	900	Proceeds	750
		P & L	150
	900		900

Debtors

B/f	122	Cash	1,460
Sales	1,520	Bad debts	12
		c/f	170
	1,642		1,642

Creditors

Cash	10,420	b/f	1,390
c/f	1,440	Purchases	10,680
Cash	210		
	12,070		12,070

Provision for bad debts

Bal c/f	17	P & L	17

5

(a) James Barker – Balance Sheet at 31 December

	£		£	£
Capital – 1.1	20,000	Fixed assets		
Profit	2,400	Tools		800
	22,400	Equipment		12,000
Drawings	2,000			12,800
Capital 31.12	20,400	Current assets		
		Stock	200	
Loan	7,500	Cash	15,000	
Creditors	100			15,200
	28,000			28,000

(b) Income Statement for the year ended 31 December

Sales		13,100
Less:		
Heat & Light	450	
Rent	1,800	
Wages	7,000	
Insurance	150	
Purchases (1,400 + 100 – 200)	1,300	
		10,700
		2,400

(c)

(i) Drawings + (Closing Capital – Opening Capital)
= 2,000 + (20,400 – 20,000) = £2,400

(ii) Income – Expenses
= 13,100 – 10,700 = £2,400

Workings

Cash

B/d	20,000	Payments	18,100
Sales	13,100	c/d	15,000
	33,100		33,100

6 (a) Net Profit

	£	£
As given		41,004
Add:		
P & L on asset disposal	470	
Increase in sales	1,575	
Reduction in purchases	10,000	
Increase sales	189	
Reduce purchases	21	
Increase sales	86	
		12,341
		53,345
Less:		
Discount (allowed & received)	1,072	
Stock write off	800	
		1,872
As adjusted		51,473
Capital employed:		
As given		352,600
Add:		
Fixtures & fittings	470	
Increase debtors	1,575	
Reduce suspense	10,000	
Increase debtors	189	
Reduce creditors	21	
		12,255
		364,855
Less:		
Discount adjustment	1,072	
Stock write off	800	
		1,872
		362,983

(b) Bonus

$$\frac{\text{Net profit}}{\text{Capital employed}} = \frac{51,473}{382,983} = 14.2\%$$

∴ excess over 10% = 4%

∴ Bonus = 4 × £300 = £1,200

7

Processors Ltd – Manufacturing, Trading, and Profit and Loss account for the year ended 31 December 1982

	£		£
Stock of raw materials 1.1.82	4,300	Production cost of goods	55,150
Purchases	25,700		
	30,000		
Stock of raw materials 31.12.82	5,800		
	24,200		
Direct labour	19,200		
Prime cost	43,400		
Factory overheads:			
General expenses (3,050 + 300)	3,350		
Indirect labour	4,900		
Rent (1,400 – 200)	1,200		
Depreciation	2,000		
	54,850		
Add WIP 1.1.82	3,900		
	58,750		
Less WIP 31.12.82	3,600		
	55,150		55,150
Stock of finished goods 1.1.82	6,100	Sales	80,000
Production cost b/d	55,150		
Goods purchased	2,700		

	63,950		
Stock 31.12.82	8,000		
Cost of sales	55,950		
Gross profit c/d	24,050		
	80,000		80,000
Administration	7,400	Gross profit b/d	24,050
Debenture interest (750 + 750)	1,500	Gain on shares sold	6,500
Directors remuneration	5,000		
Net profit c/d	16,650		
	30,550		30,550
Taxation	3,900	Net profit b/d	16,650
Dividend	7,200	Distributable reserves b/f	4,200
Reserves c/f	9,750		
	20,850		20,850

Processors Ltd – Balance Sheet as at 31 December 1982

	£	£	£
Fixed assets – Plant cost			12,000
depreciation			6,000
			6,000
Current assets			
Stock – Raw materials	5,800		
WIP	3,600		
Finished goods	8,000		
		17,400	
Debtors		26,700	
Prepayments		200	
Bank		21,400	
		65,700	
Current liabilities			
Creditors		3,000	
Accruals (300 + 750)		1,050	
Taxation		3,700	
Dividend		7,200	
		14,950	
Net current assets			50,750
			56,750
10% Debentures 1990			15,000
			41,750
Ordinary shares of 25p (20,000 + 10,000)			30,000
Share premium			2,000
Distributive reserves			9,750
			41,750

Workings

Tax

b/d	200	P & L	3,900
c/d	3,700		
	3,900		3,900

Suspense

Shares	10,000	b/d	23,500
Premium	2,000		
Disposal	11,500		
	23,500		23,500

Investment disposal

b/d	5,000	Suspense	11,500
P & L	6,500		
	11,500		11,500

8 *Trevor & Francis*

(a) Adjustments to profit

	£	£
Profit as first drafted		9,540
Add:		
(3) Licences prepaid	50	
(5) Stock	330	
		380
		9,920
Less:		
(1) Loss on buildings	500	
(2) Loss on plant	215	
(4) Bad debts	291	
(5) Stock	470	
(6) Cash	35	
		1,511
		8,409
Interest:		
Trevor (20,100 – 2,000) × 9%	1,629	
Francis (10,000 – 3,800) × 9%	558	
		2,187

Profit share:		
Trevor	3,111	
Francis	3,111	
		6,222

(b) *Balance Sheet as at 31 December 1979*

Fixed assets:	*Cost*	*Dep'n*	*WDV*
Freehold buildings	11,500	—	11,500
Plant	14,385	6,600	7,785
Motor vehicles	8,000	2,700	5,300
	33,885	9,300	24,585
Current assets:			
Stock		4,860	
Debtors		13,709	
Prepayments		50	
Bank		762	
Cash		5	
		19,386	
Current liabilities			
Creditors		11,262	
Net current assets			8,124
			32,709

Partners' capital:

	Trevor	*Francis*	*Total*
Capital 1 Jan. 1979	20,100	10,000	30,100
Profit for year	4,740	3,669	8,409
	24,840	13,669	38,509
Drawings	2,000	3,800	5,800
	22,840	9,869	32,709

9

Squirrel Antiques – Trading Profit and Loss Account for the year ended 30 April 1982

	£	£
Sales		22,900
Stock b/f	4,600	
Purchases	7,400	
Renovation costs (2,200 – 150)	2,050	
	14,050	
Stock c/f (5,100 + 800)	5,900	
Cost of sales		8,150
Gross Profit		14,750
Interest received		190
		14,940
Less: Expenses		
Rent & rates (1,450 – 150)	1,300	
Light & heat (920 + 100)	1,020	
Wages	2,700	
Sundry expenses	870	
Depreciation – F & F	640	
Vehicles	2,875	
Repairs	150	
		9,555
Net Profit		5,385

Squirrel Antiques – Balance Sheet as at 30 April 1982

		£	£
Capital:			
At 1 May 1981			16,360
Profit for year			5,385
			21,745
Drawings			4,200
			17,545
Fixed Assets (note 1)			7,685
Current Assets			
Stock	5,900		
Prepayment	150		
Cash at bank	3,910		
	9,960		
Less Accrual	100		
			9,860
			17,545

Note 1 Fixed Assets

	Cost	*Depr.*	*NBV*
Fixtures & fittings	6,400	3,240	3,160
Motor vehicles	11,500	6,975	4,525
	17,900	10,215	7,685

10

(a) ***Green Ltd – Balance Sheet as at 31 March 1983***

	£000	*£000*
Share Capital		
Authorized		
25,000 8% preference shares of £1		25
75,000 ordinary shares		75
		100

Issued and fully paid:		
25,000 8% preference shares of £1		25
60,000 ordinary shares of £1		60
		85
Share premium		10
General reserve		20
Retained profit (32 – 15 – 5)		12
		127
10% Debentures		50
		177
Fixed Assets (note 1)		125
Current Assets:		
Stock	75	
Debtors	34	
Cash	3	
	112	
Current Liabilities:		
Creditors	18	
Proposed Dividend	11	
Overdraft	26	
Accruals	5	
	60	
Net Current Assets		52
		177

Note 1 Fixed Assets

	Cost	*Depr.*	*WDV*
Freehold land & buildings	55	—	55
Plant	80	30	50
Vehicles	35	15	20
	170	45	125

(b) Green Ltd – Computation of net trading profit for the year ended 31 March 1983

	£000	£000
Retained profit 31.3.83		32
less: Retained profit 1.4.82		8
		24
Add:		
General reserve transfer	5	
Dividends	11	
		16
		40
Less:		
Depreciation – Plant	8	
Vehicles	7	
Interest	5	
		20
Net trading profit		20

11 Hillgate Ltd – Balance Sheet as at 31 December 1981

	£	£
Share Capital – authorized, issued, and fully paid		100,000
Retained profit		44,015
		144,015
Fixed assets (note 1)		98,700
Current assets:		
Stock	29,142	
Debtors (21,784–938)	20,846	
Prepayments	300	
Bank	23,101	
	73,389	
Current Liabilities:		
Dividend	10,000	
Creditors	17,493	
Accruals	581	
	28,074	
Net Current Assets		45,315
		144,015

Hillgate Ltd – Trading and Profit and Loss Account for the year ended 31 December 1981

	£	£
Sales		316,810
Less:		
Opening stock	25,689	
Purchases	201,698	
	227,387	
Closing stock	29,142	
Cost of sales		198,245
Gross profit		118,565
General expenses	32,168	
Wages and salaries (54,207 + 581)	54,788	
Rent and rates (4,300 – 300)	4,000	

Light and heat	1,549	
Bad debts (748 + 77)	825	
Depreciation	5,500	
Net profit		98,830
		19,735
Less Dividends		10,000
Retained profit		9,735
Bal b/fwd		34,280
Bal c/fwd		44,015

Note 1 Fixed assets

	Freehold premises	*Machinery*	*Total*
Cost	65,000	55,000	120,000
Depreciation	—	21,300	21,300
NBV	£65,000	£33,706	£98,700

Workings

1 Depreciation – b/f	15,800
P & L	5,500
c/f	£21,300
2 Bad debt provision – b/f	861
P & L	77
c/f	£938

Chapter 12

1

(a) ***Duswell Ltd – Cash budget***

	Jan.	Feb.	March	April	May	June	July	August	Sept.	Oct.	Nov.	Dec.
Inflows												
Debtors	7,000	8,000	8,000	10,000	12,000	13,000	14,000	16,000	16,000	16,000	17,000	19,000
	7,000	8,000	8,000	10,000	12,000	13,000	14,000	16,000	16,000	16,000	17,000	19,000
Outflows												
Advertising	1,000			1,500			1,800			2,400		
Creditors	4,000	4,800	4,800	5,600	6,000	6,000	6,000	6,400	6,400	7,200	8,000	8,000
Wages, etc.	3,000	3,600	3,600	4,200	4,500	4,500	4,500	4,800	4,800	5,400	6,000	6,000
Salaries	1,600	1,600	1,600	1,600	1,600	2,000	2,000	2,000	2,000	2,000	2,000	2,000
Production equipment				2,000	2,000	2,000						
Dividend				600								
	9,600	10,000	10,000	15,500	14,100	14,500	14,300	13,200	13,200	17,000	16,000	16,000
Net inflow/(outflow)	(2,600)	(2,000)	(2,000)	(5,500)	(2,100)	(1,500)	(300)	2,800	2,800	(1,000)	1,000	3,000
Bank b/f	7,500	4,900	2,900	(900)	(4,600)	(6,700)	(8,200)	(8,500)	(5,700)	(2,900)	(3,900)	(2,900)
Bank c/f	4,900	2,900	900	(4,600)	(6,700)	(8,200)	(8,500)	(5,700)	(2,900)	(3,900)	(2,900)	100

(b) ***Profit for the year***

	£	£
Sales (18,100 x 10)		181,000
Cost of Sales (18,100 x 7)		126,700
Gross Profit		54,300
Salaries	22,000	
Advertising	6,700	
Depreciation	5,000	
		33,700
Net profit		20,600

(c)

Non-cash items – depreciation		5,000
		25,600
Applications:		
Dividend	600	
Plant	6,000	
		6,600
		19,000
Inflow of working capital		
Finished goods increase	1,400	
Raw material increase	4,000	
Debtor increase	25,000	
Creditor increase	(4,000)	
		26,000
Bank decrease		7,400

(d) *Cash budgeting* points might include:

(i) Define cash budget as an estimate of the cash receipts and cash payments arising from the planned activities of the business, usually prepared on a month-by-month basis but sometimes covering shorter periods.

(ii) Explain that cash, like other working capital items, must be controlled so that adequate resources are available for the needs of the business but there is not any excess of resources tied up unproductively.

(iii) Point out that cash management is particularly significant as a temporary shortage may discredit or even destroy the business.

(iv) The cash budget serves not only as a planning tool inside the business but also as an essential document to use when negotiating bank finance.

Leutasch Ltd – Cash budget

	June	July	August	September	October	November
Inflows						
Shares issued	88,800					
Debtors				38,850	51,800	51,800
Total inflows	—	—	—	38,850	51,800	51,800
Outflows						
Plant	88,800					
Raw material suppliers			18,500	18,500	18,500	18,500
Wages		14,800	14,800	14,800	14,800	14,800
Overheads – Factory			7,400	7,400	7,400	7,400
Administration			1,850	1,850	1,850	1,850
Selling and Distribution			3,700	3,700	3,700	3,700
Total outflows	—	14,800	46,250	46,250	46,250	46,250
Net inflow/(outflow)	—	(14,800)	(46,250)	(7,400)	5,550	5,550
Cash b/f	—	—	(14,800)	(61,050)	(68,450)	(62,900)
Cash c/f	—	(14,800)	(61,050)	(68,450)	(62,900)	(57,350)

Leutasch Ltd – Manufacturing Trading and Profit and Loss Account for the accounting period to 30 November 1983

	£		£
Purchases	111,000	Production costs c/d	207,200
Less – stock of raw materials c/f	18,500		
Cost of raw materials consumed	92,500		
Direct wages	74,000		
Factory overheads	37,000		
Plant depreciation	3,700		
	207,200		207,200
Production costs b/d	207,200	Sales	194,250
Finished goods stock c/f	51,800		
	155,400		
Gross Profit c/d	38,850		
	194,250		194,250
Admin. overheads	9,250	Gross Profit	38,850
Sales overheads	18,500		
Net Profit	11,100		
	38,850		38,850

Leutasch Ltd – Balance Sheet as at 30 November 1983

	£	£
Fixed Assets		
Plant – cost		88,800
depreciation		3,700
		85,100

Current Assets:		
Stock (18,500 + 51,800)	70,300	
Debtors	51,800	
	122,100	
Current Liabilities:		
Creditors	49,950	
Bank	57,350	
	107,300	
Net Current Assets		14,800
		99,900
Share Capital – ordinary shares of £1		74,000
Share Premium		14,800
Retained Profits		11,100
		99,900

Workings

Raw material costs

Monthly purchases 3,700 × 5 = 18,500

Purchases commence June, so first payment to suppliers: August

Wages

3,700 × 4 = 14,800 per month

Payments commence July

Debtors

August sales 2,775 × 14 = 51,800

Finished goods stock

Goods produced	18,500
Goods sold	13,875
Stock	4,625

$\frac{4{,}625 \times 207{,}200}{18{,}500} =$ 51,800

Suspense Account

Purchases	10,000	Bal b/d	8,928
		Discount allowed	536
		Discount received	536
	10,000		10,000

3

Nick's Newsmart: Statement of source and application of funds for the year ended 31 March 1982

Sources from operations		£	£
Net profit			8,600
Add: Items not involving movement of funds			
Depreciation			600
Total funds generated from operations			9,200
Applications			
Purchase of fixtures		5,200	
Drawings		6,200	
			11,400
			(2,200)
Increase/(Decrease) in working capital:			
Increase in stock of magazines, etc		2,660	
Increase in stock of sweets, tobacco, etc		1,760	
Increase in trade debtors		2,500	
Increase in other debtors		380	
Decrease in trade creditors		600	
Increase in other creditors		(20)	
		7,980	
Movement in net liquid funds:			
Reduction in bank balance	(10,400)		
Increase in cash	220		
		(10,180)	
			(2,200)

Notes

There are a number of other possible layouts, and an alternative presentation which placed a greater emphasis on the net liquid fund movement would be very acceptable.

4

Corrigan Ltd – Statement of source and application of funds for the year ended 31 December 1981

	£000	*£000*
Source of Funds		
Profit before tax		808
Adjustments for items not involving movement of funds:		
Depreciation	195	
Loss on disposal of plant	2	197
Total generated from operations		1,005

Other sources:		
Shares issued	100	
Sale of plant	3	
		103
		1,108
Applications		
Tax	400	
Dividends	200	
Purchase of land and buildings	25	
Purchase of plant	51	
		676
		432
Increase/(Decrease) in working Capital:		
Stock – increase	236	
Debtors – (decease)	(103)	
Creditors – (increase)	(3)	
	130	
Net Liquid Funds		
Overdraft – decrease	300	
Cash – increase	2	
		432

Workings

FA Movements

	L & B	Plant	Goodwill
B/fwd	1,297	1,054	200
NBV of disposals	(5)		—
Depreciation	(40)	(105)	(50)
Additions (balancing figure)	25	51	—
	1,277	1,000	150

Profit for year	£000	£000	
Retained			213
Add:			
tax		345	
dividend		250	
			595
			808

5

Happy Holidays Ltd – Statement of sources and applications of funds for the year ended 31 October 1982

	£000	£000
Sources from operations:		
Profit for the year		12
Items not involving movement of funds:		
Loss on sale of assets	6	
Depreciation	28	
Research and development	4	38
Generated from operations		50
Other sources:		
Sale of assets	6	
Issue of shares	10	
Issue of debentures	14	30
		80
Applications:		
Purchase of land and buildings	16	
Purchase of other fixed assets	40	
Research and development	24	
Dividend paid	10	90
		(10)
Increase/(Decrease) in working capital:		
Increase in debtors	5	
Decrease in stock	(4)	
Increase in creditors	(10)	—
	(9)	
Movement in net liquid funds:		
Decrease in cash	(1)	(10)

Harry – Cash budget

	Jan.	Feb.	March	April	May	June	July	August	Sept.	Oct.	Nov.	Dec.
Cash in:												
Takings	—	—	—	2,000	3,000	—	6,000	6,000	6,000	7,000	—	
Cash out:												
Deposit	16,000	—	—	—	—	—	—	—	—	—	—	—
Mortgage payment	350	350	350	350	350	350	350	350	350	350	350	350
Wages	—	—	—	800	800	800	800	800	800	800	—	—
Food	—	—	—	400	600	800	1,200	1,200	1,200	600	—	—
Laundry	--	—	—	—	100	150	200	300	300	300	150	—
Rates	—	—	—	1,500	—	—	—	—	—	—	—	—
Electricity	—	200	—	—	200	—	—	200	—	—	200	—
Drawings	400	400	400	400	400	400	400	4,400	400	400	400	400
	16,750	950	750	3,450	2,450	2,500	2,950	7,250	3,050	2,450	1,100	750
B/f	18,000	1,250	300	(450)	(1,900)	(1,350)	(3,850)	(800)	(2,050)	900	5,450	4,350
Net movement	(16,750)	(950)	(750)	(1,450)	550	(2,500)	3,050	(1,250)	2,950	4,550	(1,100)	(750)
	1,250	300	(450)	(1,900)	(1,350)	(3,850)	(800)	(2,050)	900	5,450	4,350	3,600

(a) ***Cash budget for the six months to 31 December 1984***

	July	August	September	October	November	December
	£	£	£	£	£	£
Inflows						
Redundancy Payment	15,000					
Debtors	—	—	3,000	6,000	6,000	10,500
	15,000	—	3,000	6,000	6,000	10,500
Outflows						
Fixed Assets	8,000					
Stock Purchases	5,000	4,000	4,000	7,000	7,000	7,000
Running Expenses	1,600	1,600	1,600	1,600	1,600	1,600
Drawings	1,000	1,000	1,000	1,000	1,000	1,000
	15,600	6,600	6,600	9,600	9,600	9,600
Net movement	(600)	(6,600)	(3,600)	(3,600)	(3,600)	900
B/fwd	—	(600)	(7,200)	(10,800)	(14,400)	(18,000)
C/fwd	(600)	(7,200)	(10,800)	(14,400)	(18,000)	(17,100)

(b) ***Forecast trading and profit and loss account for the 6 months ending 31 December 1984.***

	£	£
Sales		46,500
Cost of Sales		31,000
		15,500
Expenses	9,600	
Depreciation	800	
		10,400
Net profit		5,100

(c) ***Balance sheet as at 31 December 1984***

	£	£
Fixed Assets		7,200
Current Assets:		
Stock	10,000	
Debtors	21,000	
	31,000	
Current Liabilities:		
Creditors	7,000	
Bank	17,100	
	24,100	
Net Current Assets		6,900
		14,100

Capital Introduced	15,000	
Profit	5,100	
Drawings	(6,000)	14,100
C/fwd		

Expenses (12 × 1,600)	19,200	
Depreciation	1,600	
		20,800
		21,200

(d) Arguments to be used:

(i) Once established, business yields a regular cash inflow of £900 per month – enough to clear loan in 17 months.

(ii) Forecast P & L fails to do justice to potential profitability because of low sales in first three months. Full year's profit would be:

Sales (12 × 10,500)	126,000
Cost of Sales (12 × 7,000)	84,000
Gross Profit	42,000

(iii) Forecast is sensitive to sales prediction. The applicant's experience as a sales manager qualifies him particularly well to make this prediction.

Workings

	Sales	*Cost of Sales*
July	3,000	2,000
August	6,000	4,000
September	6,000	4,000
October	10,500	7,000
November	10,500	7,000
December	10,500	7,000
	46,500	31,000

Chapter 13

1 *Macdonald Ltd*

Profit and loss account for the year ended 31 March 1982

	£	£
Sales		730,000
Cost of Sales		600,000
		130,000
Expenses		57,000
Net Profit		73,000
Bal b/fwd		6,700
		79,700
Transfer to general reserve		67,300
Bal c/fwd		12,400

Balance Sheet as at 31 march 1982

	£	£
Ordinary Shares		150,000
General Reserve		87,600
Profit and loss account		12,400
		250,000
Debentures		35,000
		285,000

	£	£
Fixed Assets		195,000
Current Assets		
Stock	50,000	
Debtors	80,000	
Cash	60,000	
	190,000	
Less current liabilities	100,000	
Net current assets		90,000
		285,000

Workings

Fixed Assets $\frac{1.3}{1} \times 150{,}000 = 195{,}000$

Current Assets $\frac{1.9}{(1.9 - 1)} \times 90{,}000 = 190{,}000$

Cash + Debtors $\frac{1.4}{1} \times 100{,}000 = 140{,}000$

∴ Stock 190,000 – 140,000 = 50,000

Equity $\frac{50}{39} \times 195{,}000 = 250{,}000$

Debtors $\frac{730{,}000}{356} \times 40 = 80{,}000$

Note: This question requires confident use of ratios, and an understanding of reserve movements.

2

(a)

	Acorn	Oak
(i) Gross Profit %	$\frac{100}{300} = 33\frac{1}{3}\%$	$\frac{50}{150} = 33\frac{1}{3}\%$
Net Profit %	$\frac{30}{300} = 10\%$	$\frac{12}{150} = 8\%$
(ii) Acid Test	$\frac{30}{29} = 1$	$\frac{17.5}{15.5} = 1.1$
(iii) Return on net assets	$\frac{30}{210} = 14\%$	$\frac{12}{108} = 11\%$
(iv) Days Debtors	$\frac{26}{300} \times 365 = 32$	$\frac{14}{150} \times 365 = 34$
Days Creditors	$\frac{29}{185} \times 365 = 57$	$\frac{15.5}{9.2} \times 365 = 61$

(b) Additional ratios computed

	Acorn	Oak
Asset turnover	$\frac{300}{210} = 1.4$	$\frac{150}{108} = 1.4$
$\frac{\text{Expenses}}{\text{Sales}}$	$\frac{70}{300} = 23\frac{1}{3}\%$	$\frac{38}{150} = 25\frac{1}{3}\%$

Although both companies have the same gross profit percentage, Acorn has a higher net profit percentage. This is because expenses are a smaller proportion of sales for Acorn, possibly because of economies of scale. Asset turnover for the two companies is similar, so that Acorn's higher return on net assets can be attributed to the tighter control of general expenses.

Oak has a slightly stronger acid test. Oak seems to both collect and pay debts more slowly than Acorn, but these differences between the two companies are not substantial.

(c) Main limitations

Ratios can only be applied to figures in the accounts. Accounts have the following limitations:

(i) Accounting conventions do not necessarily represent economic reality, because assets are not shown at 'value' and 'goodwill' is ignored. Inflation adds to these problems, particularly when comparison is made over a number of years.

(ii) Published accounts are normally published months after the year end, and so give outdated information.

(iii) The balance sheet gives a snapshot at one point in time; this may not be typical of the position of the business, particularly in an industry prone to seasonal fluctuations.

(iv) The user may be concerned with only one part of a reporting entity, and not be able to identify that segment in the accounts.

In addition the following problems arise in using ratios

(i) In focusing on ratios there is a danger of losing sight of the significance of individual amounts in isolation.

(ii) There are a number of terms used in ratio analysis which are used in a variety of ways, e.g. return on capital employed. Thus ratios have to be defined carefully.

4

(a)

	Rex	Regis
Stock turn	$\frac{945}{156} = 6$	$\frac{920}{36} = 26$
Debtors ratio	$\frac{120}{1080} \times 12 = 1.3$	$\frac{72}{1080} \times 12 = 0.8$
Creditors ratio	$\frac{191.4}{957} \times 12 = 2.4$	$\frac{137}{932} \times 12 = 1.8$
Current ratio	$\frac{528}{191.4} = 2.8$	$\frac{224}{137} = 1.6$
Liquid ratio	$\frac{372}{191.4} = 1.9$	$\frac{188}{137} = 1.4$
Working capital	£336,600	£87,000

(b) Regis appears to have a very much tighter working capital management, turning over stock more than four times as quickly and collecting debts in almost half the time compared to Rex. Regis also manages to pay creditors more rapidly. Both the current ratio and the liquidity ratio are very much lower in the case of Regis. However since Regis has a bank balance which covers:

$$\frac{116}{137} = 85\%$$

of current liabilities, there appears to be no cause for concern. Rex Ltd is holding very large cash balances, apparently unproductively. The efficiency of Regis Ltd. is highlighted if we identify the working capital turnover ratio:

Rex	Regis
$\frac{1,080}{336.6} = 3.2$	$\frac{1,080}{87} = 12.4$

The achievement is particularly impressive because Regis has a higher gross profit percentage and only slightly higher overheads.

5 *Lisburn Electrics*

Liquidity

The cash balance has increased substantially. However close examination of the working capital position raises doubts as to the chairman's claim of 'careful control of working capital'. The dramatic fall in 'days debtors' does indeed suggest a considerable tightening of credit control; however the substantial fall in stock turnover would suggest a corresponding relaxation of stock control, the net effect of stock and debtors taken together absorbing an extra £20,000 of working capital. In fact, despite the increase in cash, both the current ratio and the acid test have fallen because of the increase in creditors. Creditors' turnover has halved.

The rise in the cash balance would seem to be attributable to:

(a) A new share issue in the year.
(b) The increase in short-term credit being taken.
(c) Fixed asset replacement has apparently been less than depreciation for the year.

It would seem advisable to enquire whether there have been special circumstances affecting the working capital position at December 1982.

Performance

Although sales, profits, and dividends have all increased an examination of some key ratios suggests an unsatisfactory position.

Return on equity has fallen slightly, whether measured before or after tax. The return on total funds has been even more substantial, and we can see that the increase in gearing arising from current liabilities has cushioned the impact of this fall on shareholders.

Examining the secondary ratios we find a slight increase in the net profit percentage but substantial drop in the asset turnover, this latter being largely attributable to the failure to make productive use of the large cash balance.

The dividend cover has fallen substantially, so that in large part the increased dividend has been achieved by reducing dividend cover.

Conclusion

The large cash balance at the year end is puzzling, particularly as the company have felt it necessary to raise new share capital in the year. The company made no use of these new funds in 1982. Two points of inquiry emerge:

(a) Was there some disruption of activity in 1982 that explains the change in working capital structure and the failure to employ cash balances profitably?

(b) Are there plans for new investment to use the accumulated cash balance?

---

6 *Lisburn Electrics – Computation of rating*

	1981		*1982*	
Return on equity (post-tax)	$\frac{23}{350}$	= 6.6%	$\frac{25}{430}$	= 5.8%
Return on equity (pre-tax)	$\frac{35}{350}$	= 10%	$\frac{40}{430}$	= 9.3%
Return on long term funds	$\frac{40}{400}$	= 10%	$\frac{45}{480}$	= 9.4%
Return on total funds	$\frac{40}{470}$	= 8.5%	$\frac{45}{630}$	= 7.1%
Total asset turnover	$\frac{400}{470}$	= 0.85	$\frac{420}{630}$	= 0.67
Net profit %	$\frac{40}{400}$	= 10%	$\frac{45}{420}$	= 10.7%
Current ratio	$\frac{270}{70}$	= 3.9	$\frac{450}{150}$	= 3
Acid test	$\frac{150}{70}$	= 2.1	$\frac{250}{150}$	= 1.7
Stock turnover	$\frac{400}{120}$	= 3.3	$\frac{420}{200}$	= 2.1
Days debtors	$\frac{130}{400} \times 365$	= 119	$\frac{70}{420} \times 365$	= 61
Creditors turnover	$\frac{400}{70}$	= 5.7	$\frac{420}{150}$	= 2.8
Long-term borrowing: long-term funds	$\frac{50}{400}$	= 12.5%	$\frac{50}{480}$	= 10.4%
Total borrowing: total funds	$\frac{120}{400}$	= 25.5%	$\frac{200}{630}$	= 31.7%
Fixed asset turnover	$\frac{400}{200}$	= 2	$\frac{420}{180}$	= 2.3
Dividend cover	$\frac{23}{10}$	= 2.3	$\frac{25}{15}$	= 1.67

7 *Leek Ltd – comments*

Overall profitability

The return on equity fell in 1981 but more than recovered in 1982. The rise was assisted by the introduction of an element of long-term gearing in that year, but the return on long-term funds shows the same pattern.

Level of activity

The level of turnover generated by the resources of the business rose slightly in 1981 and substantially
but the absolute level of gross profit rose in 1982 because of the high increase in sales. Expenses have risen very little over the three years in absolute terms, dropping from 18.3 per cent to 9.7 per cent. This tight control of expenses, which more than compensated for the fall in the gross profit percentage explains the increase in the net profit percentage in 1982.

Working capital management

The level of sales has doubled over a period during which the net working capital has fallen by one-third. In 1981 both stock control and credit control appear to have been relaxed, financed by a substantial increase in the level of credit taken by suppliers and to some extent by an erosion of cash balances. In 1982 stock control was tightened but credit control was relaxed even further while the period of credit taken from suppliers was reduced and the increased working capital requirement was financed by an overdraft. Both the current ratio and the acid test reflect the dangerous fall in company liquidity.

in 1982. Over the three years new investment in plant has enabled the company to double the level of sales without any increase in property and an actual reduction in working capital employed.

Profitability of trading

The gross profit percentage has fallen steadily over the three years; presumably this is a sacrifice that has been accepted to achieve increased sales. This policy led to a fall in the level of gross profit in 1981

Financial policy

The company appears to have a policy of distributing most profit by way of dividend, retaining little. Gearing has increased substantially, particularly with the raising of the new debentures.

Recommendations

The company faces severe liquidity problems. Recommendations would include:

(a) A halt to the current rate of expansion, with a trading policy of improving the gross profit per cent rather than expanding sales.
(b) Tighter control on debtors.
(c) A change in dividend policy, retaining a substantial proportion of profit.
(d) No further expansion of plant except for essential replacements.
(e) If following the above further finance is needed then this to be raised by new equity, not borrowing.

	1980	*1981*	*1982*
Return on equity	$\frac{20}{130} = 15.4\%$	$\frac{14}{147} = 9.5\%$	$\frac{42}{150} = 28\%$
Return on long-term funds	$\frac{20}{130} = 15.4\%$	$\frac{14}{147} = 9.5\%$	$\frac{46}{190} = 24.2\%$
Asset turnover (long-term)	$\frac{300}{130} = 2.3$	$\frac{350}{147} = 2.4$	$\frac{600}{190} = 3.2$
Net profit % (long-term)	$\frac{20}{300} = 6.7\%$	$\frac{14}{350} = 4\%$	$\frac{46}{600} = 7.7\%$
Gearing – (long-term)	NIL	NIL	$\frac{40}{190} = 21\%$

Gearing – Total	$\frac{65}{195} = 33\frac{1}{3}\%$	$\frac{103}{250} = 41\%$	$\frac{170}{320} = 53\%$
Current ratio	$\frac{125}{65} = 1.9$	$\frac{150}{103} = 1.5$	$\frac{170}{130} = 1.3$
Acid Test	$\frac{65}{65} = 1$	$\frac{65}{103} = 0.6$	$\frac{70}{130} = 0.5$
Property turnover	$\frac{300}{30} = 10$	$\frac{350}{30} = 11.7$	$\frac{600}{30} = 20$
Plant turnover	$\frac{300}{40} = 7.5$	$\frac{350}{70} = 5$	$\frac{600}{120} = 5$
Working capital Turnover	$\frac{300}{60} = 5$	$\frac{350}{47} = 7.4$	$\frac{600}{40} = 15$
Days Stock	$\frac{60}{225} \times 365 = 97$	$\frac{85}{280} \times 365 = 111$	$\frac{100}{500} \times 365 = 73$
Days Debtors	$\frac{25}{300} \times 365 = 30$	$\frac{35}{350} \times 365 = 36$	$\frac{70}{600} \times 365 = 43$
Days Creditors*	$\frac{25}{235} \times 365 = 101$	$\frac{103}{305} \times 365 = 123$	$\frac{100}{515} \times 365 = 71$
Gross Profit %	$\frac{75}{300} = 25\%$	$\frac{70}{350} = 20\%$	$\frac{100}{600} = 16.7\%$
Expenses/Sales	$\frac{55}{300} = 18.3\%$	$\frac{56}{350} = 16\%$	$\frac{58}{600} = 9.7\%$

* Since cost of sales will include some manufacturing costs, the time taken to pay creditors will exceed these figures.

Workings of purchases, expenses, and dividend

Sales		300		350		600
Stock b/fwd	50		60		85	
Purchases	235		305		515	
Stock c/fwd	(60)		(85)		(100)	
		225		280		500
Gross Profit		75		70		100
Expenses		55		56		58
Net Profit		20		14		42
Tax and dividends				12		39
				2		3
Profit b/f				25		27
Profit c/f		25		27		30

Funds Statement

	1981		1982	
Source of funds:				
Profit for year		14		42
Other sources:				
Share issue	15		—	
Debenture issue	—		40	

		15		40
		29		82
Applications				
Net plant investment	30		50	
Tax and Dividends	12		39	
		42		89
		(13)		(7)
Working Capital				
Stock increase	25		15	
Debtor increase	10		35	
Creditor decrease (increase)	(38)		3	
	(3)		53	
Cash decrease	(10)		(60)	
		(13)		(7)

Note: A full breakdown of the plant acquisitions/disposals/dividends is not available.

8

(a) ***Bysouth Ltd – Statement of source and application of funds for the year ended 31 December 1978***

	1978		1977	
	£000	*£000*	*£000*	*£000*
Source of funds				
Profit for the year		30		22
Adjustments for items not involving movement of funds:				
Depreciation	16		12	
loss on sale of fixed asset	—		5	
		16		17
Generated from operations		46		39
Other sources				
Sale of fixed assets	—		3	
Issue of shares	20		—	
		20		3
		66		42
Applications				
Purchase of fixed assets	14		23	
Dividends	11		9	
		25		32
		41		10
Increase/(Decrease) in working capital:				
Stock increase	14		8	
Debtors increase	52		24	
Creditors increase	(13)		(8)	
	53		24	
Bank – decrease	(12)		(14)	
		41		10

Workings

Fixed Assets	*1977*	*1978*
	£000	*£000*
Cost b/fwd	142	153
Additional*	23	14
Disposals	(12)	—
Cost c/fwd	153	167

*Balancing figure

(b) Ratios:

	1977			1978		
Return on equity	$\frac{22}{149}$		= 14.8%	$\frac{30}{189}$		= 15.9%
Return on total funds	$\frac{22}{206}$		= 10.7%	$\frac{30}{270}$		= 11.1%
Asset turnover	$\frac{520}{206}$		= 2.5	$\frac{560}{270}$		= 2.1
Net profit %	$\frac{22}{520}$		= 4.2%	$\frac{30}{560}$		= 5.4%
Current ratio	$\frac{101}{57}$		= 1.8	$\frac{167}{81}$		= 2.1
Acid test	$\frac{66}{57}$		= 1.2	$\frac{118}{81}$		= 1.5
Days debtors	$\frac{66}{300}$	× 365	= 80	$\frac{118}{430}$	× 365	= 100
Days stock	$\frac{35}{352}$	× 365	= 36	$\frac{49}{379}$	× 365	= 47
Fixed Asset turnover	$\frac{520}{153}$		= 3.4	$\frac{560}{167}$		= 3.4
Working Capital turnover	$\frac{520}{44}$		= 11.8	$\frac{560}{86}$		= 6.5
Gross Profit %	$\frac{168}{520}$		= 32%	$\frac{181}{560}$		= 32%
Expenses /Sales	$\frac{146}{520}$		= 28%	$\frac{151}{560}$		= 27%

Sales change:

Credit	$\frac{430 - 300}{300}$	= 43% +
Cash	$\frac{130 - 220}{220}$	= 41% –
Total	$\frac{430 - 300}{520}$	= 3% +

Comment

Between 1977 and 1978 profit has increased from £22,000 to £30,000, reflecting an improvement in the return on equity and a rather smaller improvement in the return on total assets employed. If we look at the secondary ratios there has been an interesting change in the company's performance, with an improvement in the net profit percentage and a decline in asset turnover.

The net profit percentage represents the return earned on sales. The gross profit percentage has remained constant, and the improvement in net profit is attributable to a drop in expenses as a proportion of sales; this is because expenses have been held virtually level while sales have risen by 8 per cent.

The asset turnover represents the level of sales achieved in relation to the resources employed by the business. The fall in asset turnover cannot be attributable to fixed asset usage, since fixed asset turnover has remained constant. Our attention is therefore focused on working capital usage.

The 'days debtors' and 'days stock' ratio indicates relaxation both of credit control and stock control; the impact of this on working capital has been compounded by a change in the sales mix, with a 43 per cent rise in credit sales. This is shown by the funds statement, which in both 1977 and 1978 shows debtors absorbing more than the total working capital increase for the year. The principal reason for the outflow of cash can therefore be identified as the increase in debtors and stock, attributable to a combination of relaxed working capital control and a change in the mix of cash and credit sales.

9

(a) *Binns – Statement of sources and applications of funds for the year ended 31 March 1983*

	£	£
Sources of funds		
Profit in year		6,680
Adjustments for items not involving movement of funds:		
Depreciation	850	
Loss on van	300	
		1,150
Generated from operations		7,830
Other sources		
Sale of van	500	
Loan	3,000	3,500
		11,330
Applications:		
Purchase of van	6,400	
Drawings	4,130	10,530
		800
Increase/(Decrease) in working capital:		
Stock – increase	1,380	
Debtors – increase	460	
Accruals – increase	80	
Creditors – increase	(160)	
	1,760	
Net liquid funds		
Bank decrease	(960)	800

Workings

Fixed Assets

	Van		*Fixtures*	
	Cost	*Depr.*	*Cost*	*Depr.*
B/Fwd	3,200	2,400	1,100	470
Additions/charge for year*	6,400	800	—	50
Disposals	(3,200)	(2,400)	—	—
C/Fwd	6,400	800	1,100	520

*Balancing figure

(b) *Ratios*

	1982	*1983*
Return on equity	$\frac{2,920}{3,490} = 84\%$	$\frac{6,680}{6,040} = 111\%$
Return on total assets	$\frac{2,920}{4,430} = 66\%$	$\frac{6,980^{*}}{10,460} = 67\%$
Current ratio	$\frac{3,000}{940} = 3.2$	$\frac{4,280}{1,420} = 3$
Acid test	$\frac{3,000 - 1,370}{940} = 1.7$	$\frac{4,280 - 2,750}{1,420} = 1.1$
Return on total assets – assuming £4,000 'wage' to Binns	$\frac{2,920 - 4,000}{4,430} = (24\%)$	$\frac{6,980^{*} - 4,000}{10,460} = 28\%$
Increase in Profit		$\frac{6,680 - 2,920}{2,920} = 129\%$
Increase in Stock		$\frac{1,380}{1,370} = 101\%$
Increase in Debtors		$\frac{460}{1,040} = 44\%$

* Assumes £300 interest on loan

Binn's profit has increased by 129 per cent in 1983. At first sight this might seem in line with the increased capital employed in the business; assuming interest of £300 on the loan, then return on total assets has changed very little while the increased return on equity can be seen as a consequence of gearing. However in a one-man business of this kind ratios of this kind computed in the conventional way are meaningless, because they fail to take into account as an expense the value of the work put in by the proprietor. If we recompute the return on total assets assuming a notional 'wage' to Binns of £4,000 we show a dramatic increase in the return; the amount of £4,000 is a rough estimate, assuming that drawings represent what Binns regards as a reasonable reward for his labour.

We are not given turnover figures for the two years, but it seems reasonable to assume that in a business of this kind the main reason for the increase in profit is an increase in turnover, probably of a similar amount. Thus the business has faced two major demands for new funding in the year:

(a) The need to replace the van, involving a net outflow of £5,900.
(b) The increased working capital needed to support the increased turnover.

These requirements have been met in four major ways:

(a) Raising a long-term loan.
(b) Retained profit.
(c) Restricting the increased working capital requirement; although profit increased by 129 per cent, the increase in stock was limited to 101 per cent and debtors to 44 per cent.
(d) The erosion of cash balances and incurring an overdraft.

(c) and (d) are reflected in the fall in the acid test.

Further expansion would clearly be inhibited by the constraints on working capital, and a continued policy of retaining a substantial proportion of profit would seem wise.

INDEX